SOCIAL ECOLOGY AND DEMOGRAPHIC STRUCTURE OF BHOTIAS

Concept's Discovering Himalayas Series

1. People's Participation in Himalayan Eco-System Development: A Plan for Action/**M.L. Dewan** (for Revised and Enlarged edition, see Serial No. 4)
2. Nut Fruits for the Himalayas (CDHS)/**M.L. Dewan, M.C. Nautiyal** and **V.K. Sah**
3. Vedic Philosophy and Himalayan Eco-System Development/ **M.L. Dewan** and **B.D. Joshi (Eds)**
4. People's Movement for Himalayan Rejuvenation: 2nd Revised and Enlarged edition/**M.L. Dewan**
5. Water Resources in The Himalayas: Harvesting, Tradition and Change (Foreword by Dr. M.L. Dewan)/**Piyoosh Rautela**
6. Images of Women in the Folksongs of Garhwal Himalayas/ **Anjali Capila**
7. Himalayan Snow and Glaciers: Associated Environmental Problems, Progress and Prospects/**Jagdish Bahadur**
8. Traditional Health Practices of Kumaoni Women/**Anjali Capila**
9. Uttaranchal: Vision and Action Programme for a New State/ **M.L. Dewan** and **Jagdish Bahadur (Eds)**

About the Author

Chittaranjan Dash is MSc and PhD in Anthropology. He pursued the academic and research career at Utkal University, North Eastern Hill University, Delhi University and Jawaharlal Nehru University. He is currently a Post Doctoral Fellow of Indian Council of Social Science Research (New Delhi) at the Centre for the Study of Regional Development, School of Social Sciences, Jawaharlal Nehru University, New Delhi. He has been assisting the Centre in teaching MA and MPhil students. He has worked extensively on the high altitude demography, life and culture of the Bhotias, human rights, women rights and environment issues among the communities of Uttaranchal Himalayas. He received MAKA Essay Prize 1995-96, which was open to the citizens of SAARC countries organised by the Indian Council of Cultural Relations, New Delhi. He has a number of research papers published in leading academic journals.

Concept's Discovering Himalayas Series No. 10

SOCIAL ECOLOGY AND DEMOGRAPHIC STRUCTURE OF BHOTIAS

Narratives and Discourses

Chittaranjan Dash

CONCEPT PUBLISHING COMPANY, NEW DELHI-110059

Cataloging in Publication Data—DK
Courtesy: D.K. Agencies (P) Ltd. <docinfo@dkagencies.com>

Dash, Chittaranjan.
Social ecology and demographic structure of Bhotias : narratives and discourses / Chittaranjan Dash.
p. cm.
Study conducted at Pithoragarh District of Uttaranchal State, India.
Includes bibliographical references (p.)
Includes index.
ISBN 8180692272

1. Bhotia (Tibetan people)—India—Pithoragarh (District)—Population. 2. Bhotia (Tibetan people)—India—Pithoragarh (District)—Social conditions. 3. Human ecology—India—Pithoragarh (District). I. Title.

DDC 304.609 545 1 22

ISBN 81-8069-227-2

First Published 2006

Published and Printed by
Ashok Kumar Mittal
Concept Publishing Company
A/15-16, Commercial Block, Mohan Garden
New Delhi (INDIA)

Phones : 25351460, 25351794
Fax : 091-11-25357103
Email : publishing@conceptpub.com

Dedicated to

My revered teachers who enlightened me

Prof. (Dr.) Jyotirmayee Kanungo

Dr. Govind Singh Saun

and

My beloved parents who are the source of my life and success

Shri Bhimsen Dash

Smt. Puspita Dash

FOREWORD

Life activities are drawn upon mutual dependence of human beings and environment, particularly when one is dealing with a tribal population. Unlike other animals, human beings are quite capable of modifying their environment in order to accommodate themselves with the help of their cultural domain. High altitude ecological conditions pose severe challenges to human, particularly tribal people's adaptation. Invariably, human populations adapt by manipulating their demographic parameters. Dr. Chittaranjan Dash has attempted to unravel demographic adaptation of the Bhotia, a tribal population of the Central Himalayas.

Drawing demographic information from high and low altitude populations of Bhotias of Pithoragarh District of Uttaranchal, Dr. Dash has tried to establish the demographic adaptation of this tribe to varying ecological settings.

Higher child population, reduced old age population, high proportion of masculinity, smaller family size, accumulation of major agricultural holdings, higher mean fertility to compensate higher offspring mortality, etc., observed among the Bhotias of high altitude, are nothing but demonstration of their positive adaptive demographic attributes.

Notwithstanding the small samples of both the Bhotia populations, the detailed analyses in the book have been able to project the above aspects vividly.

This book should be able to provide a good comparative demographic reading to the students and researchers in the field of Anthropological Demography, Population Studies, Human Geography and Human Ecology.

28 November 2004
New Delhi

Prof. A. K. Kalla
Head, Department of Anthropology
and *Dean, Faculty of Science*
University of Delhi

PROLOGUE

Mountains are a world apart. Various streams of civilization and cultures that spread over a long distance were unable to climb an altitude of few hundred metres. The achievements of great civilizations reach these mountains imperfectly and with too many distortions. Consequently, mountains have always been considered a laggard in the achievement of human civilization. Continuous and persistent lag not only put these mountains at the receiving end of human achievements, but also subjected them to the processes of marginalisation and subordination. The domination of the mountain world is so complete that these have been used and constructed to meet the needs imposed by the world outside it. Himalayas in general and Uttaranchal Himalayas in particular are no exception to this.

Uttaranchal Himalayas have a chequered history of attaining prominence and disappearing into oblivion many times since the time of Vedas when it was first mentioned in the Hindu religious texts. Since then it has experienced many ups and downs, but the most significant changes experienced by this region were introduced by the British colonizers, and paradoxically these changes continue to exist even today with minor modifications.

It was the colonizers who introduced the process of spatial differentiation and transformed the processes of social stratification. Hill stations, cantonment towns, health resorts, etc. emerged as islands of development and modernisation in the midst of areas of deprivation and marginalisation. Most of these developed centres were located in the Lesser and Middle Himalayas. At the other extremes of the spectrum were the rural and tribal areas of Great and Trans-Himalayas that exhibited the ugly face of colonial rule. These areas emerged as proletarian reserves. Bhotias inhabiting the Greater Himalayas for most of the time of the year faced series of difficulties and hardships with the graduation of colonial rule. They were subject to a lot of restrictions and curtailment in their transhumance ways of life, which received a final blow after the Chinese aggression in 1962. Hereafter, the Bhotias have remained confined to Indian Himalayas only. Most of them migrated and settled into areas that were considered alien to the Bhotia ways of life so far. These, in turn, had secular repercussion on every sphere of the personality of the region. However, there was also a brighter side of all these developments. Uttaranchal Himalayas once again emerged as the centre stage of discourse cutting across different disciplines. Dr. Chittaranjan Dash is one of those scholars who ventured into one of the least treaded areas as far as scholarship in India is concerned. This book tries to record and analyse the impact of altitudes on the demographic structure of the Bhotias in the district of Pithoragarh.

This is a complex issue and it can be attempted from the point of environmental determinism as well as from social-ecology approach. Dr. Dash has placed his entire argument in favour of an interdependent organism-habitat relationship as against the one-sided approach adopted by the environmental determinism. It is an ensemble approach where changes in different attributes of demographic structure are placed in the explanatory discourses of altitudinal variations as an integral part of the high altitude ecology.

There are many highlights of the study, as every aspect of this sensitive yet complex problem needed a deep insight into the subject, and this book stands out as an example in the field of interdisciplinary studies. The stringent environmental settings of the Greater Himalayas have always been considered depressing as far human habitation is concerned. This book dispels such notions and brings out the argument in favour of the social, institutional and technological adjustment that the Bhotias have been able to articulate through their social ecology. Their tradition, food habits and social associatedness are all reflective of their adjustment and modification of their respective environment. These in turn, have resulted into demographic response like age and sex composition, survival level, fertility pattern, etc. The entire book presents an integrated argument and any one-line conclusion will amount to serious injustice to the scholarly efforts carried out by Dr. Dash, and the people under analytical discourses. To do justice to the scholar and theme under investigation, the book must be read in its entirety.

29 November 2004
New Delhi

Dr. B.S. Butola
Professor
CSRD, School of Social Sciences
Jawaharlal Nehru University

PREFACE

High altitude ecology poses a severe challenge for human adaptation. Since the work of Monge in 1942, an understanding of how people live and work in high altitudes have become a topic of scientific research. The principal objective of the present research work is to study the altitudinal differences in the demographic compositions of the Bhotia tribal people adapted to high and low altitude environments in the district of Pithoragarh in the Kumaon region of Uttaranchal Himalayas.

The present book is based on the empirical evidence gathered through fieldwork among the Bhotia tribe. The book incorporates eight chapters. Chapter 1 interrogates the concepts like social ecology, high altitude environment, demographic structure, etc. It outlines the human habitations in Himalayas, review of literature, Scheduled Tribes in Uttaranchal and scope of the book in the present context. Chapter 2 depicts an account of spatial ecology of the region and its land and people. It mentions the ethnographic profile of the Bhotia tribe and the state of their transition. Chapter 3 presents the anthropological episteme in the material and method. It highlights the sample survey, preparation of the interview schedule, fieldwork process, etc. It defines the demographic compositions, fertility measures, methods and statistical tools used in the book. Chapter 4 contexualises the attributes of demographic structure of the Bhotias. It includes age-sex compositions, family structure and marital status of the Bhotia tribe. Chapter 5 deals with the human resources such as education and occupation. It also presents the present economic status of the Bhotia tribe settled in the high and low altitudes of Uttaranchal Himalayas. Chapter 6 exposes the fertility pattern and the inner dynamics of high altitude ecology. It highlights the pregnancy history of the Bhotia women, mean value analysis, the survival level, fertility measures, etc. Chapter 7 exclusively deals with the fertility determinants, transcendence and immanence among the Bhotia community. It incorporates several biosocial aspects and their association with fertility. Chapter 8 presents the analytical discourses on the above matter in the form of critical summary, to conclude the book.

In coming up with this book, I owe thanks to a number of persons. First of all, my sincere regards are extended to the revered teachers Dr. (Mrs.) Jyotirmayee Kanungo, Professor of Anthropology, Utkal University and Dr. Govind Singh Saun, Deputy Director, Indian Council of Social Science Research, New Delhi who provided all academic and logistic support to carry out higher studies in High Altitude Tribal Demography.

Boundless regards are due for Dr. A. K. Kalla, Professor and Head, Department of Anthropology and Dean, Faculty of Science, University of Delhi and Dr. Balbir Singh Butola, Professor, Centre for the Study of Regional Development, School of Social Sciences, Jawaharlal Nehru University who showered knowledge and blessings on me. Their efforts have led to and shaped my academic acculturation.

I extend my gratitude to Prof. Aslam Mahmood, Chairperson and Dr. Sachidanand Sinha, Associate Professor, Centre for the Study of Regional Development, School of Social Sciences, Jawaharlal Nehru University and Dr. R. K. Pathak, Professor of Anthropology, Punjab University, Chandigarh. They generated academic inquisitiveness in me and went through the manuscript, and many aspects dealt in the book have been modified through a series of interactions and debates.

Friends are my resource, which is meaningless if not mobilised in personality and career building. Dr. Rajib Lochan Sahoo, Archivist cum Manager, CRDC, College of Agricultural Banking, Reserve Bank of India, Pune; Dr. Rajesh Dev, Lecturer in Political Science, Women's College, Shillong; Dr. Prasenjit Biswas, Reader in Philosophy, Assam University, Silchar; Dr. Sukalpa Bhattacharjee, Lecturer in English, North-Eastern Hill University, Shillong; Dr. Archana Srivastava, Research Associate and Mr. Debidatta Aurobinda Mahapatra, Senior

Research Scholar, School of International Studies, Jawaharlal Nehru University are among many others, with whom, I interacted without any hesitation in developing arguments in support of the textual and contextual formation of the book.

Parents are the most important persons in my life. The scope is expanded further to my younger brother Mr. Manasranjan Dashmishra, PhD Scholar, School of Economics, Devi Ahalya Viswavidyalaya, Indore (under the supervision of Prof. Ganesh Kawadia); only sister Mrs. Padmaja Sahoo and brother-in-law Dr. Rajib Lochan Sahoo who are the perennial source of inspiration for any success in my life. Narayan Padmamurty, my nephew, has an important role in life. I drew many theoretical concepts by observing and enjoying his infancy and childhood. Sangita, my wife, receives special credit by helping me in all aspects to bring out this book into the present form.

Special regards and affections are offered to Dr. Sugathan, a Philosopher and Freelancer, his wife Dr. Usha, Researsh Associate, School of International Studies, Jawaharlal Nehru University and their daughters Leenu and Anu. They being my neighbours have always encouraged and persuaded me.

I acknowledge the faculty, scholars and staff at the Centre for the Study of Regional Development, School of Social Sciences, Jawaharlal Nehru University and Department of Anthropology, Utkal University for providing me all academic and infrastructure support needed for taking up this volume.

It would be appropriate to acknowledge the Indian Council of Social Science Research, New Delhi for providing funds to carry out this kind of research on the people inhabiting one of the most remote altitudinal peripheries of Himalayas in India.

I express respect and sympathy to the people on whom I tested the academic queries. I apologise myself before the people for investigating and drawing information that are purely personal.

Last but not the least, I am very much obliged to Mr. Ashok Mittal, Managing Director, Concept Publishing Company, New Delhi for publishing this book. I am also thankful to the authors and researchers whose works and ideas I have used and critically analysed while doing my present humble academic and literary exercise.

30 November 2004
New Delhi

Dr. Chittaranjan Dash
Post Doctoral Fellow
Centre for the Study of Regional Development
School of Social Sciences
Jawaharlal Nehru University, New Delhi

CONTENTS

LIST OF COLOUR PLATES

(Between Page No. 104-105)

LIST OF FIGURES

LIST OF TABLES

1

SOCIAL ECOLOGY AND DEMOGRAPHIC STRUCTURE

Interpreting Social Ecology

Generally it is considered that tribal communities inhabit the inhospitable, difficult and isolated areas. Unlike non-tribal communities, they have a direct and perfect symbiotic relationship with their environment. The overwhelming concentration of tribes in the hilly, rugged and peripheral areas of a country like India also proves that tribal way of life with difficult terrain and inhospitable environment conditions have become synonymous with each other. Their life is a saga of constant adjustment to such environment. The harsh and unpredictable environment throws ever-increasing challenges before the tribes, which they have responded by adapting and adjusting to their environment through modification of their institutional, technological and biological attributes in a given environment. This book tries to understand the interrelations between the impacts of altitude and the demographic structure of the Bhotia tribal society. This issue can be approached through various angles. However, the approach of social ecology is preferred over others, as it places equal emphasis on the attributes of environment and human response in an interdependent and interactive framework.

Ecology is the study about the relations between organisms and their environments or of the organism-environment nexus, and has been used as an independent variable in the study of aspects of simple or tribal societies (Mencher, 1994:42).

Environment influences all organisms and the environmental characters are in turn expressed in the behavioural pattern of organisms. An intricate network of interactions binds up organisms with one another. Therefore, it is understood that ecology is a science, which studies the interaction between different organisms and their respective environments for the purpose of survival including reproduction.

Social ecology refers to the total interacting process of human being with the rest (whether organic or inorganic and living or non-living matters) of the environment. Human being is not just a social animal, but a society-creating animal, which has an identifying feature, *i.e.*, culture creation; for this reason, the human being is different from the rest of the species in the kingdom of *animalia*. Human needs are derived out of the long and continuous interaction with the nature. The rate of dependency is so high that the survival of human being without the help of others becomes a question. Therefore, the whole set of ecological aspects in the context of studying human being constitutes 'social ecology'. In other words, the study about the sum total of what human beings depend on the nature, both organic and inorganic materials, is known as 'social ecology.' It is true that, to a considerable extent, social facts can be adequately explained with reference to other social facts alone (Godelier, 1986:6). However, in many instances social facts can properly be understood in reference to the natural environment within which humans, like any other species, live, survive and reproduce.

While humans are unique among the earth's creatures in their elaborately developed cultures, they do not stand above or apart from nature. The ecological infrastructure powerfully conditions the evolution and direction of human economic life, political relations, social structure and ideology. At the same time, human intervention itself reshapes the natural environment in its own image (Guha, 1994:5). Social ecology, then, rests on the awareness of the interdependence between the biophysical and socio-cultural domains. Social ecology also shapes the socio-cultural and reproductive behaviour of the human beings.

Anthropologists studying small societies have traditionally exhibited a greater interest in ecological questions, relying as they do on methods of intensive field work among peasants and tribal cultures so obviously dependent on nature. Moreover, in-depth and emphatic studies of the social institutions of small societies have led anthropologists to develop a healthy respect for the ecological sensibilities of local communities. Thus, anthropologists have documented in great detail and in a variety of regions, the indigenous knowledge systems, conservation mechanisms and adaptations to the biophysical world of tribal and peasant societies. They have also studied the ways in which a particular society's adaptation to the nature and its influence on internal and external social relations are carried out (Guha, 1994: 8).

Human ecology is concerned with sociological problems in their fullest breadth. It overlaps, therefore, all the spheres of learning that concern the social life of human beings. The interaction of population and environment is seen as culminating in a system of relationship between differentiated parts, giving the population its unit character and enabling it to maintain its identity (Howley, 1968:330). 'Cultural Ecology' is the study of the processes by which a society adapts to its environment. Its principal problem is to determine whether these adaptations initiate internal social transformations or evolutionary change. It however, analyses these adaptations, in relation with other processes of change. Its method requires examination of the interaction of societies and social institutions with one another and with the natural environment (Steward, 1968:337). Although, the culture of any society constitutes a holistic system in which technology, economics, social and political structure, religion, language, values, and other features are closely interrelated, but the different components of a culture are not similarly affected by ecological adaptations. Societies change through a series of structural and functional transformations (Steward, 1968:341).

In this context, it can be discussed that the high altitude[1] ecology poses a severe challenge for human adaptation. The availability of the most vital elements like Oxygen is reduced at high altitudes. The stress at high altitude includes hypoxia,[2] high solar radiation, severe cold, aridity, rough terrain, limited nutritional base, high wind, etc. (Clegg *et al.*, 1970:488-91; Mazess, 1975:168; Moore and Regensteiner, 1983:286). These physical elements collectively determine the impact of environment on individuals and populations (Baker, 1969:1149-50 and 1978:317). Acclimatization to high altitude ecology reaches its highest degree of efficiency in the human beings born there and raised in such environment. It is important to consider that all adaptive mechanisms among the native residents of high altitudes show a harmonious integration and have attained a physiological 'steady state', a condition that is not found in newcomers, even after a prolonged exposure (Hurtado, 1964:1). The human habitations in the Himalayas[3] are spread over different altitudes. The high altitude habitations have arid or semi-arid climate, and settlements here are very small in size compared to the low altitude ones. The settlements down the hills are either agglomerated or dispersed type and situated on the hill slopes or on the valleys. The size of the settlements at low altitude is quite bigger than the high altitude settlements (Raha, 1987:xix). The Figure 1.1 shows world's major areas of elevation above 2500 m from the mean sea level (MSL).

The population considered the fittest, is the one, when it contributes minimum required number of offspring to the next generation. The genetic as well as the cultural survival of a population varies with the type of environment it is exposed to. The net adaptive forces work in favour of the population structure, when there is a perfect adjustment of the population with the environment. The present book outlines the nature of interrelationship between the high altitude ecology and the population structure. The population structure is studied through its age-sex structure, gender and dependency ratio, bio-social events like menarche, marriage and menopause, fertility and mortality. The social conditions of human being like educational attainment, marital status, economic prosperity, etc. are also taken into account.

In all societies, reproduction is imbued with social significance and cultural meaning. Adult social identity is

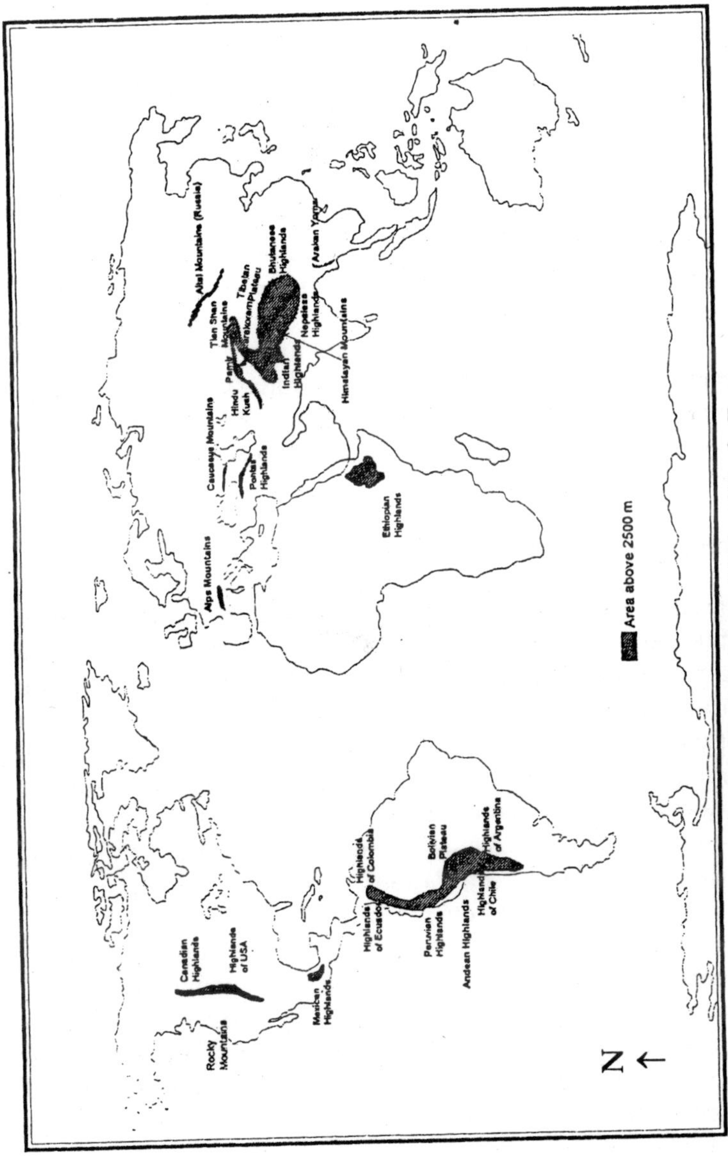

Fig. 1.1: World's Major High Altitude Zones

inevitably tied up with issues of marriage and parenting. There are negative outcomes for female in terms of their reproduction (*e.g.*, poor health from repeated childbearing, increased risk of death for high parity mothers). In some societies, changes associated with the modern world have eroded traditional practices that allowed birth spacing. Family planning programmes have tended to operate very much in terms of a western model of conjugal pair whose decision-making is a rational expression of self-interest. Women do not live as social isolates; they belong to families, kin groups, status groups, classes, villages, nations, all of which encompass power relations that may impact on fertility, directly or indirectly. Women in societies with patrilineal kinship, who live in their husbands' families, will be very differently empowered in their domestic relations than women in matrilineal and uxorilocal societies (Robinson, 2001:47-8).

Demographic Structure: An Overview

A French mathematician Achille Guillard first used the term demography in 1855. In Greek, the term 'demography' means 'description of the people'. However, demography is the empirical, statistical and mathematical analysis of human populations. According to Hauser and Duncan (1972:1-3), demography is the study of the size, territorial distribution and composition of population, changes therein and the components of such changes, which may be identified as natality, mortality, territorial movement (migration), and social mobility (change of status). For Bradley (1996:319) 'demography is an interdisciplinary, policy-oriented science concerned with understanding and measuring population change'. Moreover, demography tries to explore the wider spectrum of human communities and in doing so the demographers lay special emphasis on the relative measurement of size, composition and distribution of population through time and space (Sarkar, 1993:299-300).

In the late seventies and the eighties, anthropology began to be strongly influenced by demography. The underlying objective, however, was not to reduce anthropology to statistical demography but to understand the demographic variables leading to changes in facets of the social structure (organisation) of preindustrial societies (Srivastava, 1994:434). With the tremendous growth of historical demography in the past 30 years, several useful bridges have been built between anthropology and population studies. The academic boundaries between the two subjects have increasingly come in for reconsideration (Kreager, 1993:334). Moreover, Hauser and Duncan (1972:6-10) made distinction between 'demographic analysis and population studies'. Demographic analysis is confined to the study of components of population variation and change. Population studies, on the other hand, are concerned not only with population variables but also with relationships between population changes and other variables like social, economic, political, biological, genetic, geographical, and the like. The early demographers did not limit themselves to improving census and vital registrations; they outlined a programme for collecting community level data (a 'statistique ethnographique' as they called it) which, they argued, was necessary to making sense of changing trends in births and deaths (Kreager, 1993:34-5).

Demographic structure of any population group is key to all population related disciplines, which not only feeds with quantitative but also qualitative information. The demographic composition describes well the population situation at a particular point of time and place, and the different variables affect the population dynamics, which are responsible for a community to determine its stability and sustainability. Though birth and death are important patterns in affecting the demographic structure of a population, particularly the size, birth is more important over death as an adding factor. The picture of birth in demography is represented by the concept of fertility, which is essentially the biological one but it varies in different living conditions. Therefore, human fertility constitutes an essential aspect of the studies in modern sociology and demography.

Fertility, prior to the onset of the modernity, was generally uncontrolled. 'Traditional populations accept children, whatever God or fate has given them'. But with the advancement of time and development of science and technology the attitude towards family size and the approach to the study of fertility pattern has changed, because now it does not remain as a normal biological process, but is considered affected by different variables like social, cultural, economic, particularly family planning or effectiveness of contraception and environmental conditions. Depending on these variables, different models have been developed on the proximate determinants of fertility and the most influential model is the Bongaart's model (Wood, 1990:217-8). Keeping in view the importance of the fertility in demographic structure at the present juncture, there is an urgent need to study the demographic structure, focusing the fertility pattern of the population groups in India at micro-level for better understanding, and particularly of those populations inhabiting at different altitudes for description of the population situation in varying environmental conditions.

Altitudinal Demographic Studies: A Review

The first kind of research work on high altitude goes to Monge's effort (1942:81-2) observing difficulties in reproduction experienced by Spanish women at Andean high altitudes. Since his observation, an understanding of how people live and work in high altitude has become a topic of scientific research and a plethora of works based on altitudes came up from different scholars all over the world. Yet enough is to be known to suggest the influence of altitudes on demographic structure. However, some studies are before us to examine. The number of males born compared to females is reported higher while the mortality of male infants and children is much higher, leaving an adult population with an excess of females, which means that females outnumber males during adulthood (Baker, 1978:319-22; Weitz, *et al.*, 1978:185). It was reported on high altitude Sherpas of Upper Khumba in Nepal that at birth, females continue outnumbering males all through and at least unto the age of 14 years (Gupta, 1980:104-5). The study in Himalayas as such shows that age-sex structure is insignificant between high and low altitudes (Gupta, 1980:104). Some others found a constriction at the base of age-sex pyramid indicating a decline in fertility and lesser number of younger individuals in the Sherpas of Upper Khumbu in Nepal (Gupta *et al.*, 1987:102-2). The population structure seems to be affected more by culture than by features of the physical environment (Weitz *et al.*, 1978:194).

Sex ratio (females/males × 100)[4] at birth has strikingly been low in high-landers as compared to low landers (Baker 1969:1151 and 1978:320-1; Weitz *et al.*, 1978:184-5; Bangham and Sacherer, 1980:325). However, the sex ratio has been found increasing during early years of life due to differential mortality at high altitude (Baker and Dutt, 1972:370-2; Weitz *et al.*, 1978:194, Dutt, 1980:109-12). With the exception for early childhood, the trend of mortality as observed for infants continues in the later childhood periods, resulting in equal sex ratio by adulthood (Baker, 1969:163).

Masculinity proportion is the percentage of males in a population. As some researchers reported that the sex ratio at birth at high altitude was found low compared to low altitude. It may, therefore, be said that the masculinity proportion will show higher value, as it is a measure of population composition. It thus appeared to be more old age people among the Andean high-landers than in the general population (Baker, 1978:320). Contrary to this, highland Bods in the Western Himalayas have a young profile with less old people (Prakash, 1990:50-60). As the age composition differs in the reported research works, the index of aging (*i.e.* the relative numbers of older people in the population) also varies accordingly. The index of aging is low in those populations in which a high proportion of people are below 15 years of age (Chachra and Bhasin, 1998:413). The dependency of population is based on the fact that every member of a society is a consumer and only some members are producers (Thomson and Lewis, 1965:11). The age group of 15 to 59 years is considered economically active (Hauser, 1976:60-61) and the dependency ratio is calculated in relation to this active age group.

Menarche and menopause are two important biological events that are greatly responsible for the overall fertility (Chatterjee, 1994: 271-2) of a population. In case of women the active reproductive period begins with the onset of menarche and continues till the attainment of menopause. These two biological events are greatly influenced by race, heredity and environment (Valsik *et al.*, 1973:99-103), nutritional intake and sociological factors that include awareness, education and economic conditions (Satyanarayan and Naidu, 1979:163-5) and social origin (Pattnaik, 1985:3). It has been reported that the two biological factors responsible for lowering and controlling fertility are late menarche and early menopause (Frisch, 1975:19-22).

Age at menarche is delayed at high altitude females as compared to low altitude females (Clegg, 1978:77-8; Bangham and Sacherer, 1980:324-5; Beall 1983:365; Laurenson *et al.*, 1985:66-7). Retarded age of menarche at high altitude has been casually related to low oxygen pressure (Weitz *et al.*, 1978:179). A delayed onset of menarche can potentially reduce completed fertility rate, as age at menarche is a biological indicator of the beginning of the reproductive span. It has been observed that age at menopause is only marginally influenced, if at all, by the stress of high altitude environment and age at menopause does not influence completed fertility rate (Beall, 1983:368-9).

Age at marriage is a social indicator of the beginning of the reproductive span. But it is the birth of the first child that makes the real beginning of fertility. Some of the investigators have reported that there is higher mean age at first childbirth in high altitude (Laurenson *et al.*, 1985:65-67), whereas other researchers observed that the mean age at first childbirth does not vary greatly with altitude (Abelson *et al.*, 1974:24-26).

The idea of correlating fertility and altitude was first reported by Stycos (1963:257) and then the relationship between altitude and fertility was demonstrated by James (1966:97-101), who found that this variable was a more powerful explanation of differences in fertility than any other variable and he suggested that the hypoxic effect of high altitude resulted in reduced fertility. Both mean number of pregnancies and live births are significantly lower in the woman at high altitude (Kashiwazaki *et al.*, 1988:836), whereas the observation of Basu *et al.* (1979:144) is contradictory to this finding, *i.e.*, the mean number of live births and child/woman ratio are higher in high altitude. However, mean number of survival and total fertility rates are reduced at high altitude (Gupta, 1980:108). The study carried out by Parkash and Malik (1990:176) shows a clear-cut difference between high and low altitude Bods, where almost all the values of fertility measures, such as crude birth rate, general fertility rate, total fertility rate, completed family size, mean number of children and child/woman ratio are found higher for the high altitude natives than the low altitude counterparts. The difference in number of live births is related to socio-cultural factors, which varies with altitude (Stycos, 1963:267-70). The use of reproductive life histories together with socio-economic and cultural data allows a more complete examination of factors affecting fertility (De Jong, 1970:114-9). The low fertility of the population at high altitude is partly due to the interaction between social factors that delay the age at marriage and those that promote nulliparity. Both these factors function to maintain a large pool of woman of marriageable age, and voluntary celibacy (as Buddhist nuns of highland Nepalese groups) is common enough to significantly reduce the reproductive capacity of the population (Goldstein, 1976:230-3).

Recent observations cast doubt on the single factor concept, particularly with respect to fertility, showing that the debilitating effects on reproduction are not simply due to hypoxia but also because of ethnic and socio-economic factors (Goldstein *et al.*, 1983:45-7). Studies suggested that Tibetan populations generally have high fertility at high altitude compared to other Tibetan populations living at moderate altitude (Goldstein, 1981:721-2) and higher fertility among the high altitude Bods than the low altitude counterparts in Western Himalayas (Parkash and Malik, 1990:175). The direct effect of hypoxia reducing fertility in the Andean and Eastern Himalayan populations has also been called into question by the contradictory findings (Goldstein *et al.*, 1983:28-30) and the issue is controversial (Abelson, 1984:702-3; Goldstein *et al.*, 1984:419-23, 1984a:703-5 and 1984b:996-7). Hence, the relative contributions of these factors and of hypoxic altitude to reproduction remain unclear (Kashiwazaki, 1988:839-43). Moreover, fertility is affected by a number of factors including education, income, dietary habits, occupation and practice of family planning methods.

Human Habitation in Himalayas

Ever since the dawn of civilization in India, the socio-cultural history of the land is replete with references to the Himalayas. History is eloquent that hordes of diverse ethno-linguistic communities crossed over the Himalayan ranges into the sub-continent turning it into a land of multiple socio-ethnic characters. Socio-cultural norms and ways of life having their origin in or beyond the Himalayas have influenced the people's life patterns especially the religious system of this land from the earliest times to the present day (Mahanta, 1997:3-7).

The Himalayas, a complex mountain system in southern Asia, containing the highest peaks in the world and one of the youngest ranges of mountains, is at the same time the most expansive. The main range, which lies between the valley of Indus on the west and the unexplored gorges of Brahmaputra on the east, covers mainly Pakistan, India, Nepal and Bhutan. Among them, India bears more than 60 per cent of the Himalayan range. Himalaya is a Sanskrit word meaning, 'abode of snow' (Carter, 1992:200-1). Figure 1.2 shows the geographical location of the Himalayas. The Indian Himalayan region extending over 2,500 km from north-west to north-east covers 11 states, *viz.* Jammu and Kashmir and Himachal Pradesh in the Western Himalayas; Kumaon and Garhwal divisions of Uttaranchal in Central Himalayas; and in the Eastern Himalayas as Darjeeling district of West Bengal, Sikkim, Arunachal Pradesh, Nagaland, Manipur, Mizoram, Tripura and Meghalaya.[5] According to Census 2001, the Himalayan region occupies 12.6 per cent of the total geographical area of the country and the total human population in this area is 3.7 per cent

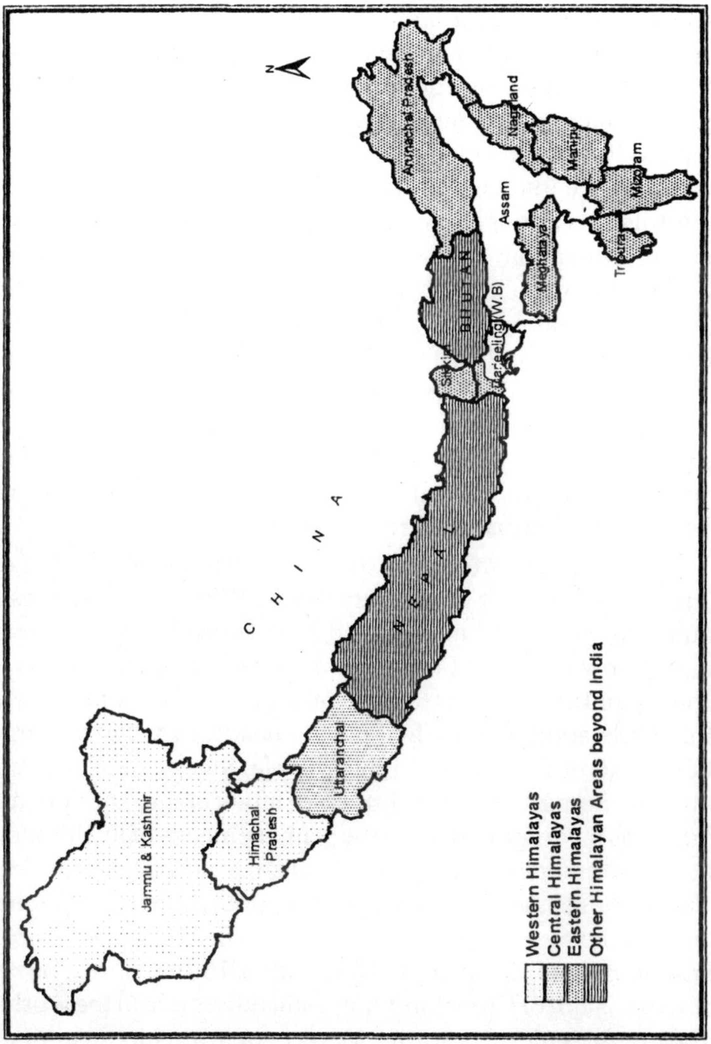

Fig. 1.2: The Himalayas: Geographical Location (India)

of the country's total population. Appendix 1 shows the area and human populations in different Himalayan states.

The vast mountainous tract of the Himalayas in India has acted as a shelter for a large number of ethnic groups with diverse culture, identity and social formation. They master the difficulties created by the inhospitable environment of the rugged, unkempt and mountainous terrain of the Himalayas. They dwell and adapt themselves accordingly for their survival. The difference in their culture exists not only in their material life but also in various other aspects of their life such as economy, social organization, political activities, religious beliefs and practices and even in their value-judgement (Raha, 1987:xix). The total Himalayan range has been broadly divided into Western, Central and Eastern Himalayas on the basis of its geo-cultural diversity. The Western Himalayan region is known for a spectacular integration of Hinduism, Buddhism and Islam; the Central Himalayas for a dominant Hindu culture based on stringent caste principles and the region of Eastern Himalayas is known for its tribal culture (Samal, 1993:87).

These people are found living in varied ecological and cultural environment of the Himalayas. While some of these ethnic groups live in almost arid high altitude regions that remain snow clad for at least five months in a year, some live in the foothill areas amidst thick vegetaiton with heavy monsoon rain. While some people live on the beautiful valleys, some others live on the rugged, inhospitable, steep slopes of the mountain. Some follow transhumance mode of life. Though the Himalayas have agriculture as the primary means of livelihood, others lead a mode of life with pastoralism or animal husbandry as the source of livelihood; others have various other occupations like trade, cottage industry, craft, business, service, etc. Here, while some are Buddhists, some are Hindus, some have embraced Islam or Christianity, and still others live in the world of their own deities and spirits. Many people are monogamous but some practise polyandry and some follow polygyny. Thus, no doubt, the Himalayas provide a very formidable and interesting field for anthropological research (Raha, 1995: xviii-xix).

The human habitations in the Himalayas are spread over different altitudes. The high altitude habitations have an arid or semi-arid climate. The vegetation growth here is quite low. People inhabiting in the high altitude zone include the Monpa, the Khamba, the Ramos, the Pailibe, the Boojar Bori, the Bokar, the Tagin, the Sulung, and some others in Arunachal Pradesh. In Sikkim, they are mostly the Bhutia. In Kumaon and Garhwal areas of Uttaranchal they are Bhotias and Anwals residing in high altitude valleys. In Jammu and Kashmir the Bodh or Bhot, the Argon, the Dard, the Mon, the Gara, the Beda and others of Leh and Zanskar areas and the Shia Muslims of Kargil are high altitude dwellers. The Bodh of Spiti, the Zad of Kinnaur, and the Pangwala of Pangi valley (Chamba) belong to the high altitude zones of Himachal Pradesh.

A large number of tribal groups reside in the low altitude zones. In Eastern Himalayas they are the Aka, the Apatani, the Miniang, the Sherdukpen, the Pasi, the Padam, the Nocte, the Wancho and others in Arunachal Pradesh; the Kachari, the Ahom and others in Assam; the Ao, the Angami, the Konyak, the Chakhesang, the Kuki and others in Nagaland; the Mao, the Maram, the Tangkhul, the Sema, the Simte and others in Manipur; the Mizo and others in Mizoram; the Tripuri, the Uchai, the Noatia, the Riang and others in Tripura; the Garo, the Khasi, the Jaintia, the Synteng, the Pnar, the War, the Lyngngam and others in Meghalaya; and tribal (the Bhutia and Lepcha) and caste groups (the Nepalese) in Sikkim and Darjeeling district of West Bengal. In the Central Himalayas mostly the Hindu Garhwali and Kumaoni caste groups and tribes like the Jaunsari, the Raji, the Bhotia, the Boksa and the Tharu live besides Muslims. In the Western Himalayas, there are Muslims, various Hindu castes and some non-Mongoloid tribes (Raha, 1987:xx-xxi).

Bhotias, Bhotiyas, Bhutiyas, Bhots, Bods, Bodhs, Bots and Bottos are labels ascribed to a number of tribes residing on the tough terrains of Himalayas along the Indo-Tibetan border (Kashyap, 1998:35-6). Some are settled at low altitude and some have high altitude settlements.[6] Etymology of the label Bhotia is as 'Bod, the native name for Tibet, corrupted by people of India into Bhot, has given rise to the name Bhotiya to the border tribes between the two countries'. As a result, there are certain tribal groups labelled as Bhotia. Table 1.1 shows the listing of Bhotia tribes in different states.

Table 1.1: Bhotias in Different States

Year of Declaration	*State*	*Communities/Tribes Listed*
1950	West Bengal	Bhutia, Sherpa, Toto, Dukpa, Kagatey, Tibetan and Yoma
1950	Tripura	Bhutiya
1950	Himachal Pradesh	Bhots/Bodhs
1967	Uttar Pradesh (Now Uttaranchal)	Bhotia
1978	Sikkim	Bhutias (including Chambipa, Dopthapa, Dukpa, Kagatey, Sherpa, Tibetan, Tromoph and Yolmo
1989	Jammu and Kashmir	Bot and Botto

Source : Kashyap, 1998: 35-6.

Moreover, the high altitude settlements are very small in size. The people are mostly mongoloid and depend more on pastoralism, but less on agriculture. They lead a nomadic or transhumance mode of life. Cultivation is done on small patches of plots and irrigation mostly depends on snowfall as water sources like springs and streams are very few and rainfall is insignificant. With the development of modern communication and transport systems, they are now coming in regular contact with the people down the hills and plains; thereby, the long preserved traditions have been indicating a sign of rapid change. On the other hand, the settlements, down the hills are either agglomerated or dispersed type and situated on the hill slopes or on the valleys. The size of the settlements is quite bigger than the high altitude settlements. The inhabitants in this part of the

Himalayas are mostly agriculturists and some tribals from the Eastern Himalayas practise shifting cultivation, while a few others are hunters and gatherers. The people inhabiting hills have larger interaction with the people of the plains and this has compelled them to imbibe 'the culure of plains' (Raha, 1987:xxii).

Scheduled Tribes in Uttaranchal

The term 'tribe' is a magical word from whose enchantment anthropologists have been unable to break free despite their better judgment. English usage mingled terms like 'tribe', 'kindred', and 'lineage' quite indiscriminately (Southall, 1996:1329) while the British definition tended to regard 'tribe' as primitive and backward community (Dasgupta, 1997:99-100). There is a tendency to define a tribe in terms of a common territory, a common dialect, cultural homogeneity and the practice of marrying within the group. However, the Constitution of India does not define a tribe, excepting by way of listing some communities 'primitive' and 'backward' as 'Scheduled Tribes' in accordance with the provisions of Article 342 of the Constitution that came into force in 1950. According to the Census of India, there are 650 Scheduled Tribes for which data have been published for various states and union territories. This total of 650 does not mean that there are 650 different Scheduled Tribes (STs) in the country. Many of them have been counted more than once as they occur in different state lists (Sachchidananda and Prasad, 1996:xx). However, according to Anthropological Survey of India, there are 426 tribes and 165 sub-tribes in India (Dasgupta, 1997:99).

The scheduling of tribes[7] started in independent India with the passage of Scheduled Tribe (Constitution Order) in the year 1950. It however, ignored the existence of any Scheduled Tribe in Uttar Pradesh till 1967. The Constitution of India notified, on 24 June 1967, the communities, *viz.*, Bhotia, Buksa, Jaunsari, Raji and Tharu (Kashyap, 1998:33) as Scheduled Tribes of the state. Among the five scheduled tribes, Buksa and Raji are two primitive tribal groups. Tharu is the largest tribe (41.7 per cent) followed by Jaunsari (29.8 per cent), Buksa (14.1 per cent), Bhotia (13.9 per cent) and Raji (0.5 per cent). According to the Census 2001, the state of Uttaranchal has 256,129 tribal population (3 per cent of population belong to the Scheduled Tribes), which accounts just 0.3 per cent of the total Scheduled Tribe population of the country. The Kumaon Himalayan region has 138,021 tribal population (53.9 per cent of the ST population of the State) that accounts for 2.5 per cent of the total population of the region. The sex ratio of ST population of the state of Uttarachal is 970, which is well below that of the Kumaon region (981).

In lieu of the conclusion, social ecology connotes to the total interacting process of human beings with the rest of the environment, whether organic or inorganic and living or non-living. In other words, the whole set of ecological aspects in the context of studying human beings is 'social ecology'. The ecological infrastructure powerfully conditions, the evolution and direction of human economic life, political relations, social structure and ideology. Social ecology even shapes the socio-cultural and reproductive behaviour of the human beings. Anthropologists studying small societies have traditionally exhibited a greater interest in ecological questions, relying on the methods of intensive fieldwork among peasants and tribal cultures dependent on nature. They have also been studying the ways in which a particular society's adaptation to the nature influences its internal and external social relations including the childbearing process and survival of the population. In fact, a population is considered the fittest, when it contributes minimum required number of offspring to the coming generation. Therefore, social ecology relates in all its dimension and scope to each and every affair of human beings in the social and physical world.

The high altitude possesses a severe challenge for human adaptation. The stress at high altitude includes hypoxia or tension due to the lack of proper amount of Oxygen, severe cold, aridity, rough terrain, limited nutritional base, high wind, etc. High altitude zones are those zones, where the elevation is above 2,500 m from the mean sea level. Below this line, the low altitude zones begin. In Himalayas, the human habitations are spread over different altitudes. The high altitude habitations have an arid or semi-arid climate and settlements are very small in size compared to the low altitude. The entire belt of Himalayas from east to the west is occupied by many tribal groups (41 per cent). The nature of human settlement varies from region to region. The demographic studies try to explore the information about the size, composition and distribution of population through time and space. The structure of population depends on the fertility, mortality and migration, which collectively depend on the biophysical nature of the environment. As fertility is a contributory factor to the population structure, this is imbibed with socio-cultural significance and meaning. Both the nature of the environment and the level of development of a society determine the level of fertility. The socio-cultural parameters, *viz.* education, economy, occupation structure, etc., are some of the determinants, which influence the fertility and demographic structure of a population. Therefore, in this context, the efforts have been made to understand the demographic composition of the Bhotia tribe in high and low altitudes of Uttaranchal Himalayas.

This book incorporates many perspectives and ideas that are relevant in the field of population and society. The classification and interpretation of the Bhotia populations on the basis of high and low altitudes remove the academic confusion of high altitude depressing effect on demographic events like fertility, and it brings clarity on the socio-cultural and economic dimensions and their effect on fertility of these Himalayan populations. It explores the ideas about the settlement pattern of the Bhotia tribe in high and low altitudes. It brings out the survival level of the Bhotia populations adapted to Uttaranchal Himalayas. This approach not only widens the vision and understanding of the readers on these aspects, but it would also engage the planners and policy makers in re-describing their findings in a new light.

Notes

1. There is no such pinpoint definition or answer to exactly demarcate the 'high' altitude from the 'low'. However, most individuals experience some high altitude effects at altitudes of 2,500 m and over; and for the purpose of describing the effects of altitude, the '2,500 m contour line' may be taken as a general divider between 'high' areas of land as opposed to 'low' (Pawon and Jest, 1978: 17-8).
2. Although all high altitude environments have in common a reduced barometric pressure, and hence reduced partial pressure of oxygen, that means, the percentage of Oxygen in the ambient air is the same at high altitude as it is at the sea level, but the barometric pressure, which depends upon the molecular concentration of the air, decreases with increase in altitude. This, in turn, means that the partial pressure of Oxygen in the ambient air at high altitude is reduced. Otherwise, this is the decrease in Oxygen availability or hypoxia. For example, reduced atmospheic presure at 1,500 m is 630 mm/Hg; at 2,500 m 570 mm/Hg; at 3,000 m 520 mm/Hg; at 3,500 m 493 mm/Hg; and at 4,500 m, near the upper limit of human habitation, it is 430 mm/Hg. The partial pressure of Oxygen in inspired air is proportionately reduced, ranging from 149 mm at sea level to 80 mm at 4,500 m (Clegg *et al.*, 1970: 488-90).
3. On the question whether the word Himalaya (singular) or Himalayas (plural) should be used, one official report agrees that it would be appropriate to use the plural form—hence 'Himalayas'—as it covers a wide range of areas from Ladhakh to North-Eastern region including many distinctive socio-cultural boundaries (Planning Commission, 1993:1). However, in case of Uttaranchal the plural form, Himalayas and in case of Kumaon the singular form, Himalaya have been used as the latter covers a small portion of the total Himalayas and maintains a cultural uniqueness.
4. In the texts of many authors, sex ratio is mentioned as males/females × 100. For the purpose of comparison, sex ratio is described here as females/males × 100.
5. Geologically, Meghalaya is an extension of Deccan Plateau in the Northeast separated by Yamuna fault. But on the basis signature on the surface, relief, climate, vegetation and more importantly economy and culture it is considered as a part of Himalayas. Moreover, its proximity to the Himalayan mountain system too accounts for the prevalence of characteristics of Himalayan environment here.
6. In Uttaranchal the altitudinal zones are an important component of ecological setting. It is particularly relevant in case of the Bhotia tribes, who have traditionally inhabited the valleys and higher ridges of Middle and Greater Himalayan ranges. The Bhotias represent a

synthesis of time and space, meaning thereby, the Bhotias move to the valleys with the onset of autumn season and they move to summer pastures (*Bugyals*) in Greater Himalayas in the summer. Thus, the life cycle of Bhotias revolves between the valleys and the *Bugyals* when Mercury fluctuates. This has significant impact on the demographic structure, social customs and traditions.

7. There is a conceptual ambiguity about the tribe and Scheduled Tribe. Census of India has two categories of identifying or categorizing the Scheduled Tribes. The first category indicates the people as Scheduled Tribes and the second category refers to those people live in the Scheduled Areas. The communities or castes living in the Scheduled Areas of Himachal Pradesh are considered the Scheduled Tribes. When these people move from Himachal to Jammu and Kashmir, they are not included in the ST categories. As opposed to this in the North-Eastern states except Assam and Tripura people living in the Scheduled Areas are included in the ST category except the non-tribals. Furthermore, the ST people who are migrated to tea plantation areas in Assam from Central India are not included in the ST categories.

2

SPATIAL ECOLOGY OF THE REGION
LAND AND PEOPLE

Uttaranchal State

The creation of the new state of Uttaranchal has practically fulfilled the political dream of the local people after a prolonged struggle. One could observe a clear-cut cultural dichotomy between the Uttar Pradesh plains and the Uttaranchal hills. On November 9, 2000 the new state became fully operational. Uttaranchal consists of the parts of Central Himalayas, which have been carved out from the former state of Uttar Pradesh. It has a well-recognized geographical and socio-cultural unit. According to the Census 2001, it covers a geographical area of 53,483 sq. km inhabiting 8,489,349 persons with a density of 159 persons per sq. km. The state of Uttaranchal is bound by the neighbouring countries like Nepal in the east and Tibet in the north, Himachal Pradesh in the west and Uttar Pradesh in its south. Uttaranchal is one of the 28 Indian states, lying between 28° 44′ and 31° 29′ north latitude and 77° 35′ and 81° 2′ east longitude. With the two administrative units of Garhwal and Kumaon commissionaries, the area includes 13 districts, namely Uttarkashi, Chamoli, Rudraprayag, Pauri Garhwal, Tehri Garhwal, Dehradun and Hardwar in Garhwal administrative division, and Nainital, Almora, Champawat, Pithoragarh, Bageswar and Udham Singh Nagar in the Kumaon administrative division. These two divisions are also marked by cultural and linguistic differentiation along with marked developmental pace. The Figure 2.1 shows the political geography of Uttaranchal.

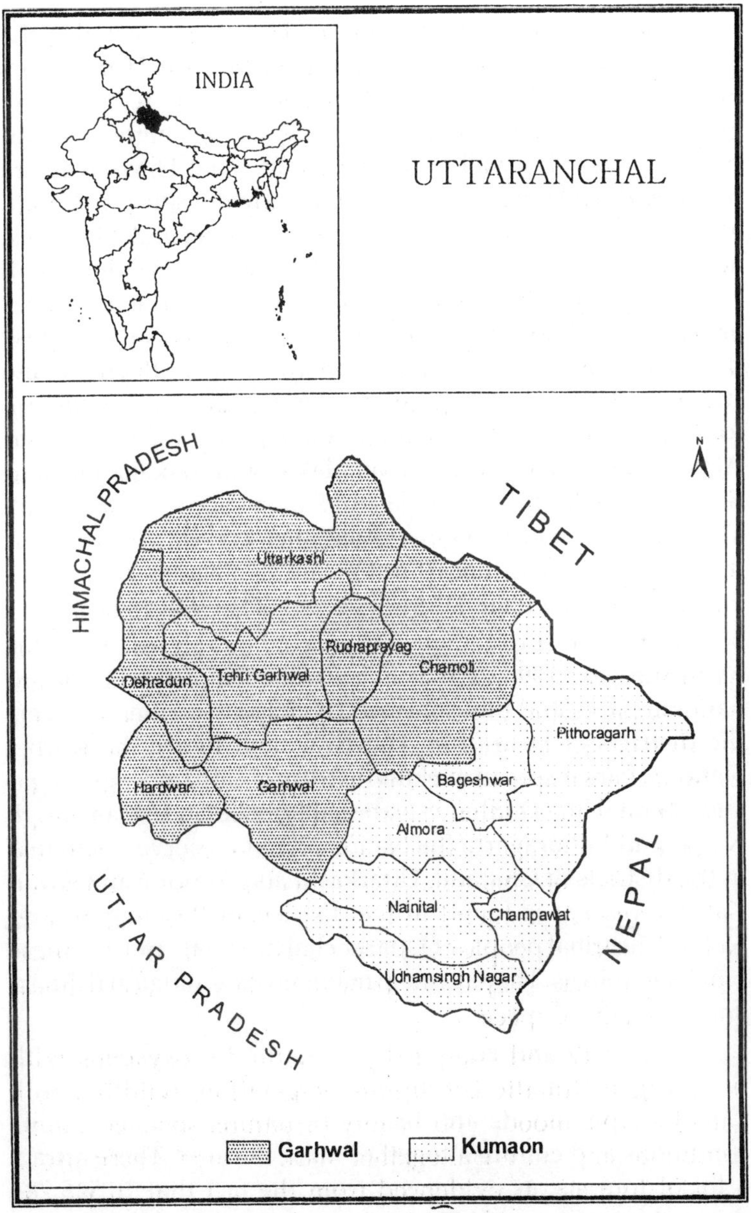

Fig. 2.1: Uttaranchal

The physiographic division of Himalayas includes the Trans-Himalayas, Great Himalayas, Middle Himalayas, Siwaliks, Doons, *Bhabar* and *Tarai* regions. There are many perennial rivers, which open from the glaciers of higher reaches of Himalayas. The valleys in the Uttaranchal Himalayas are fertile and well irrigated. Hence, these are densely populated. Most of the urban centres have come up after independence across the river valleys. Uttaranchal is also famous for most of the confluences (*prayags*) of the rivers. These confluence places are considered holy places in Hindu mythology. Some of these important places are known as *Devprayag* (the confluence of the two important rivers Bhagirathi and Alakananda), *Rudraprayag* (of Mandakini and Alakananda), *Karanprayag* (of Pindar and Alakananda), *Nandprayag* (of Mandakini and Alakananda) and *Bishnuprayag* (of Bishnuganga and Saraswati, *i.e.*, Swetganga). There are many more religious places such as Kedarnath (famous for Lord Shiva), Badrinath (Lord Vishnu), Gangotri, Yamunotri, Panchachuli (see Plate 1), Aum Parvat (see Plate 2), etc.

In the forest coverage, Uttaranchal has almost 3,498,400 ha in the year 1998-99 that helps to develop five important national parks and bio-reserves. The Rajaji bio-reserve covers the districts of Dehradun, Hardwar, and Pauri; the Korbet National Park is spread over the districts of Udham Singh Nagar and Nainital; the Dudhawa National Park lies in Udham Singh Nagar and Pithoragarh; the Nandadevi bio-reserve is situated in the districts of Chamoli, Uttarkashi and Almora; and Sarju-Kali bio-reserve is found in the districts of Pithoragarh and Nepal. The tribal people of Uttaranchal dominate most of these bio-reserve areas. They also help maintain the ecological richness and diversity of species.

A variety and complexity of natural ecosystems with unique geo-climatic conditions, vegetation, wildlife, soil, kaleidoscopic moods and beauty of nature, socio-economic conditions and culture altogether mark the area. These attract a lot of tourists, as evidenced from the fact that 10,548,784 domestic tourists and 54,701 foreign tourists visited Uttaranchal during 2000-01. This not only enhances the government purse but also gives a lot of employment and exposure to the native people. The local products like handicrafts and other items are sold to the outsiders. This way, it gives rise to make the local items popular among other communities. Uttaranchal, being a source of major religious river systems and a place of many pilgrimages of Hindus, attract a lot of outsiders every year. Uttaranchal has been found important not just being a place of pilgrimages, but it touches two international boundaries. From this point of view, the Government of India has included Uttaranchal in the special status category. Through numerous passes, from time immemorial, it has provided socio-cultural, trade and commercial linkages for India and Tibet with other parts of Asia.

The Kumaon Himalaya

The present-day Kumaon Himalayan region includes six districts, *viz.*, Almora, Nainital, Udham Singh Nagar, Bageshwar, Champawat and Pithoragarh. The Kumaon Himalaya is situated approximately 28° 44′ and 30° 49′ north latitude and 78° 43′ and 81° 2′ east longitude. The total area of the Kumaon region is 21,035 sq. km populated by 3,565,383 individuals. The density of population of the region is 170 individuals per sq. km. It is bound by Tibet in the north, Nepal in the east, Uttar Pradesh in the south and Pauri Garhwal and Chamoli districts of Garhwal Himalaya in the west.

The geographical boundaries of the present-day Kumaon (or Kumaun) are totally different from the ancient and medieval Kumaon. Till 16th century, Kumaon locally called 'Kumu' was an area including Champawat and its suburbs. In the medieval period, during the reign of King Akbar, Kumaon Suba was adjacent to Badaun, on northeast including the *Tarai-Bhabar* area of the present Kumaon, Nazimabad, Kanth and Gola Gokarnath. Up to the year 1753, Katyur, Dhaniyakote, Paliyakote, Askote, Sore and Saira were not the parts of Kumaon. Later, during the rule of Gorkhas (1790-1815), Kumaon region was extended up to the river Kali in the northeast and Nanda Devi on the west. During the British period, Kumaon included Almora, Nainital, Tarai and Garhwal. In the year 1891, three districts were formed, such as Garhwal, Nainital and Almora. The year 1948 marked the establishment of one more district, *i.e.*, Tehri Garhwal. It is only after the Chinese invasion in 1962 that Pithoragarh, Chamoli and Uttarkashi tehsils were converted into independent districts (Dhoundiyal and Dhoundiyal, 1997:17-8). The present Kumaon includes six districts as mentioned above.

Geographical Classification

Geographically, Kumaon has three distinct areas—Hills (Mountain), *Bhabar* and *Tarai.* The hill areas are situated at a height between 560 m and 7,800 m from the mean sea level (MSL). This region constitutes four-fifth of the total Kumaon region and is densely forested with *Chir, Baanj, Deodara,* etc. The Bhabar area lies between 300 m and 560 m height. The forests of this area are treed with *Saal, Shisham, Toon,* etc. The Tarai area is situated south of the Bhabar and is relatively more fertile than the two regions (Singh, 1971:15-21). In this Himalayan region, the climate is temperate, with wide variations in temperature. In January, the temperature varies from 12.5°C to 17.5°C and in May from 27.5°C to 32.5°C with high extremes of 35°C or more. The period from April to June is the hottest duration with hot winds blowing from west. In the northwest districts, winter is quite severe. Even the temperature goes down –5°C. The maximum monthly rainfall in the state is received during the months of July and August. November and April are the driest months. In winter, rainfall is less. The Uttaranchal region, except the snow bound areas, receives heavy rainfall of more than 1,200 mm.

People in Kumaon

Randhawa (1970:1-5) has divided Kumaon into four zones based on climatic conditions and the people living therein. These zones are trans-Himalayan Tibetan desert zone, inner Himalayan Bhotia alpine zone, middle Himalayan Khasiyan zone, and outer Himalayan Kumaon zone. The trans-Himalayan Tibetan zone is a plateau situated at an average height of 15,000 ft and the people living in this zone, in general, resembles to the people living in Tundra. The Bhotia zone extends from 10,000 ft to 15,000 ft and is inhabited by semi-Mongolian tribe known as Bhotias. The Khasiyan zone extended from 3,000 ft to 10,000 ft and is inhabited by the Khasiyas. The outer Himalayan zone is constituted of lower foothills below Ranikhet, Almora and Pithoragarh and the Brahmins occupy this zone; they are the immigrants from the plains brought by the Chand Rajas as their priests, advisers, etc.

Population Configuration

According to the Census 2001, the Uttaranchal state accounts for less than one per cent (1,603,242) of the total population of the country. The area of Uttaranchal is 53,483 sq. km (1.7 per cent of the total area of the country). The area of the Kumaon region is just 39.3 per cent of the state and inhabited by 42 per cent of the state population with a density of 170 individuals per sq. km that is above the figure for the state Uttaranchal (159). The decadal growth rate in the state during 1991-2001 is 19.2 per cent, which is lower than that of the country (21.3 per cent). The decadal growth rate of the Kumaon region is 16.9 per cent in the same period. The sex ratio of Kumaon region is found to be 980 that show the status of the women is quite comfortable than the state, where the sex ratio is 962 females in 1000 male population. This is above the national figure (933). The country has 15.9 per cent children below seven years of age. The state of Uttaranchal has 0.8 per cent of the total child population of the country. The Kumaon region has 42.9 per cent children in 0-6 years of age. The sex ratio of the children in the state is 908, which is well below the figure of the country (927). However, the sex ratio of the children in Kumaon is 917, which is slightly better than that in the state. Appendix 2 shows the area and population configuration in Uttaranchal.

The state of Uttaranchal has three per cent of population belonging to the Scheduled Tribe, which accounts just 0.3 per cent of the total Scheduled Tribe population of the country.

The Kumaon Himalayan region has 53.9 per cent of the ST population of the state that constitutes 2.5 per cent of the total population of the region. The sex ratio of ST population of the state of Uttaranchal is 970, which is well below that in the Kumaon region (981). The state of Uttaranchal also accommodates around one per cent of the total Scheduled Caste population of the country, of which Kumaon region bears 43.5 per cent of the state SC population. The state has 71.6 per cent people as literate, of which 83.3 per cent are male and 59.6 per cent are female. The figures for Kumaon region do not vary much with those of the state. The region has 72.4 per cent people as literate. The male literacy rate is 86 per cent and the female literacy rate is 59.5 per cent.

Uttaranchal is one of the three newly formed states. It is economically backward. In Uttaranchal, the total percentage of workers (main and marginal) is 36.9 per cent, of which 46.1 per cent are male and 27.3 per cent female. In the Kumaon region, the percentage of workers (main and marginal) is 40.9 (male 45.4 per cent and female 35.8 per cent). The percentage of main workers in the state is 27.4, of which the male workers constitute 37.9 per cent and the female workers 16.4 per cent. In the Kumaon region, 28.7 per cent people are main workers of which 35.5 per cent are male and 21.4 per cent female. The percentage of non-workers in the state is 63.1 (53.9 per cent male and 72.7 per cent female). In the Kumaon region, it is more or less same *i.e.*, 59.1 per cent (54.6 per cent male and 64.2 per cent female). As far as the cultivation is concerned, the state of Uttaranchal has 50.1 per cent cultivators, which is well above the national figure (31.7 per cent). In the state, there are 34.3 per cent male cultivators and 77.8 per cent female cultivators. In the Kumaon region, there are 59.8 per cent cultivators, of which 44.6 per cent male and 77.1 per cent female depend upon cultivation. The state has just 8.3 per cent and the Kumaon region also has 7.1 per cent people as agricultural labourers, which are well below the national figure (26.5 per cent). The women's work participation rate in the state is 36.9 per cent, which is below that of the Kumaon region (40.9 per cent).

Development Status

The infrastructure development in Uttaranchal has been very poor and below the national average. As it is a newly formed state, the attention of the Central Government has to shift from the dominant states to the states in periphery. However, the state has been identified as a problematic region, as it borders with two neighbouring countries. Uttaranchal has 16,826 villages, 86 towns and 13 districts. Only 9,868 (58.6 per cent) villages were electrified. The forests are the most important resource base in the region. The importance of rich forest cover has special significance for the extensive subsistence pastoral economy of the Bhotias. This in turn, is also the important element of the traditional knowledge base and tribal ecology, as the Bhotias are exclusively dependent upon forest for meeting the basic necessities of their life. Appendix 3 shows the intra-regional variation in the levels of development of Uttaranchal.

Agriculture is the mainstay of the people in Uttaranchal. The Gross Cropped Area (GCA) in the state was 1,306,200 ha in the year 1998-99, of which the Kumaon region shared 50.9 per cent. Only 42.2 per cent of GCA was under the irrigation coverage in the state. The Kumaon region had 32 per cent of Gross Irrigated Area in the same year. In the state, the area under foodgrain is almost 75.6 per cent. In the Kumon region, it is around 82 per cent. The area under rice to the area under foodgrain is 30.8 per cent in the state of Uttaranchal. However, 65.8 per cent of area under rice falls in the Kumaon region. More area is used in the state for the wheat production. Particularly, the inclusion of Udham Singh Nagar into the Kumaon region makes the situation better for the state. The average use of fertilizers in the Kumaon region is 48.1 kg/ha, which is quite low in comparison to the usage at the state level (101.4 kg/ha).

Total road length in the state was 17,457 km in the year 1996-97. Of this, a stretch of 7,842 km road was in the Kumaon region. The road density was 0.4 km per sq. km. There were 2,683 Post Offices in the state in 1998-99. Out of these, only 1,185 (44.2 per cent) Post Offices were situated in the Kumaon region. In the banking sector, there were altogether 857 bank branches in the state in 2001-2002. Only 343 (40.0 per cent) branches were situated in the Kumaon region. The Credit-Deposit Ratio was more in the Kumaon region (28.7 per cent) than in the state (26.0 per cent). In Uttaranchal, there were 16,990 primary schools and 266 secondary schools. In Kumaon region, there were 7,173 (42.2 per cent) primary and 113 (42.5 per cent) secondary schools in the year 2002-03. There were 40 primary students per teacher in the state, while it was 25 students per teacher in the Kumaon region. In the health sector, there were 3.3 Primary Health Centres per one lakh population in the state and 3.8 Primary Health Centres in the Kumaon region. The number of hospital beds available per lakh population was around 120 in the region. The number of hospitals was around 12 per lakh population in the state and the region as well, in the year 1994-95.

Field Area: District Pithoragarh

The District Pithoragarh was constituted on 24 February 1960 with 32 pattis (30 pattis from tehsil Pithoragarh and two pattis from tehsil Almora). In December 1968, the district was included in the Kumaon division to comprise districts such as Nainital, Almora and Pithoragarh. Recently, Bageswar, Champawat and Udham Singh Nagar were included in the Kumaon region when reorganization of area took place to form the state of Uttaranchal. Pithoragarh is situated in the northeast of Uttaranchal and forms the north-eastern part of Kumaon region. It lies between 29°27′ and 30° 49′ north latitude and 79° 44′ and 81° 2′ east longitude. Tibet has bound it in the north, Nepal in the east, district Champawat and Almora in the south and the districts Bageswar and Chamoli in the west (see Figure 2.1)

According to the geological formations of the district, it may be divided into four broad belts, *viz.* (1) the innermost Siwalik hill ranges, (2) the Lesser and Middle Himalayas, (3) the Inner Himalayas, and (4) the thin belt bordering the Tibetan Himalayas. The bigger part of the district lies under perpetual snow and considerable area is rocky and barren. Some of the important rivers that flow through the district are Saryu, Ladhiya, Ramganga, Goriganga, Kali, Dhauli and Kuti Yanti.

The total area of the district is 7,100 sq. km. Administratively, it consists of five tehsils and eight development blocks. There are five important towns in the district, such as Munsiyari, Dharchula, Didihat, Gangolihat and Pithoragarh. Around 40 per cent of the district area is under the cover of forests (see Appendix 2 and 3).

Climate

The altitude of the district ranges from 500 m to 7,200 m and the climate, therefore, largely depends on the elevation and varies accordingly. The period from October to January is the coldest and the temperature varies between 10°C and –5°C. Cold wind begins to blow by 3.00 p.m. each day and the outdoor activity is then abandoned, as the temperature comes down to 7°C and then decreases subsequently in the night. Most of the rain occurs during the monsoon period. The average rainfall ranges between 1,000 mm and 1,500 mm in a year. The monsoon period lasts from June to September, which is climatically the most depressing time of the year in this Himalayan district. Heavy rains cause landslides and roadblocks, stopping all communications and making travel hazardous.

Flora and Fauna

The vegetation of the district varies considerably according to the climatic zones, from coniferous forests in the lower levels, through birch and rhododendron woods and then scrub and alpine pastures, before giving way to bare rock and snow. The forests are confined to the river valleys and the southern parts of the district. In Saal forests, the chief tree, Saal (*Soriya robusta*) is found up to a height of about 1,220 m. The Saal logs are chiefly used for house building purposes. Some other trees in these forests are Amaltas (*Cassia fistula*), Amrud (*Pridium guava*), Awla (*Phyllanthus emblica*), Haldu (*Adina cordifolia*), etc. The Chir (*Pines roxbergii*) trees are found up to a height of 1,800 m. The other varieties of trees include Banj (*Quercus incana*), Chandan (*Litsaca chinensis*), Chironji (*Buchananilati folia*), Marpankhi (*Thusa compecta*), Debdar (*Cedrus deodara*), etc. The trees, which grow at high altitude, are Bhojpatta (*Betula utilis*), Chamakhodik

(*Carpinus viminea*), Silverfur (*Abeis pindraw*), Sprus (*Picea moninda*), Rai (*Pesia moranda*), Kilmoda (*Berberis aristata*), etc. Between the altitudes of 3,250 m and 4,000 m, the dominant species are the conifers. During the past few decades as deforestation is becoming evident in the Himalayas, the wild animals of the district have greatly been declined in number and variety. The Sambar (Jarau) and Kakar (barking deer) are widely distributed in the low and high altitude regions of the district. The musk deer have now almost become extinct and the snow leopard is quite rare. There are tigers found in the district. The district is very rich in birds.

Livelihood

The livelihood of the people in the district mainly depends on agriculture. Animal husbandry including sheep and goat rearing, weaving and spinning of woollen materials, etc. supplement the livelihood of the people. As the slopes are very steep and the terrain hilly, soil is found to be very poor and stony, and only a small percentage of land is irrigated. So, the size of the fields is very small and the food produced here is not sufficient for the subsistence of the people. The chief Kharif crops are paddy, *jhangora*, *maiza*, *mandua*, pulses, potatoes, and tomatoes. The Rabi crops include wheat, barley, masur, peas, linseed, and mustard. Though agriculture is the mainstay of the people, the food produced is not enough for the entire year. To compensate for the deficit food requirements, the people have to look for other avenues of income such as making baskets (made of rigual, *i.e.*, a larger variety of grass) and woolen goods like *thulma*, *chutka*, *kalin*, and *dan* (these are a kind of carpets done by hand). Potatoes and carpets are the commodities largely exported from the district.

Demographic Account

As per the Census 2001, the district Pithoragarh holds 6.1 per cent of the state population with a density of 65 individuals per sq. km. There are 1031 females in 1000 males, which show a better female status in the district. The decennial population growth in the period 1991-2001 was found 10.9 per cent. The literacy rate is found 75.9 per cent, with male and female literacy rates at 90.1 per cent and 62.1 per cent respectively with a gender gap of 28 point. The percentage of workers is 43.0 (male 43.4 per cent and female 42.6 per cent). The percentage of main workers is 26.8, with male 31.1 and female 22.7. However, the percentage of marginal workers is 16.2 with male 12.4 and female 19.8. The total percentage of non-workers is 57.0 with 56.6 per cent male and 57.4 per cent female. The percentage of cultivators is 67.6 with male 47.7 and female 87.2. This shows that the female population in the district is more engaged in agriculture. However, there are a few agricultural labourers (*i.e.*, below 1.5 per cent). The percentage of ST population is 4.2 in the district, which constitutes 7.5 per cent of the state level ST population, with a sex ratio of 1046. The percentage of SC population is 23.0 in the district, which constitutes 7.0 per cent of the total SC population of the state with a sex ratio of 990. The female work participation rate is 43.0 per cent, which is higher than that in Kumaon Himalaya (40.9) and the state (36.9) (see Appendix 2).

The amenities reflect the infrastructure development of the area. The district covers just 13.3 per cent of land of the state. It is reported that 267,700 ha area of the district is covered by forest (1998-99). The Gross Irrigated Area to the Gross Cropped Area is just 9.3 per cent. Fertilizer consumption is 5.4 kg/ha. In the year 1997-98, 1,564 villages had electrification. Road density of the district was 0.2 km/sq. km in the same year. The Credit-Deposit Ratio was only 17.5 per cent in 2001-02. However, there were 1457 primary and 123 secondary schools in 2002-03. There were 4.3 Primary Health Centres, 120.7 beds and 14.2 Hospitals available per lakh population in the year 1994-95 (see Appendix 3).

People: The Bhotia Tribe

In the Kumaon Himalaya, the Bhotia people are found to inhabit Dharchula (see Plate 3) and Munsiyari tehsils (see Plate 4) of Pithoragarh district. There are also a very thin percentage of Bhotias in other districts of Kumaon region (due to migration from their higher ridges to permanently settle down at some urban places), not only in Almora but also beyond Uttranchal.

Other two important Himalayan districts of Uttaranchal counting from west to the east, bordering Tibet (now a province of China) are Uttarkashi and Chamoli (these two districts are in Garhwal Division) where the Bhotias do inhabit. The people themselves resent being referred to as Bhotias and prefer to be known by their indigenous names, such as *Sauka* and *Rang* in Kumaon Himalaya; *Jad*, *Tolchha* and *Marchha* in Garhwal Himalaya. Ethnically, they are separate groups but put under the name Bhotia since 1967 by the Government of India, scheduling them as the tribe 'Bhotia' in Uttar Pradesh (now Uttaranchal).

The term 'Bhotia' denotes the people living in the Bhot region of Himalayas, *i.e.*, the northern most part of Uttaranchal. This is a generic term for several groups of people. Etymologically, the word Bhotia is popularly believed to have originated from the term 'Bhot' or more correctly 'Bod', which means Tibet. However, this nomenclature is not free from controversy. Some are of the belief that Bhotias are Mongoloid in origin and hence immigrants, while some others regard them as a crossbreed probably between Khasas and Hunas. Some others are of the opinion that the Bhotias are of Tibetan origin (Joshi and Pande, 1997:64). While some others suggest that they might represent the Tonganas (Joshi and Brown, 1986:59-6). Raipa (1974:1-3) again looks them as the descendant of Kinnauras and Rajkiratas, who lived in this region since Vedic period. Moreover, the Bhotias have experienced various stages of ecological succession in the cultural landscape. The history before 10th century is only legendary. They have been mentioned as the Kiratas, Kinners and the Ganas of Shiva who later on mingled with the Khas, Nag, Shak and others (Raypa, 1992:74-5). There is only speculation about the origin of Bhotias, since, they have no written history. Some considered them remnants of an ancient civilization still preserved in the isolated valleys of Kumaon (Randhawa, 1970:15-6). Some Bhotia people are of the opinion that they belong to an ancient Rajput clan who lived in the Indian plains and fled into the high mountains during a period of religious speculation at the time of Muslim conquest of India. However, some contradict this, and view that they are an aboriginal people called Sauka who always lived in these valleys and never moved in from anywhere. The consensus in all four valleys is that they belong to the Kshatriya caste and are descendants of the Rajputs (see Plate 5). Their family name is taken from their villages, and their middle name is always Singh to show their Kshatriya status (Hoon, 1996:67); for example, Jawahar Singh Nabial, Bala Singh Hiyanki, Sher Singh Pangtey, Laxman Singh Brijwal, Chandra Singh Gwal, etc.

Bhotia Habitats in Pithoragarh

The Bhotia of Kumaon, who like to introduce them as *Sauka* or *Rang*, live in the northern high altitudes of Pithoragarh, a district that was earlier a part of Almora district. In Kumaon, the word 'Bhot' signifies the country within the snowy ranges, south of the Tibetan border inhabited by the Bhotia. Tibetans, refer to Bhotias as '*Mons*' or '*Monpa*', meaning 'others' (Hoon, 1996: 66-7). The human settlements in the Bhoti (*i.e.*, the land of Bhotias) region of Kumaon are confined only to four valleys, namely Johar, Darma, Chaudans and Byans (Mehra and Tiwari, 1955:10). The Johar valley is in Munsiyari tehsil, whereas the other three valleys are under the jurisdiction of tehsil Dharchula. Rivers such as Goriganga, Dhauliganga and Kaliganga drain these valleys. The impact of climatic conditions on the life of Bhotia is obvious. The higher reaches of these valleys remain wholly covered with snow for nearly six months in a year (with the snowfall beginning from the end of September up to the last week of February). The severity of winter compelled with the heavy snowfall makes it impossible for the people to live there, and hence they have to come down southward to their winter homes in the warm places. Thus, transhumance became a regular feature of their life. Figure 2.2 shows the geographical location of the Bhotia habitats in the District Pithoragarh.

Munsiyari Bhotia

The valley of Goriganga from Milam to Munsiyari is known as the Johar valley. The Bhotias who are the inhabitants of this valley are known as Johari Bhotias or Johari (see Plate 6). They are also known as Saukas and belong to village Milam and other villages in the valley, such as Martoli, Burphu, Mapa, Tola, Luwan, Sumtu, Laspa, Panchhu, Bilju, Dhapa, etc. The Johari Bhotias show the influence of their Kumaoni neighbours

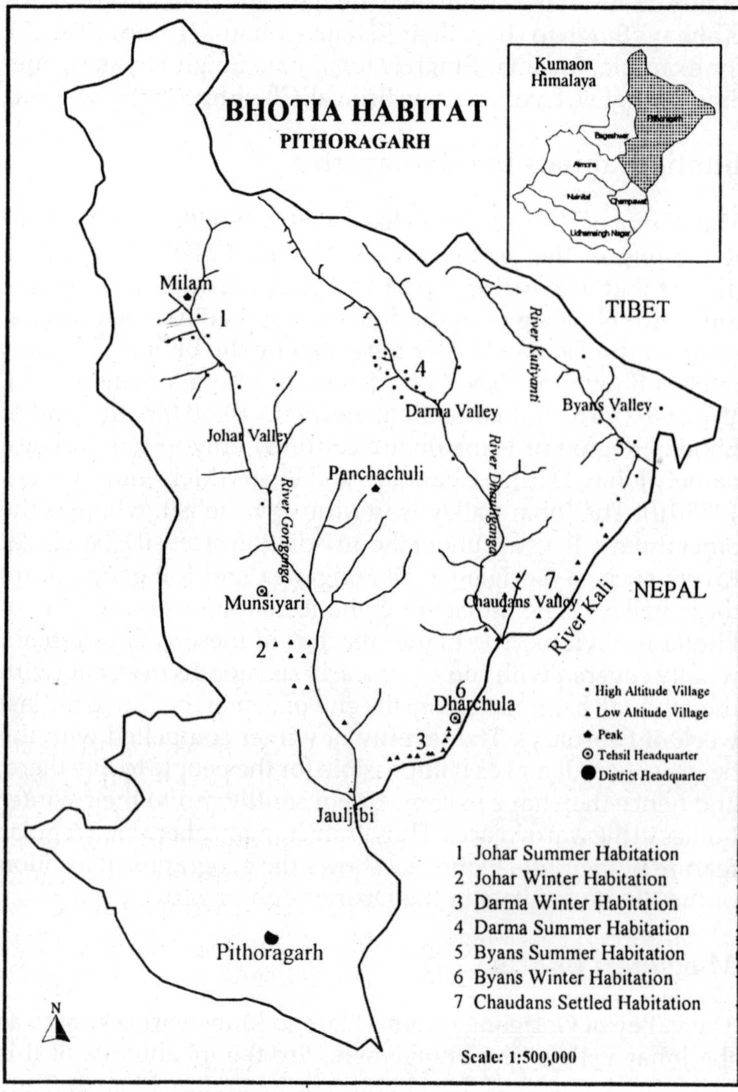

Fig. 2.2: Pithoragarh: Bhotia habitat

in their general customs and language. Now, the people from the Johar valley are settled at low altitude villages surrounding the urban unit Munsiyari. Therefore, they are identified as the Munsiyari Bhotias who have delinked their activities at high altitude. Figuires 2.2A and 2.2B show the Bhotia villages in summer and winter habitations in Johar valley.

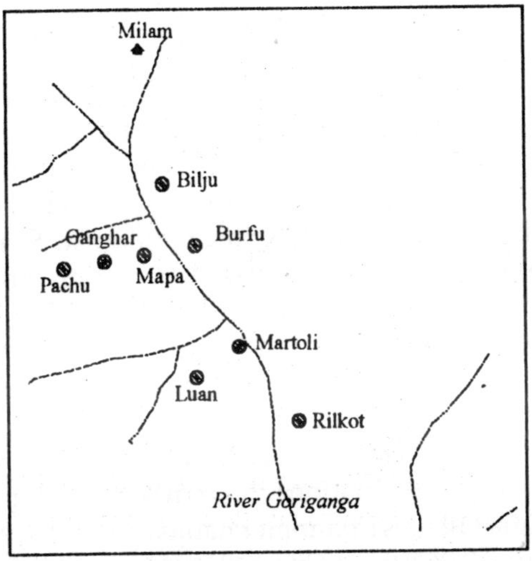

Fig. 2.2A: Johar Summer Habitation (1)

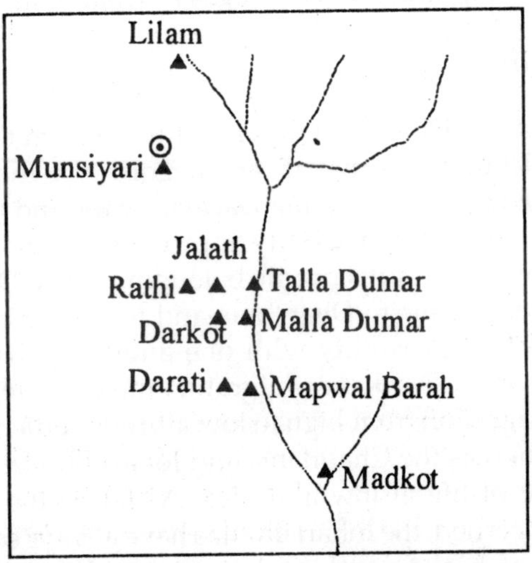

Fig. 2.2B: Johar Winter Habitation (2)

Dharchula Bhotia

In the tehsil Dharchula, Bhotias live in three valleys (see Plate 7). Up streams along Dhauliganga from Tawaghat (this place is 19 km beyound Dharchula), known as Darma valley; some important villages in this valley are Sobla, Tejam, Dar, Bongling, Sella, Goe, Sipu, Dugtu, Marchha, Baling, Nagling, Philam, etc. It is at Tawaghat that the eastern Dhauliganga flowing from northwest joins the river Kaliganga, which flows southwards separating Nepal in the east. Upstream of the river Kaliganga, the villages along the western side constitute the valley, Chaudans. The villages that constitute Chaudans valley are Pangu, Tonta Gaon Roto, Rimjhim, Himkhola, Sosa, Sirkha, Sirdang, Rung, etc. As one extends further upstream along the river Kaliganga, we find villages such as Budi, Garbiyang and Napalchu. Along the sides of the river Kuti Yanti that flows from northwest towards southeast direction, the villages found are Gunji, Nabi, Rongkong and Kuti. All these villages constitute the Byans valley. Figures 2.2C and 2.2D show Bhotia villages in summer and winter habitations in Darma valley. Figures 2.2E show the Bhotia villages in summer habibations in Byans valley. However, figure 2.2C also indicates the Byans winter habitation. Figure 2.2F shows the Bhotia villages in Chaudans valley.

Relationship

The Bhotias from Dharchula differ culturally from the Bhotias of Munsiyari though they have been categorized as the Kumaoni Bhotias. Marriages between the Darma, Byans and Chaudans Bhotias are common and socially approved. This is due to the fact that in winter months people belonging to the Darma and Byans valleys migrate to Dharchula and its nearer places and also live in close proximity with one another (Chachra and Bhasin, 1998:408). They have a migratory mode of life, basically a seasonal migration from high to low altitude settlements and *vice versa*, whereas the Chaudansi and Johari Bhotias have the settled mode of life at low altitudes. As far as the marriage system is concerned, the Johari Bhotias have always considered themselves of higher rank and status, and refuse marital relations with the Bhotias of other regions (Upreti, 1968:18-9).

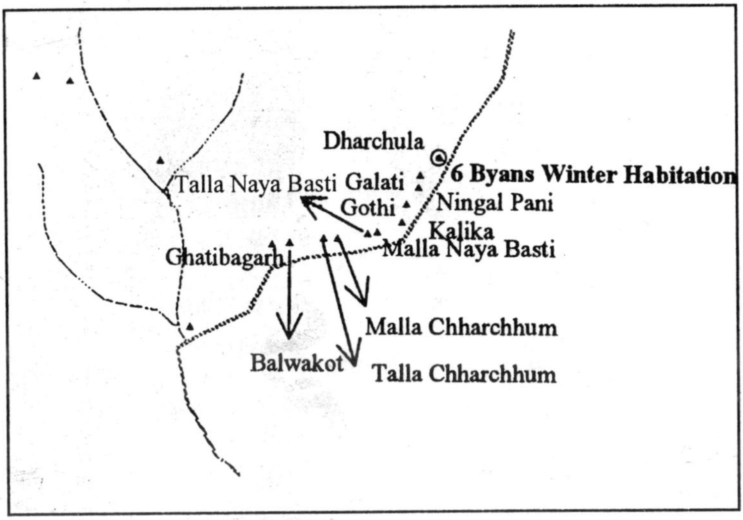

Fig. 2.2C: Darma Winter Habitation (3); Dharchula and Byans Winter Habitation (6)

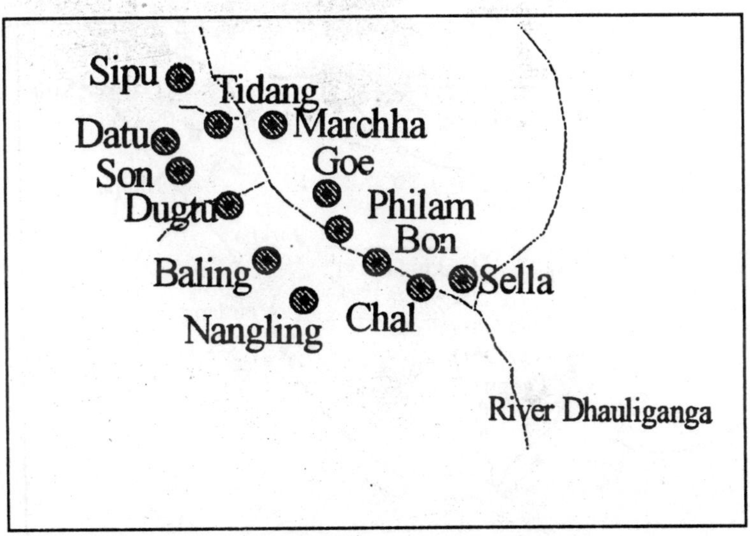

Fig. 2.2D: Darma Summer Habitation (4)

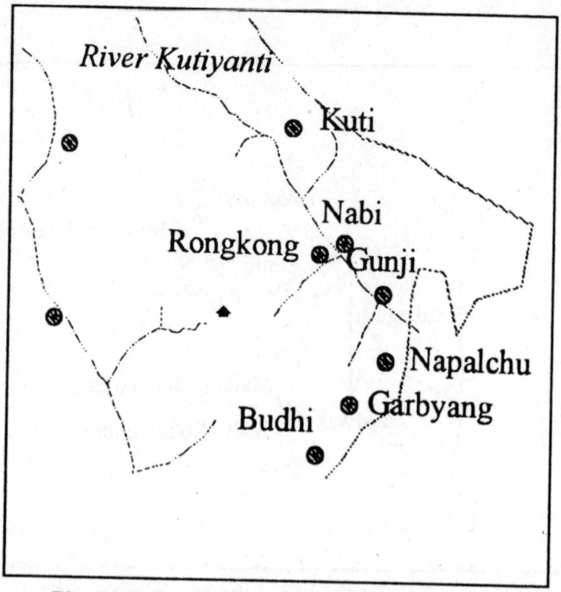

Fig. 2.2E: Byans Summer Habitation (5)

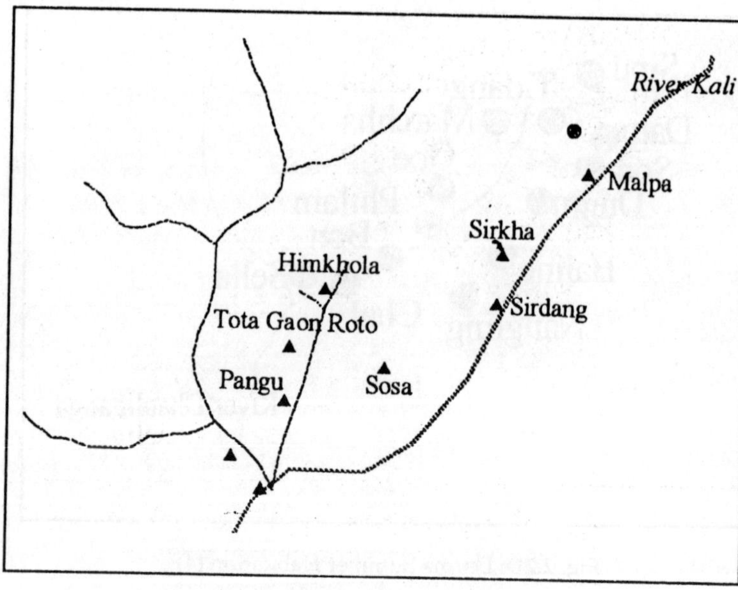

Fig. 2.2F: Chaudans settled Habitation (7)

Now, things are a little changed and people more often look for the personal achievements than the community itself. According to Shrivastava (1966:196-97), the Bhotia tribe in Pithoragarh is structurally divided into the following units:

The Bhotia Community

⇩

The several valleys inhabited by different groups of Bhotias named after the valley

⇩

The Local group (Village)

Surname often derived from the name of the Village

⇩

Clan (Garkha)

Sometimes, it may be same as the local group when the members of one clan inhabit an entire village.

⇩

Lineage (Ranth)

⇩

The Family

⇩

An individual Bhotia

The most important structural unit is the valley. For the outer world and the community, a person is identified with the name of the valley where he inhabits. The valleys, besides being culturally identifiable, are the main socio-political units in Bhotia social organization. The order, in which the Bhotia people are ranked, is *Johari, Byansi, Chaudansi and Darmi.*

Trade as Traditional Economy

The Bhotia played an important role as a bridge and buffer community between Tibet, northern India, and Nepal. Due to their strategic domicile, the Bhotias had adopted trade and monopolized it through the barter trade relationship with the Tibetans. They exchanged agricultural produce, grains, sugar, spices, hardware and broadcloth from the lower Himalayas and Ganga plains in India for salt, wool, borax, gold dust and precious stones, sheep, horses, etc. Sheep and goats were of vital importance to the average Bhotia traders, which were used as the pack animals capable of negotiating very difficult routes leading from the Bhotia valleys to Tibetan trading centres (Srivastava, 1966:174). It is a well-known fact that throughout the long history of Kumaon, Bhotias maintained their monopoly in trade. There were various reasons for it. The conditions like geographical proximity of their region to Tibet, their mutual intelligibility with the people across the border, and the tradition of pastoralism among them had invariably placed the Bhotias in an advantageous position in relation to their trade. Besides these, there are some favourable attributes of Bhotia personality like industriousness, spirit of adventure, courage to face the hardship, etc. Again, the trade activities required frequent travels through difficult terrain round the year. This consequently imposed a semi-nomadic pattern of life, a condition with which their emphasis on trade and mobile life had largely overshadowed their agriculture (Brown, 1987:130-2).

Each Bhotia trader had a special correspondent in Tibet with whom the trade transactions used to take place. Over the years, it turned to be the feeling of a strong relation and friendship between one Bhotia trader and his special correspondent in Tibet. Therefore, it effectively, helped the Bhotia to hold their monopoly in their profitable trade pursuit that mainly accounted for the enviable economic prosperity of the Bhotia in past. The Kumaoni Bhotia used to have their trading contact with Tibetans in two different places, such as Gyanima and Taklakot as the international marketing centres. The Bhotia from Johar valley used to attend the Gyanima centre and the Bhotia from Darma, Chaudans, and Byans used to visit Taklakot centre, the reason being their convenience and shortcut route to the Tibetan marketing centres.

Termination of Trade

The trade had been the most vital economic assignment of the Bhotia until the closure of the border. They used to export Indian goods for their Tibetan consumers and import Tibetan items for the people of India. The fortunes of the Bhotia changed drastically with the Chinese assumption of control over Tibet in 1959 and the Sino-Indian war in 1962. The Indo-Tibetan border was sealed and trans-Himalayan trade came to a grinding halt. The disruption of traditional trade relations between Bhotias and Tibetans by the Chinese authorities was hence, a severe blow to large sections of the Bhotia community. Not only, it deprives professional traders of their livelihood, but it also had an adverse effect on the livelihood of several other professions that were indirectly dependent on the continuance of trade (Das, 1982:209).

The Bhotia had always taken trade for granted. It was well beyond their wildest dreams that it would end and they were totally unprepared for it. With the stoppage of trade, the cattle wealth of Bhotias lost its significance as the beast of burden. Now they use their sheep and goats only for obtaining wool and selling it to the butchers for meat. After the cessation of trade, most of the Bhotia people have abandoned their villages en-route summer settlements; for example, the Johari Bhotias are now centred around the place Munsiyari (an urban unit) at lower altitude in their winter settlements. They lived as a closed society, interacting with the mainstream only for the purpose of trade, and they lacked that social culture, which is necessary for existence in competitive society. In fact, they had never also thought of educating their children properly. They could not rely on agriculture as the second line of defence which was severely handicapped due to the lack of fertile lands and being extraordinarily high altitude. Dairy farming, too, did not have much to offer, as it had always remained a neglected sector. The pack animals like sheep and goats were of little use for Bhotias after the termination of trade and hence were sold off.

The woollen industry, which was their main source of earning after trade, also suffered considerably in the years following the cessation of trade. The supplies of imported Tibetan wool were of insufficient quantities, and finally, ended. To keep their industry alive they had to depend on domestic supply that was very much short of their requirements. Moreover, there no longer remained a demand for the non-Bhotias who used to be the freight shepherds and used to carry merchandise for the Bhotia traders to and from Tibet. Being hereditary traders, they had also developed a habit to reinvest their profits in items of trade supplied goods to Tibetans on credit basis as well, and hence, they had very little cash at the time of stoppage of trade. This acted as a deterrent in immediately developing their economic strength. Therefore, the cessation of trade with Tibet has forced them to reorient the course of their socio-economic life (Chachra and Bhasin, 1998:408). Now, they have been adopting a multitude of economic activities, such as shop keeping, contract taking, liquor vending, etc.

Seasonal Migration or *Kuncha*

The term *Kuncha* implies a family and livestock caravan that migrates to the high altitude villages in summer to cultivate crops and graze their animals. The vagaries of climate in the higher valleys like, violent wind, landslides and avalanches have compelled the Bhotias to adopt to the seasonal migration. In addition to this, the trade with Tibet was the primary motivation for transhumance among the Bhotias, with components of agro-pastoralism integrated into that economy. This practice is being followed since generations and involved the migration of the entire village community from the summer habitation to winter habitation and *vice versa* (Hoon, 1996: 83-7). In winter, when there is heavy snowing on the high altitudes and that remains snowbound for about six months from October or November to March or April, the Bhotia people stay at their low altitude habitations. The migration to high altitude settlements (see Plate 8) takes place in the month of April or May from the low altitude settlements (see Plate 9), and in the month of September or October, they start coming back to their respective winter habitations at low altitudes.

The seasonal migration could be attributed to economic as well as the climatic factors. Agriculture, the principal economic activity takes place at high altitudes along with some other economic activities, such as collection of medicinal plants, roots, leaves etc., for the consumption in rest of the year at their winter habitations. The path leading to high altitude settlements have no proper road communication; pack animals are the only means of transportation. For this purpose, Bhotias had to maintain large herds of these animals and for feeding them, they had to incessantly search for grazing pastures (*Bugyals*) (see Plate 10). Whenever, they went to Tibet for trade, they left their animals under the supervision of anwals,[1] who in fact, take care of these animals and graze in the pastures at high altitudes and on their return they used to do the same at low altitudes. Thus, the agro-pastoralism and transhumance with the Bhotias were not independent practices but a consequence of trade activity (Dangwal, 1997:428-32).

Agriculture and Landholding

Involvement in long distance trade determined the lifestyle of the Bhotias, and it is obvious that any such change in the scope for such trade must have developed over generations. With the closure of the Indo-Tibetan border, the Bhotias have had to look to other avenues of livelihood. They continue to practise agro-pastoralism based on transhumance and nomadism. Therefore, the traditional Bhotia economy had three components such as trade, postoralism and high altitude agriculture. The Kumaon and Uttarakhand Zamindari Abolition and Land Reform Act of 1960, which was really meant to release bounded labour and to eliminate exploitation of poor tenant farmers by the Zamindars (Landlords) all over India, allotted agricultural lands owned by the Bhotia in the winter villages to tenant farmers without appreciating the transhumance nature of their lifestyles. The Bhotias ended up losing all their landholdings in the winter valleys simply because they had leased them out to tenant farmers who lived in the winter villages all year round. Now, the Bhotia people do have their agricultural lands only confined in higher reaches (Das, 1992:212-5).

All activities concerning agriculture, except ploughing, are done by the female folk. The higher valleys produce only one crop a year, and that is either buckwheat, barley or potato. The crops have higher yields but of inferior quality. The Bhotias now depend less on agricultural produce. One settled valley out of four, *i.e.*, Chaudans does have a few holdings in the low altitudes that too, limited to a few Bhotias. In the low altitudes, both Rabi and Kharif crops of paddy, wheat, barley, maize, potato, buckwheat and chua are grown. The high altitude lands are quite conducive for the cultivation of some of the crops like ogal (*Fagophyrum esculentum*), phapar (*Fagophyrum tataricum*), etc. Besides, some vegetables like cabbage, peas and radish are also grown for their consumption (see Plate 11).

Spinning and Weaving

The womenfolk are highly skilled in manufacturing all sorts of woollen cloths. The woollen products like blanket, carpet, shawl, and clothes have had a good market in Kumaon and Nepal. The non-availability of raw wool from Tibet has severely affected the industry. They used to import raw wool from Tibet and, after keeping the best of the lot for themselves, sold it to the mills and merchants from Kanpur, Delhi, Punjab, etc. This industry provides a significant contribution to their total amount of earnings (see Plate 12). Womenfolk dominate this industry (see Chapter 5) in compare to other occupations.

Food and Drinking Habits

The food habits of Bhotias seem significantly complementary to the indigenous production potential and nutritional value. The intake is largely in the form of protein rich diet including mutton, beans and pulses; ghee and butter prepared from the milk of cow, goat and sheep; and carbohydrates from wheat, maize, rice, potato, etc. The green vegetables are absent in their diet but the wild varieties of vegetables and leaves including mutton and chicken are taken sufficiently and kept dried for the future consumption especially in the winter months. The diet of Bhotias mainly consists of rice and mutton. Though the rice is not produced in upper valleys, it is the staple food of Bhotias as cooking of rice comparatively takes less time, labour, and fuel.

The babies are breast fed for longer period. For the pregnant woman, no special and rich food is provided; but after delivery, nutritious food is given to them. The tea churned with butter and salt is common and this special drink among them is known as *Jya*. It gives warmth to body and protects throat from infections. Now-a-days, they take rice, wheat-floured *chapati*, pulses, and vegetables with all condiments. The common tea is also taken. Both men and women use *Chakti* (*i.e.*, the locally available beer) (see Plate 13). It is taken on regular basis for warming up the body to escape from the cold. It is prepared out of rice or wheat. This is an important item in Bhotias' religious and cultural life and also in entertaining the guests. It has attained so much importance that no ceremony or ritual can take place without it. The liquor they consume is known as *Barchhyang*. However, now-a-days, English wine has been entered into the life of Bhotias (see Plate 14).

Religion

The Bhotias follow Hinduism. Nevertheless, due to their continuous isolation and with the absence of the Brahmins, the primitive animism is not absent. Their religion seems to be influenced much by 'Shivaism'. The 'Linga' shaped idols represent as Shiva in their temples. They worship Hindu Gods and Goddesses and observe Hindu festivals (see Plate 15). However, side-by-side, they worship spirits and every natural object like mountain peaks, rocks, rivulets that represent some deities. They also believe in supernatural powers. This belief left impressions on their religious ceremonies and festivals. Since long, they also encountered the Tibetans; but Buddhism could not influence the Bhotias. The pilgrimage to Kailash-Mansarowar and establishment of Narayan Ashram in Chaudans valley in 1935-36 by Narayan Swami have also strongly infused the Hinduism and prevented the Christianity to flourish (see Plate 16). Some of the deities are *Byasirkhi* (the Byans Rishi), *Shyang Se* (the Greatest God: Lord Mahadev), *Gabla* (who helps in trade), and *Mati* (the Goddess earth). Durga and Nanda, along with the Devi who protect the Bhotias from diseases, are also worshiped.

Concept of Dhalang

On many occasions the ceremonial activities are being observed by worshiping Lord *Shiva*. The idol of Lord *Shiva* as *Lingum* is made out of the paste of *Phapar* (*Fagophyrum tataricum*) flour known as *Dhalang*. After the completion of rituals, the *Dhalang*, which was worshiped, is being distributed among the members of the family and villagers as *Prasadam*. While making the paste of *Phapar* for the purpose of *Dhalang*, nothing is added except water (in such a proportion to make it more condensed, which could be made into the shape of *Lingam*) and therefore, it is tasteless.

Language

The Bhotias in the district Pithoragarh of Kumaon Himalaya speaks an unwritten language belonging to the Himalayan branch of Tibeto-Burman family (Trivedi, 1995:263). Moreover, the language also varies among the Bhotias in different valleys (Hoon, 1996:73). *Ranglo* is spoken among the Bhotias in Dharchula tehsil and *Johari* in Munsiyari tehsil. However, some aspects of the Bhotia language including vocabulary resemble Mundari language (Raypa, 1992:74). Hindi is now becoming the common language. Bhotias both males and females can speak Hindi, Kumaoni, Nepali and Tibetan. They use the *Devanagari* script for writing purposes. Now among them, there is an attempt to develop a separate script for their language.

Education

Until the Indo-Sino war in 1962, the spread of education was very low, that too, limited to the elementary education only.

The geo-cultural and political changes have now compelled them to seek education and jobs. But during the last two decades, education among them have been spreading fast along with higher education; having Scheduled Tribe status, scholarships and free education facilities are being provided. Some Bhotias are occupying better positions like IAS, IFS, doctors, lawyers, engineers, etc. (Raypa, 1992:73-4). The attraction towards education certainly would bring them a better life and higher standards of living (see Plate 17). Even the present Chief Secretary of the State of Uttaranchal, R. S. Tolia, is himself a Bhotia from the district Pithoragarh.

Housing Pattern

The isolation and geomorphology of the land have compelled them to have an agglomerated pattern of settlement. Bhotia houses in the Kumaon region are generally double storied. The walls are built with stones and the steep slanting roofs are covered with slates. This kind of roof is suitable in the region frequented by storms and snowfalls. The windows and doors are less in number and small in size. A typical Bhotia house may have four rooms: two rooms each in the ground and first floors (see Plate 18). The staircase, which leads from outside to the first floor generally bifurcates the house. In the first floor, there are two rooms: one each on both sides of the staircase are meant for sleeping, sitting, gossiping, entertaining guests, having wine, etc. Of the two rooms in the ground floor, one is for the kitchen cum storehouse and the other one is generally for cattleshed. Now-a-days, the houses are constructed with the cemented bricks and provisions for separate kitchen, latrine, bathroom, and cattleshed are taken into consideration (see Plate 19).

Dress and Ornaments

Bhotia males and females were always found to wear woollen clothes that were made locally. The spinning of wool, weaving it into clothes and even stitching used to be done by them. The male dress consists of coat, trouser, and cap. The women's dress consists of an upper garment, a skirt from waist to ankles, a conical shaped cap dropping backwards, and a cotton girdle at the waist (see Plate 20). Now, almost all women are being found to wear *Sarees* instead of traditional dress. The Bhotia women are also fond of ornaments. They have a unique pattern of arranging the ornaments in gold and silver in different parts of the body, such as ear, nose, neck, waist, and ankle. Today, there is a drastic change in dress pattern and ornaments. The boys use the modern dress, such as long pants, shirts, jeans, etc. and the girls use the *salwar* and *kamij* and even jeans. The clothes they use at present are all mill-made and include both woollen and cotton (see Plate 21).

Rites de Passage

Birth

The birth of a baby in the Bhotia family marks a high kind felicitation with joy and happiness. The mother and the baby are both confined to a separate room. The 11th day of birth is particularly celebrated with rituals. The relatives and villagers are invited to participate in the ceremony. If the person is poor, only the nearest kinsmen are invited. The prayer is first offered to the dead ancestors and ancestral God. Then the prayer is offered to other Gods and Goddesses. This ceremony is performed for the babies irrespective of sexes. The elderly people bless the baby. Food, wine, and other edible things are distributed along with dance, singing songs and other entertainments. Finally, the name to the baby is given by the villagers collectively or the oldest of the clan men in the village among the Dharchula Bhotia or sometimes by the priest among the Munsiyari Bhotia. Some related intermediary ceremonies are also observed for the baby, as it grows up (see Plate 22).

System of Marriage

The Kumaoni Bhotias are divided into four sub-groups based on their presence in the valleys, *i.e.,* they are named after the valleys. Each of the sub-groups is again divided into several clans and lineages, which regulate marriage alliances and indicate ancestry. The Bhotias practise endogamy at the territorial level and exogamy at the clan/lineage level. The Darmi, Byansi, and Chaudansi practise cross-cousin marriage. Marriage is arranged through negotiation and during negotiation the status of the concerned families and the education of boys and girls are important priorities among other criteria. Marriage among them is monogamous. Earlier, they used to practise marriage by elopement and now it has thin appearance. The vermilion mark, a necklace, and a nose-ring made of gold are the marriage symbols among some of the Bhotia sub-groups. The dowry is not encouraged in the marriage. Divorce is granted on grounds of adultery and maladjustment but it has very rare occurrence. The marriage is now solemnized at the bride's residence according to Hindu rites and in a style similar to the Rajputs. It is an important social occasion in the Bhotia life. The bridegroom's party consisting his cousins, villagers and friends along with the drum party, visits the bride's residence. Preferably, these days, marriage ceremonies are being organized in their winter settlements at low altitudes, the reasons being proper road communication, availability of electricity, telephone and other facilities. The elderly people from both sides perform rituals. Drinks, dance, and songs go around for a couple of days.

Concept of 'Rang-Bang'

The Bhotias of Byans and Darma have an interesting marriage system, *i.e., Rang-Bang,* a dormitory in which the girls have the opinion of selecting their life partners (Mehra and Tiwari, 1955:14). In every village, a house, or some spot is set apart, which is called *Rangbankuri,* meaning the place of *Rang-Bang*. Here, the boys and girls meet and spend the night singing, drinking, and smoking. The main objective of the *Rang-Bang* is to arrange marriages. In due course of time, it has lost its importance (see Plate 23).

Death

Generally, the death is observed in the pattern followed by Hindus. It used to be observed with all rituals within a week or

2-3 months after the death. It is so, because earlier the duration of trade-trips was uncertain and the migration period depended on climatic conditions. However, the dark half of the lunar month is always chosen for the death ceremony. The brighter half of the month is selected for other rituals and worshipping. However, the priest is consulted among the Johari Bhotias. Among them, it is continuously observed up to 11 days since the day of death of a person. During the period between death and death ceremony, shaving or cutting hair among males, wearing of ornaments by females, and ceremonial performances in the family are prohibited. The son-in-law and maternal uncle play important roles in the death ceremony. Like other life activities, in the death, the local deities and ancestors are worshipped. Wine, *Dhalang*, sweets, rice, incense, oil-lamp, and a strip of white cloth are the main offerings to the spirit of a dead person (see Plate 24).

Status of Bhotia Women

The Bhotias, like many other tribal communities, display relatively higher level of social harmony between gender and age. Unlike the women subject to various forms of deprivation and hegemonies in the so-called developing societies, they enjoy relatively less differential status among the Bhotias. Women are not just the partners of men in tribal society. They are the major economic help to the family and society, an indigenous society works as a corporate group. Women are very much dearer to the nature not because of their biology but because of their social position and nature of assignments (Sayers, 1982:95-99). The tribal women are valued much more than their male counterparts in every aspect. The total crafting mechanism, ethics, ethos and expertise in the knowledge about their immediate environment lie with the women. They also contribute in educating and socialising the young generation in the family level and therefore, they are considered as the carrier and instructor of the social customs and ethics. Women assume multiple identities within the household and society, depending upon the role assigned at different stages in life. Sometimes, they become daughter, sister, wife or mother. All these stages of identity cast an impressive outcome through the attachment and association with the other members in the family and society.

Generally, the women section of Bhotia tribe is highly respected and treated with dignity based on equality of rights in the broad spectrum of social network. The women are not looked down upon. Their voice in the family and society is well regarded (see Plate 25). There is a strict practice of monogamy; however, the widow remarriages are not discouraged. They not only remain inside the house to treat the guest serving the country liquor, but also, they participate in the generation of economy either in the form of crafting or participating in the paddy field along with the men folk or even to help extending the seasonal migration. In the cultural and ceremonial practices, the attendance of the women adds special grandeur and aesthetics with melody of songs, dance and music (see Plate 26). The free will of the unmarried girl to choose the life partner is witnessed through the public pronouncement in the institution of *Rang-Bang*. This tradition is not seen frequently with the scope of modernisation narrowing the vigour and magnitude of cultural life. Absence of dowry also denotes ascribing equal status to women section. Bhotia women equally take part in the village Panchayat, ceremonies and festivals along with men. However, when one goes deep to understand the status of women inferred from the proverbs, it is seen that there is some discrepancy and incoherent aspects prescribing them sometimes so high and sometimes so low status.

The realms of women's activities extend well over the fortress of the domestic wall, as the Bhotia women meaningfully contribute in rearing the livestock of the family. Their acquired skill in rearing sheep, goat, mule, etc., is some of the rare yet exclusive contribution in the material culture and social capital of the household and community. The sight of Bhotia women flocking the herd of sheep and goat in the *Bugyals* (summer pastures in the Himalayas) and forests of Greater Himalayas is testimony to this fact. According to Hoon (1996:181), the Bhotia women work harder than men except ploughing. Women work hard all the time and their work is especially hard in winter when they have to spend greater energy on subsistence, gathering fuel and fodder. Women contribute the major share of the family labour and produce woollen clothing and bedding for the family. Women also cooperate with the other family members during financial stress and help crossing over the crisis by providing the finance help which they have had earned by selling the local wine or the woollen products. Women thereby make a monetary contribution towards household expenses (Hoon, 1996:201-2). Therefore, in this situation, there is an effort to examine the context and usages of the proverbs[2] bestowing attributes of status to the women in Bhotia society.

Role and Importance of the Mother

'Chamei lakte na, du lakte kalan.'[3] This proverb reflects the role of mother in the family. The process of socialisation begins in the family itself. As the mother is very close to the offspring, she has more responsibility than any other members of the family including the father. If we refer to the core meaning of the proverb, it implies that the mother is the first agent in the process of upbringing and imparting values of socialisation to her children. The children, particularly the daughters, go rough in a sense of breaking the rules and conduct assigned to them by the society, when the mother fails to perform her duty. This indicates that the whole responsibility of the socialisation process lies with the mother. The society also deserves from the mother, that to act according to the norms and conducts prescribed by the genius abounding all members. As daughter is considered to be the future mother, the carelessness of mother can distort the whole normative behaviour and social structure, and hence the society.

In another instance, a proverb like *'Bate hosinde pura mulya, nati hosinde phe mulya'* [4] infers that the mother in the family is considered as nucleus and all other members revolve around her. The affiliation that the mother shows for her children and *vice versa* is the emotional involvement, which has been evolved through the mother-infant dependency along the line of socialisation. According to the proverb, it is found that if the father is dead, the children are semi-orphan and when the mother is dead, the children are considered fully orphan. Therefore, the society assigns a central role to mother and women as a whole.

Women and Management

Women are considered as good managers. In their daily routine work, they perfectly nurture and nourish the interest of members and satisfy the demands of everyone in the family. They do not hesitate to sacrifice the time and energy for other members. They also try to mitigate the passion and sexual desire of their male counterparts. In this process, they submerge their happiness and anguish. At times, they come out openly to rescue their people not only in the paddy field but also in harvesting the crops. Along with the domestic modes of production, they also manage the family with perfect involvement harmonising cultural ethics and keeping good relations with the neighbours. It is expected that they are to be good in the use of language and gesture while dealing with other members in village or outside. In this context, the Bhotia society cites an example such as '*Bideh mirang shiri akho phl, ya mirang siri lun-kho phl.*'[5] This means that a woman can be considered a better housewife from her way of talking and use of gestures. At the time of scarcity of 'food and money' at home, she can arrange these from others in the village. She knows how to mould people to one's concern. Those do not have this quality are considered as 'load and pressure' to the husband and family as well. In another instance, '*Chamei ja sipu liu chyan, chham-kho ren*'[6] means, thereby, those girls or women who know the art of weaving, for them every type of wool is good. Those who do not know the art of making things, they only question at the quality of the wool. This indicates that they do not have right to question at the quality but they are supposed to manage all kinds of things given to them. If they can perform well with this, they are accredited and highly praised. The society in fact demands from them that they are to be good managers and should know the art of handling the situations which may be conducive or otherwise.

Character and Temperament

'Chamei rinsya dangmachyan danyar sai, madang machyan kho-khu shina.'[7] The Bhotia society deserves that the daughter and daughter-in-law are to be protective and conscious about their status and their interaction with other members in the family and the society in general. This proverb deciphers that if the daughter and daughter-in-law are beautiful in their attitude and character, then it can bring Gods and Goddesses on earth. If they are bad and unsociable, it amounts to bringing demons on earth. This provides a strict code of conduct for these sections of womenfolk for probably keeping them within the custody of parents as long as they are young. The other version could be restraining them from some kind of activities, which may even bring insult and mental injuries in the form of earning bad name to the family. Therefore, the unmarried daughters and the newly married women are supposed to maintain some distance from the type of people like the youths, which may bring adultery. Another interpretation given to this proverb is the women's temperament. They are expected to be good in their approach. The society even expects from them to be reserved and should have enough patience. These not only will help them to build a good personality, but also train them to be better adaptive to handle all type of situations in life. In another instance, we find that *'Mirang shiri guimati thanglang, teyi mati madang.'*[8] The meaning of this proverb depicts that, even if, efforts are taken up by the women to remain good in front of others, their fault has to be discovered by the people in the society. Therefore, the women should always be conscious to keep their character good and convincing.

Attitude towards Daughter-in-law

As such in the Bhotia society, the status of the daughter-in-law is kept high. Traditionally, their society prefers the practice of living in joint family. In joint family, the role of daughter-in-law is so important that in every matter her consent is taken into consideration as she is provided with the charge of maintaining the kitchen; for example, *'Mulin rani.'*[9] The daughter-in-law is treated as the queen or goddess of the hearth. Therefore, in order to familiarise her with the family tradition and rules, it is the duty of the son to make her aware about it. In this context, another proverb has been given importance. *'Namsya yad mlyi shiri yad likn,'*[10] which means, it is not the daughter-in-law who spoils the family, it is the son who spoils the family, for the reason being the son is unable to make the newly coming bride aware of the family norm, culture and tradition.

Stereotypism

In patriarchal society like Bhotia, the birth of a girl means she is made for other family. This connotation is so deeply rooted that it does not allow the girls to flourish in life in a sense to go for education and excel in exercising their intellectual endeavour in like their counterparts in some developed urban settlements. For example, *'Chamei jate miga nasho.'*[11] This means the girls are born to go out one day to other families after their marriage. They are meant to remain with their parents till the marriage takes place. This indicates that the stereotypic cultural settlement has been traditionally narrowing the scope for the proper improvement of life, liberty and expression of the girls in particular and the women in general. The whole process can be understood in a sense that the structural adjustment is nothing but cultural partiality that has been construed selectively giving favouritism to male domination.

Belief

Like other tribal societies, the Bhotia society is backed by some beliefs and assumptions. Traditionally, they had mercantile relations with Tibet in Trans-Himalayas and tarai region in the plains of India. So the men folk are found to be out of station most of the time in a year. Thus, in general, a feeling has been developed in treating and providing hospitality to a guest visiting the village. *'Mirang shiri chim ja yecha fle, ura shiri gai desu chyi fle.'*[12] It believes that 'as you sow so shall you reap.' If a woman treats the guests properly in her place, then she may expect that her husband who remains out of home most of the time will be treated better by others in the same way. In this context, it is observed that the development of this belief in the society has taken place for pragmatic reasons. It is found that the worries about their men who are out for earning livelihood trouble the psychology of women. This shows that there is some kind of maturity among the women in understanding the situation and their concern for husbands' absence. The treatment, which is extended to guests not only serves to overcome the psychological stress and strain, but also aids generating inter-group cohesion and harmony. This even helps enhancing the traditional business network and ties with the people visiting the village for becoming the new customer of the Bhotia craft products. Therefore, it can be estimated that the women's contribution is invaluable in the domestic level of production, which in fact goes unnoticed among other sections of the society.

Negative Attitude towards Women

In Bhotia society, the women do enjoy privileges yet they are subject to criticism and mockery. They are refrained from doing certain activities, which may earn defamation, when they violate the stringent prescribed code of conduct of the patriarchal society. This is just like giving concessions on the one hand and taking it away on the other. The myth regarding the women's status, which generated over the time, is the creation of those people who wanted to control the women in order to keep them under the shadow of paganism, extracting all possible comfort and luxury to satisfy their wants by using them as commodity of life and dance to the tune of their order. There are some instances cited below where the women have been looked down upon, serving to the pyre of male chauvinism. For example, '*Mirang shiri jyim fldan kotya chyim.*'[13] This signifies that the plan chalked out by the women remain with them for a while, as constructing a house at the hilltop because they have no foresight. In another instance, we find that '*Mirang shiri dankho katha mahoshi, nikhi dankho mar mahoshi.*'[14] The women cannot keep the matter secret with them that has been either discussed in the family or told her to do so. In the proverb, it is mentioned that they cannot digest matters or keep matters of importance with them secretly, like the dogs cannot digest the substance like ghee.

Again it is like *'Mumiyar jyewa jyonru thajukshilo, sa spang chi chi minan tha-jukshi lo.'*[15] This proverb interprets that let there be no birth of comets in the sky, so also there should be no birth of stepmother. Though the stepmother is biologically not related to the children yet socially chosen up to fulfil the role of a mother. The idea, which prevails in the mind of common people about the role of the stepmother that she does bother to not love and care the step children. In some other instances in the Bhotia society we find that *'Mirang shiri geche wang ji nimse, prakhageche shyarji nimse.'*[16] It is possible to predict the age of a woman just looking at her face. Likewise, it is possible to predict the age of a man with the help of his fame. Similarly, *'Chiti side mirang shiri, syangthe bandu.'*[17] The core meaning of this proverb is as the leaking pot troubles us, similarly the weeping women troubles the whole family, relatives and guests. The women in the Bhotia society are assumed and expected to be stronger enough to help the family in a number of activities like seasonal migration, agriculture, rearing the sheep, goat and cattle, etc. For climatic conditions and overcoming the vagaries of nature of high altitude Himalayas, the women should be as strong as the male counterpart. Therefore, the women should be self-dependent and self-sufficient in order to overcome the natural threats and social compulsion.

The analysis of the proverbs in the Bhotia society infers a good deal of facts about the cultural life of women. Their status is constructed in such a manner that they are to be fit with and fulfil the saga of patriarchal demands. The role and importance of mother in the society is primarily to nourish and nurture the infants. This process is seen as the gate way to socialise the young generation. The daughters are to be guided, especially, as they are the future mothers, and the whole motherly responsibility lies on them. They are supposed to learn perfectly the norms and the puritan ethics of the society. The entire effort of the society lies in making them as good managers in the family and society as a whole.

The cultural stereotypism implies that the women are supposed to behave and act in a particular manner in such a way that it is not go against the wish and demand of patriarchal society. They are refrained from certain activities, which hamper the benefits of the men folk. The cardinal principle of elderly generation is emphasized to pesture control and authority over female. The norms, mores, customs, social sanction etc., in the society are framed in such way to have a control over the women and prove the authority over them. Therefore, the role and image of females as such have social construction.

Bhotias in Transition

Most of the tribal communities in India live in the most vulnerable ecosystems, *viz.*, the tropical rain forests, mountains and semi-arid lands. As a result of adverse ecosystems, these people live in poor social and economic conditions. They suffer from lack of basic health, education, employment, etc. Therefore, their rights are related to land and resources or culture, language and education or development. The living standard of these communities, in general, is extremely low. The long run implication of such situation has been concerned with conflicts in relation to ethnicity, minimal rights, self-determination, participation in government and control over economic development (Das, 2001:11). Life for the Bhotia has changed drastically in the last five decades. During this period, they have undergone various stages of socio-political changes and faced diverse cultural environments. In such natural and cultural surroundings, they have been undergoing a peculiar type of ecological adaptation determined by their faculties and needs.

In the mixed socio-cultural environment, the problems and claims of communities do vary from each other. To look at this, we find that the Bhotias are a Scheduled Tribe community and receive reservation facility in jobs. Whereas, the Raji people have tough time to survive with their primitiveness and aloofness even if they enjoy the same facilities like the Bhotias. On the other hand, non-tribals of the region, who are economically backward, feel discriminated by the government's reservation policy. Their claim is to declare 'the whole region backward' irrespective of the types of communities living there, so that they could also get benefits equal to the tribal and SC communities living there.

In this situation, it becomes more interesting to know as to how these people have been able to maintain their identity despite the threat perception. The question of identity formation, like in other tribal places of India, is very important for the Central Himalayan Bhotia zone, because several ethnic groups make this region hackneyed. The process of identity formation of the hill people has also come through many stages, and the human rights issues have not been used as a tool for the development or to have access to the resources both socially and politically by communities as a whole. All of them survive with independent institutional systems with a different level of development. The Bhotias and the Jamindar Thakurs, due to historical reasons, have been progressing at a speed bit more than others, and with the new power structure the Bhotias occupy relatively a stronger position than the rest. It has cropped up into a subjective feeling of deprivation, among the non-developed communities who have not got the benefits of political and economic transformation.

It is evident from the fieldwork that most of the Bhotia households do not have land at low altitude, however, they have land at high altitude. It is observed that only the Thakurs possess more agricultural land in comparison to others. The seasonal migration among the Bhotias may have contributed to the prevailing situation. It has led to a situation of uncertain future for them living there. Unless the ownership of land rights, tenancy rights and minimum wages are assured, the inequalities will continue in the form of indebtedness, bonded labour, poverty, hunger, etc. Till date, the land question in tribal areas remains unresolved (Pathy, 2003:2832-33). When dominant caste groups entered to this place, it turned the region into a complex social dynamism. They remoulded the existing framework and created a new pattern of social interaction. Competition and capture of land introduced new lines of stratification. The tribal-nontribal reorganization was crucial by-product of these readjustments (Biswas, 1994:25-6).

In the post-independence era, the Bhotias are becoming politically more conscious as well as they are aware of their rights and privileges as a tribal group. It has led to a formation of elite among them. The entry into the primary level of education is an indication of their ethnic consciousness. The reasons are firstly, the most advantageous aspect appearing in their occupation, *i.e.*, the occupational shift from transhumance and nomadism to settled life and secondly, benefits due to the scheduled tribe status (awarded to them by the President of India in 1967). These two major factors coupled with their hardworking nature have brought enormous prosperity and awareness among them. Now, there is a move to go to schools, sending children outside the region for higher studies, and finally try for good jobs. The common Bhotia parents now prefer sending their children to school instead of sending them for cattle grazing or some other domestic work. Despite hard terrain and rough climate it is common to see children going to schools and playing games. This transformation has brought them close to their country people and the world where they live in. They seem to be aware of their rights and social duties. This has been possible with the spread of education that develops personality, understanding, tolerance and togetherness (see Chapter 5).

The formation of developmental organizations like *Simant Bhotia Janjati Utthan Samiti* (Border-Bhotia Development Society), *Rang Samaj Kalyan Sanstha* (Rang Social Welfare Organization), *Johar Sanskritik Sanghatan* (Johar Cultural Association) and the state level cultural meet on the 24 May 1998 at Pithoragarh by the Bhotias from Munsiyari and Dharchula blocks were some of the examples to know how the people were united to maintain commonness among themselves. The open seminars subsequently on the issues like their social, cultural, educational, economic and constitutional rights and demands for the formation of Uttaranchal were quite remarkable (see Plate 27). Among them the individual consciousness has slid towards mass consciousness that indicates their understanding of rights. This type of cultural meet usually strengthens to preserve the we-feeling and social solidarity. They are proud of their material attainment along with folk tradition and tribal culture. This fine blend of tradition and modernity has put the Bhotias among one of the most progressive tribes of India.

The Rajis of the same region still survive with the primitive condition. A very little move has been occurred in all aspects of human development. Even no agricultural land is found to be in their possession. Their condition is quite unhygienic and they suffer from many diseases due to malnutrition. Due to all these, they are in the verge of extinction. If we compare the Bhotias with that of the Rajis, we find that the former is in a rapid developing stage, whereas the later is yet to know them fully. The Rajis bother least about their own rights. The rest of the world for them still looks like another planet. They do not want to come out from jungles and discourse with the outer civilization. School is something a distant dream for the Raji children. Perhaps, the web of socio-cultural taboos plays important role in their life and they have remained captive to it.

With the gradual infiltration from Nepal and some migration from Indian plains, the Bhotias' traditional social structure has also got influenced. There has been a switching over to the process of sanskritisation side-by-side westernisation adopting customs, dress, language and way of life of the dominant Hindu population. The Bhotia elites are now afraid of the process of fast change occurring in their society, and the cultural admixture is due to the contact with the larger society around. Now, they are more conscious about their own cultural identity (see Plate 28).

Even among the Bhotia sub-communities, there seems to be inter-valley conflict and feeling of one's superiority. Though the language and culture slightly vary from one valley to another, the formation of elites within them shows distrust towards their fellow beings. The Bhotias moreover, have strong feeling towards their respective clans. The dominant clans such as Garbiyal, Kutiyal, Nabiyal, Hiyanki, Pangti, Martolia, and Dharamasaktu etc. in fact, have wide control over the resources. They represent themselve better in the village as well as valley-based political system. Moreover, the population strength of a clan and its influence on the local politics are directly correlated.

Therefore, the dominant clansmen have taken the advantage by availing all the opportunities in social, political and economic spheres, sometimes even by arousing differences among the rest (see Plate 29).

The non-Bhotia communities in this region show a lot of variations. These people are educationally, socially and economically backward. A few cases are found where the individual consciousness has arisen, but the degree of motivation to understand their rights is not visible. The possible reasons are as follows:

(*i*) Most of the educated people migrate to the urban places or plains for employment, leaving their house in the village,

(*ii*) The hilly terrain, which is rather unproductive for agriculture keeps the people busy round the year just for gathering their survival needs, and

(*iii*) Traditional way of farming and scarce avenues for employment have become compelling factors for the people to be content with scarcity or venture out for green pastures.

The spinning and weaving activities are the inherent profession of the Bhotias. These activities are also seen among the scheduled caste people. According to them, this was a profitable occupation for the women as well as men. But this activity is getting comparatively slow pace and some of them have even left this profession because of either its low demand or its old and traditional pattern of designing. It needs a radical improvement by modern techniques and training. Revival of this profession will be much beneficial to women in the direction of their employment and economic prosperity. This will enable them to be productive by using simple tools, local materials, and other commodities and services to barter with one another leading to full employment and self-sustaining growth (Joshi, 1996:468-9).

Majority of the people in this region do have problems about their health. The reasons may be due to non-availability of food, hard labour for hours together in activities such as agriculture, trekking in the hills, collection of firewood and cooking of food with bio-fuel and rare medical facilities. Therefore, nutrition deficiency diseases are common among the women and children. High birth rate (among the Bhotias, 24.17) and spontaneous abortions (0.17) are common things for the women leading to weakness and lower life expectancy (Dash and Kanungo, 2002:143-5). Furthermore, malnutrition and environmental degradation affect everybody. So the problems are there and yet we claim to be making progress (Paul, 2000:2).

Similarly, alcohol is a part of the Bhotia life. The Bhotias have access to prepare *chakti* (local tribal wine) at home and it is the privilege enjoyed by them being a tribal community. In practice, this cultural tradition has been converted into a commercial activity. Some people have converted it as an invisible source of economy. The *chakti* is easily available in almost every Bhotia household. In some places, the habitats of tribals and non-tribals are not far off and they pay visit to the Bhotias residence to consume *chakti*. As a result, these poor people spend their respective daily earnings, sidelining essential needs of family members. Thus, what is considered to be a right of someone (*i.e.*, getting the privilege of making wine) is proving wrong for others, *i.e.*, easily available to others for consumption (see Photograph 23).

Another point to be noted in general is that the children are considered to be the helping hand for their parents. Going to jungle with cattle heads, carrying grasses and leaves for the livestock, etc., particularly by the girls are their routine work. The parents believe that 'more hands tend to more wages for the household'; simultaneously, they also forget that 'more hands mean more mouths to feed'. This is basically due to the lack of education and awareness among the parents. Who is responsible for this and how to solve this problem are still question marks. In the direction of protection of basic rights of the children and women, easy availability of electricity and solar energy for each and every household should be taken as a priority by the government. This would certainly help the communities as a whole to have facilities of mass media like TV, by which the illiterates and common people will have access to the right to information and knowledge. It would help to achieve the national goal of small family and simultaneously they will be aware of 'what is happening in and around the country', which seems to be very important for them and the nation as well (see Plate 30).

To sum up, Uttaranchal is a new state and one of the 28 states of India. It is also a state having status of Special Category. The state is strategically important having two international boundaries, Tibet (China) in the north and Nepal in the east. The area is altogether marked by a variety of natural ecosystems with unique geo-climatic conditions, vegetation, wildlife, soil, kaleidoscopic moods and beauty of nature, socio-economic conditions, and cultures. The state has two administrative divisions *viz.* Garhwal and Kumaon. These two divisions are also marked by cultural and linguistic differentiation along with the unequal developmental pace. The state has five tribal groups such as the Tharu, the Jaunsari, the Buksa, the Bhotia and the Raji other than the caste groups like the Brahman, the Thakur, Other Backward Castes and Scheduled Castes. In the state, the Bhotia tribal groups are spread in three major districts such as Uttarkashi, Chamoli and Pithoragarh. In the district of Pithoragarh, the Bhotia habitats are confined to the Munsiyari and Dharchula tehsils.The Bhotia people have a long historical background. They had been traders for many centuries, connecting Tibet in the trans-Himalayan region with the plains and tarai region of India until the Indo-Sino war in 1962, which ultimately sealed the borderline. As a result, there was a severe crisis to their economic activities. This has even remoulded the old age mercantile activities to that of settled life and agricultural practice, which put their settlement across high and low altitudes of the Central Himalayan region. The high altitude Bhotias carry out seasonal migration to the higher ridges during summer. The migration process is not just simple mobility of the people in between summer and winter habitations but the mobility of schools, post offices, hospitals, etc. They have distinct culture, language, territory, clan leadership, housing pattern, which identify them as tribe, though the influence of dominant Hindu culture has affected the people at large. The educational upliftment is a new phenomenon and has been introduced to them as an alternative for institutional employment in government and private sectors. The status of the women by and large is at par with the men, but not in every situation, as the society is predominantly patriarchal. Their interactive network within members in the society and outsiders is quite open and impressive. However, the Bhotias are at crossroads.

Like many remote and tribal parts of our country this region is quite backward, and people still witness poverty, unemployment, illiteracy, illness, malnutrition, poor growth and deprivation. These factors loom large as the major sources of internal conflict. Even the conflicts, which appear to be social or linguistic, have some underlying economic element in it. As development, in economic terms, is a national objective, it may have little relevance for the small communities who are at the periphery, as they do not understand their rights in economic matters, and what is important that can make them aware about developmental programmes. There are, no doubt, some special incentives and facilities to the tribals like the Bhotias, which have proved very helpful in their development, to bring them to the mainstream of the nation and finally in the promotion of national integration. Therefore, for such communities some more attention toward basic necessities like access to food and nutrition, education, land reform, improvement in the agricultural process, and prospectus for rural employment is very essential at this hour. Then only, the process of undue migration to urban centres could be curtailed and viability of village life along with the vigour of social interaction could be restored. It will help to strengthen the basic rights of the people, particularly women and children living in this region, who have otherwise been facing a tough life.

Notes

1. Anwals are otherwise known as shepherds. In the past, they were those poorer section of the Bhotia community, who had not been able to carry out their own business due to poverty and opted the work as shepherds for the wealthier section of Bhotias. These anwals used to live with the herds in the grazing grounds (*Bugyals*).
2. It is mentioned in the text that the proverbs symbolize wisdom, rather than communicating simple knowledge or information. Therefore, it would be difficult to find an equivalent meaning or synonymous concept symbolizing wisdom. On the contrary, one acquires wisdom

through the process of socialization and sharing the cognitive expression of culture group. In this book, the author has tried to share the wisdom of the culture group through the process of constant interaction with the Bhotia tribal community at the cultural, social and cognitive levels. Therefore, the translation of proverbs used in this text is not based on the recognized translation but by sharing the cognitive experiences for more than a decade.

3. The children, particularly the daughters, go rough, if the mother fails to perform her duty.
4. If the father is dead, the children are semi-orphan. If the mother is dead, the children are fully-orphan.
5. A woman can be considered as a better housewife from her way of talking and making gestures, as she can mould people to one's concern. Those do not have this quality are considered headache to husband and family.
6. The girls or women who know the art of weaving, for them every type of wool is good. Those who do not know the art of making things, they only complain quality of the wool.
7. If the daughter and daughter-in-law are good in their attitude and character, then it can bring Gods and Goddesses onto the earth. If they are bad and unsociable, it amounts to bringing demons onto the earth.
8. If a woman tries to rectify her character for several times, yet at least one defect of her is traced. Therefore, she is supposed to maintain her life carefully.
9. The daughter-in-law and the women in general are treated as the 'queen of the hearth'.
10. It is not the daughter-in-law; it is the son who is bad because he spoils the family.
11. The girls are born to go out to other families after their marriage.
12. If a woman treats the guest properly in her place, it is hoped that others would also extend her husband in the same way in foreign places.
13. This interprets that the plan taken by women remains with them for a while like constructing a house at the hilltop. Women have no foresight.
14. Women cannot digest a secret matter, which means they cannot keep matters of importance secretly with them like dogs cannot digest the substance like ghee.
15. Let there be no birth of comets in the sky, so also there should be no birth of stepmother.
16. It is possible to predict the age of a woman just looking at her face. Likewise, the age of a man is predicted through the help of his fame.
17. As the leaking pot troubles us, similarly, the weeping woman troubles the whole family, relatives and guests.

3

MATERIALS AND METHODS

The anthropologists have been struggling to develop an anthropological episteme for understanding the tribal community. There are two important schools of thought particularly advocated by Maurice Godelier and Claude Meillassoux. Godelier (1986:29-33) is of the opinion that the tribal societies can be explained through the existing epistemic tools; mainly the structural model of analysis is sufficient to undertake the study on tribal society. As opposed to this, Meillassoux (1981:52-7) is of the opinion that the structural parameters of the contemporary societies are incompatible to analyse the pre-class social formation, such as the tribal society. The Bhotia society of Pithoragarh is also a case study to this fact. In the present study, the episteme developed by Meillassoux is found more appropriate, where the subject specific episteme is used. Some of the important aspects are briefly discussed here. It should be mentioned that the study conducted on the high and low altitude[1]. Bhotia populations in order to understand their whole life processes covers their social, biological and demographic activities.

Demography deals with empirical studies whose data are collected by the observation and recording of events about the human beings in a society. In this conceptualisation, society is viewed as a natural system and human being as an object of observation. This thought implies that, for anthropological demography, both quantitative and qualitative aspects of data are vital. In this sense, fieldwork or the idea of anthropologist-demographer going in person to the actual location, where the study is conducted and the data collected through first-hand methods, acquires paramount importance. Although most demographic data can be obtained from National Census, National Registers of Birth and Death and Sample Registration System, these systems do not provide an adequate understanding of the factors operating at a particular point of time at the micro-level or at the level of community. These systems are also not capable of giving an in-depth understanding of the community as a whole as it can be observed by the first-hand field study. Therefore, the need for a systematic and micro-level study of the population has been emphasized.

Sample Survey

Sample is a part of the population.[2] Sample surveys or specially designed surveys are often conducted in a numerically 'smaller' population in which census type of information is collected along with other characteristics that are relevant to the study of demographic variation, which are even according to the focus of the study. The sample surveys used in demography involve taking a sample of the population and are based on the assumption that they contain within themselves, but on a smaller scale, the same characteristics, phenomena, relationships and processes, which the larger group does. In other words, it is the use of part of population to represent the whole. There are many advantages of the sample surveys. Apart from being cost efficient it can be organized and executed relatively quickly and can gather much detailed information than a census. Methods used in the census operations like specific techniques of field procedure, interview and processing of data are also utilized in the sample survey. The sample surveys are mainly used for in-depth micro-level studies with a view to highlight the regional/sub-regional variation and specificity. Anthropological demography, thus, works on data from communities that have definite social and cultural boundaries. This enables the researcher to understand social issues and dynamics and their impact on the issues central to the framework of the study.

The present study attempts to analyse the impact of altitudes on the demographic structure in general and fertility patterns in particular of the Bhotia tribe residing in the Kumaon Himalayan region of Uttaranchal, India. The current investigation was also conceived in a comparative framework to observe and analyse the differences in the high and low altitude Bhotia settlements. Nevertheless, during the pilot survey it was found that, within these two broad categorical settlements, significant variations existed. Therefore, in this study, altitudes (high and low) have been referred to as independent variables and the demographic events and components have been considered as dependent variables.

Interview Schedule

Keeping in mind the aim of the present study, it was decided to use a schedule as a fieldwork tool, which would supplement the interview process for data collection. A semi-structured schedule was designed, which contained both closed and open-ended questions. In fact, in the interview schedule data were collected in two levels. In the first level, information on each resident of the household was collected. This included age, sex, marital status, occupation, and relationship to the head of the household, etc. At the second level, information relating to marriage history and complete reproductive history was collected from the 'fully married' women[3] of the household. The information collected in the schedule could be put in the following headings:

1. *General Information*

(*a*) Name, age and sex of the respondent.
(*b*) Name of the village, valley, block and tehsil.
(*c*) Altitude category of the village settlement (*i.e.*, high or low on the basis of altitudes mentioned in the village).

2. *Household Information*

(*a*) Name of the household head
(*b*) Type of the family

(*c*) Type of the residence.
(*d*) Total number of household members and information about each one.

(*i*) Age, sex and marital status of each household member
(*ii*) Altitude and village/town where the birth of each member took place.
(*iii*) Educational level.
(*iv*) Occupation.
(*v*) Income.

3. *Marriage History and Biological Events*

(*a*) Age at menarche and the altitude where it occurred.
(*b*) Age at marriage (both husband and wife).
(*c*) Age at menopause and the altitude where it took place.

4. *Reproductive History*

(*a*) Total number of conception(s) with reference to altitude.
(*b*) For each conception:

(*i*) Age at conception.
(*ii*) Result of the conception: Miscarriage, abortion, stillbirth, or live birth.
(*iii*) Birth order and sex of the child.
(*iv*) Total number of surviving children.
(*v*) Use of contraceptives or family planning.

5. *Fertility differential*

(*i*) Variation in the fertility pattern influenced by the socio-cultural, biological and environmental factors.
(*ii*) Use of family planning methods.

Fieldwork

The fieldwork was carried out in between the years 1998 and 1999. The fieldwork process basically focused on the collection of data at random from the Bhotia households at high and low altitude settlements with the help of interview schedule, genealogy and observation methods. Case studies had also been taken when necessary. The 'fully married' woman of the household was identified as the ultimate unit of the study, as she could be considered a fairly accurate record keeper of all vital events in the family, namely about the conceptions and other related things confined to the household. According to Goldstein *et al.*, (1983:32) a 'fully married' woman is the one who has not been divorced and is neither infertile nor a widow. Nevertheless, the interview process not only considered her but also her husband who collectively acted as the primary respondents. The cross checking to the reply was all through a continuous phenomenon. For example, sometimes, involving other members of the household into the discussion especially related to socio-cultural and economic aspects, was appreciated.

Rapport Establishment

Data were collected after establishing rapport with the ego (respondent),[4] her husband, other household members and community in general. Links were also established with the village headmen, local authorities, and others who mattered in the society. Greater participation in joys, sorrows, ceremonies, functions, gossips and sharing their local dishes helped a great deal in establishing rapport (see Plate 31).

Age Recording Assessment

The age of a woman is one of the most important items of information collected in any demographic survey, because many demographic statistics and especially fertility estimates depend on accurate reporting of woman's age. In the present research work, the age recall method was used while sketching the genealogy for assessing the age at menarche, menopause, marriage and first childbirth of the mother and at the time of abortion, stillbirth, live birth and death of a child as well. The age of children at present and at the time of death and the husband's age at present and at the time of marriage were also recorded. For women who did not know their age at the time of data collection and were unable to recall their age at their various life events, the reference calendars were used to locate the woman's birth in relation to the dates of major local events. In case of any doubts appeared, more related questions in reference were asked to the husband and other senior family members. Cross checks in the schedule decreased the chances of error in the age recording (see Plate 32).

The Sample Size

Demographic data were collected on 262 households, which included 110 high altitude and 152 low altitude Bhotia households. It is necessary to mention here the difficulties encountered in the efforts made to collect data on this Himalayan isolated tribal group. Uneven topography, harsh climate, sparsely distributed village hamlets and households, low literacy levels of the respondents, language problem, poor transport facilities and moreover, where the considered household has a 'fully married' woman or not are some of the many factors that resulted in consumption of enormous time and energy in data collection. It is important to mention here that there are five sub-groups of the tribe Bhotia, such as *Rang, Johari, Tolchha, Marchha* and *Zad*. They are individual indigenous groups and do not have any cultural similarities other than the name Bhotia scheduled as Tribe by the Government of India in 1967. The sub-groups *Rang* and *Johari* are found in the districts Pithoragarh, basically in two tehsils, *viz.*, Dharchula and Munsiyari respectively. They are collectively known as *Rang* or *Sauka* and concentrated in four valleys, such as Darma, Chaudans, Byans and Johar. Presently, the sample was gathered from the high and low altitudes of Kumaon Himalayan Bhotia tribe in the district Pithoragarh. To have a fair representation, the villages were selected at random according to the classification of altitudes (*i.e.*, high and low altitudes). The villages situated at an elevation above 2,500 m were taken as the high altitude villages (Moore and Regensteiner, 1983:285) and those lying below this elevation were considered as the low altitude villages. The categorisation of altitude of Bhotia villages and the sample size of the present study are mentioned in the Table 3.1.

Table 3.1: Sample Size of the Present Study

Classification	*Sl. No.*	*Village*	*Sample Size No.*	*Sample Size %*	*Total Bhotia House-holds*	*Altitude of the Village (in Metre) (Above MSL)*
High Altitude	1	Kuti	26	65.00	40	3,871
	2	Nabi	25	59.52	42	3,566
	3	Goe	14	31.11	45	3,116
	4	Philam	10	62.50	16	3,206
	5	Boun	15	29.41	51	3,200
	6	Sipu	09	40.91	22	3,657
	7	Marchha	11	55.00	20	3,413
		Total	110	42.80	236	3,432.71*
Low Altitude	1	Madkot	13	43.33	30	1,303
	2	Darati	18	64.29	28	1,810
	3	Dumar Talla	27	60.00	45	1,750
	4	Dumar Malla	15	83.33	18	1,780
	5	Mapual Barah	07	58.33	12	1,780
	6	Jalath	07	23.33	30	1,930
	7	Darkot	10	18.87	53	1,870
	8	Rathi	04	57.14	07	1,890
	9	Pangu	29	70.73	41	2,240
	10	T. G. Roto	22	78.57	28	2,255
		Total	152	51.18	292	1,860.80**
Total (Including 17 Villages)			262	47.92	528	2,508.06***

* Average Altitude of 7 villages at High Altitude.

** Average Altitude of 10 villages at Low Altitude.

*** Average Altitude of Combined 17 villages at Low and High Altitudes.

Out of 236 households, 110 households (46.6 per cent) were from the seven high altitude villages with an average altitude of 3,432.71 m. They are Kuti, Nabi, Goe, Philam, Boun, Sipu and Marccha. During the data collection process in high altitude villages, their respective villages in the winter habitation were consulted for better comprehension in understanding the people. The respective villages are Kutiyal Kheda for the village Kuti, Nabiyal Kheda and Khotila for the village Nabi, Ghatibagarh for the village Goe, Talla Chharchhum for the village Philam, Malle Chharchhum for the village Boun, Talla Nayabasti for the village Sipu and Malla Nayabasti for the village Marchha. Ten villages, such as Madkot, Darati, Dumar Talla, Dumar Malla, Mapwal Barah, Jalath, Darkot, Rathi, Pangu and Tonta Gaon Roto were taken for the data collection process in low altitudes (the average altitude of ten villages is calculated to be 1,860.80 m) with a sample of 152 households (51.2 per cent) out of 292 Bhotia households. Altogether, the sample size is 262 (49.6 per cent) out of 528 households from 17 villages with an average altitude of 2,508.06 m.

There was a sum total of 262 women consulted for the demographic records in the respective life time, which included 110 women from the high altitudes and 152 women from the low altitudes (see Table 3.2). The present study concentrates only on those women whose husbands were alive, had normal marital life, and not divorced or become widow and at least they had one live birth each at the time of fieldwork. The fully married Bhotia women had been chosen in the present study to observe the continuity in their reproductive cycle. The study focuses on the women within the reproductive ages ranging

Table 3.2: Distribution of Consulted Women by their Present Age Group

Sl.	*Age Group*	*High Altitude*		*Low Altitude*		*Combined*	
No.	*(in Yr.)*	No.	%	No.	%	No.	%
1	20-24	23	20.91	20	13.16	43	16.41
2	25-29	15	13.64	27	17.76	42	16.03
3	30-34	20	18.18	23	15.13	43	16.41
4	35-39	20	18.18	32	21.05	52	19.85
5	40-44	10	9.09	18	11.84	28	10.69
6	45-49	11	10.00	21	13.82	32	12.21
7	50+	11	10.00	11	7.24	22	8.40
8	Total	110	100.00	152	100.00	262	100.00

from 20 to 49 years. However, the women of 50 years and above do not influence the fertility measures except the completed fertility rate or completed family size.

Demographic Analysis

In the present study, the core of the analysis is based on altitude categorizations, *viz.*, high altitude (HA) and low altitude (LA). Importantly, demographic parameters have been calculated mainly referring to *Demographic Analysis* (Pressat, 1972), *Introduction to Demographic Analysis* (Wunsch and Termote 1978), *The Dictionary of Demography* (Pressat 1985) and 'Population Study: Measures' (In Bhasin and Bhasin, 1997: *Human Ecological Studies—Schedules and Programme*). The collected first hand data have been analysed using the demographic measures and population indices mentioned below.

Population Composition

Population composition is an important aspect while studying demography. It refers to age-sex composition of a population. It expresses the timing and tempo of a demographic process that varies with age of individuals. Individual age is rarely employed in demographic analysis. Population composition has numerous socio-economic implications on the population. For example, the predominance of younger generation in the society may cause economic burden on the family and society or greater number of adult population will exert pressure on the government to provide them with jobs. Similarly, a greater number of elders require an extra care like medical facilities, dependency homes, etc.

Age-Sex Structure

The composition of a population is done according to the number or proportion of males and females in each category. The age-sex structure of a population is the cumulative result of past mortality, fertility and migration, and demonstrates considerable variability caused by differences in these phenomena. Most of the works revolve around age groups, variously defined but frequently embracing five years (0 to 4 completed years, 5-9, 10-14 and so on). The age-sex structure of a population is well represented graphically by population pyramid. Keeping this aspect in mind, various population composition measures used in this study are described below:

(a) Sex Ratio: It is the ratio between number of females and number of males in a population. In some countries, however, it is defined as a ratio of males per 100 or 1000 females in the population. It is calculated as:

$$\text{Sex Ratio} = \frac{\text{Total number of females}}{\text{Total number of males}} \times 1000$$

The most often quoted ratio is the sex ratio at birth, though, in a more general way, ratios can be calculated for any events attributable to one or other of the sexes (sex ratio of conceptions, sex ratio of deaths, etc.). In determining sex ratio of the whole population, measurements are usually counted for each age group in order to study how the ratio varies with age. Discrepancies will appear in this profile when sex-specific migratory movements affect the population. Since males tend to be more mobile than females, countries of immigration usually have a lower sex ratio than the countries of emigration. A notable exception to the general pattern of sex ratios is the Indian subcontinent, where heavy female mortality has traditionally led to an excess of males at almost all ages.

(b) Masculinity Proportion: It is the ratio of number of males to the total population. This proportion indicates the net manpower available with the population. Every nation is interested in knowing about the available manpower resources, so that they can be put to various developmental assignments. It is calculated as:

$$\text{Masculinity Proportion} = \frac{\text{Number of Males}}{\text{Total Population}} \times 100$$

In societies where the privilege over resources is based on the line of patrileneal system of inheritance, it is ardent for the modern democratic governance to make the legal system based on equal opportunity. Thus, the masculinity proportion is an important demographic parameter to help the society and system in this manner.

(c) Index of Aging: It is the ratio of total number of population aged 60 years and above to the child population of 14 years and under. It is calculated as:

$$\text{Index of Aging} = \frac{\text{Persons of age 60 years and above}}{\text{Children of age 14 years and under}} \times 100$$

Index of aging helps to identify the proportion of elderly persons over the younger generation. In developed countries, the prevalence of low fertility over a period of time changes the demographic structure supporting the economically active population and reducing the size of younger generation. Alternation in the age structure of a population in the direction of an increase of old persons is usually reflected in an increase in the average age of the population. Such alternation generally takes the form of an increase in the number of elderly, a fall in the number of children and relative stability in the central age group. Given such regularity, demographic aging is normally studied with reference to three broad age groups representing the population of working age and young and old dependents.[5] Indeed, since the central age groups are generally little affected by aging, it is common to address the issue by simply presenting the proportion of aged 60 plus over the younger age groups (children below 15 years). A further oft-quoted statistic is the dependency ratio, which relates the size of the old and young age categories to the size of the central age groups.

(d) Dependency Ratio: Dependency ratio is defined as the ratio of dependent segments of children (0-14 years) and aged persons (60 years and above) to economically viable segment (15-59 years). It is otherwise, a ratio of the economically dependent parts of the population to the productive part. The total or overall dependency ratio is some times analysed into its two constituent parts—the burden of children and of the elderly; these are called the *child dependency* or *young age-dependency* and the *old-age dependency* ratios respectively. Countries, which are rapidly growing, have more young populations that show the highest dependency ratios.

(*i*) Total Dependency Ratio (TDR) =

$$\frac{\text{Children of 0 - 14 years + persons of 60 years and above}}{\text{Persons of 15 - 59 years}} \times 100$$

(*ii*) Young-age Dependency Ratio (YDR) =

$$\frac{\text{Children of 0 - 14 years}}{\text{Persons of 15 - 59 years}} \times 100$$

(*iii*) Old-age Dependency Ratio (ODR) =

$$\frac{\text{Persons of 60 years and above}}{\text{Persons of 15 - 59 years}} \times 100$$

The interpretation of the measure is made difficult by the fact that the size and nature of the burden of aged dependents is often quite different from that of the children. The economic and social consequences of aging are clearly considerable, particularly with regard to the increasing burden of dependency. There is a major distinction between young and old dependents. Although educational provision for children is a major government outlay, the cost of an aged dependent to the state is much larger than the cost of child, owing to the much greater healthcare needs of the old. Other than burden to the state exchequer, it is indeed a great burden to the family itself, where the government is unable to provide them (dependents) with the opportunities and protection (particularly in the developing countries).

Fertility Measures

In the present study, the fertility rates are calculated with reference to married women only, since the universe and the sample size of the study are relatively small and childrearing begins only after marriage. Since illegitimacy becomes a bone of contention and unacceptable to the members of the society, it is very rare on part of the women to give birth to illegitimate child. Giving birth to a child before marriage, for a woman, is a rare phenomenon. Thus, the rates are calculated referring to the married women only. An advantage, which is found in this, is that one can observe the fertility pattern and behaviour of the married women (in their reproductive age), not of all women including the unmarried ones in the reproductive age groups who are distributed in the age-sex structure. This can identify the fertility behaviour of women better in the high and low altitude settlements.

(a) Crude Birth Rate (CBR): It is the ratio of live births in a specified period (usually one calendar year) to the average population in that period (normally taken to be the mid-year population). The value is conventionally expressed per 1000. It is a general measure of fertility and an indicator of birth rate of a population.

$$\text{Crude Birth Rate} = \frac{\text{Number of live births in a year}}{\text{Total population in that year}} \times 1000$$

As with any crude rate, it is influenced both by the level of the process it attempts to measure fertility and by the age-sex structure of the population. Nevertheless, the relative number of women of childbearing age in the population, as a whole does not vary greatly in most populations; so, crude birth rate is less affected by variations in the age-sex structure.

(b) General Fertility Rate (GFR): It is the ratio of number of live births in a specified period (often a year) to the average number of women of childbearing age (usually taken as 15 to 49 years) in the population. It is commonly given as a value per 1000. It shows how many women in the childbearing age have contributed to the existing population through births.

$$\text{General Fertility Rate} = \frac{\text{Number of live births in a year}}{\text{Number of women in ages 15 - 49 years}} \times 1000$$

It is slightly superior to the Crude Birth Rate, because, in this, only potential mothers who could bear a child are considered. Using this index, distortions in Crude Birth Rate due to peculiarities in the age structure can be eliminated. It is still a relatively unsophisticated guide to fertility taking no account of the Age-Pattern of Fertility[6] or Marriage Patterns.

(c) Age Specific Fertility Rate (ASFR)[7]: It is the number of live births occurring to women of a particular age group per year, normally expressed per 1000 women. It represents the number of live births to the total number of women in a specific age group (usually five year age groups from 15-19 to 45-49 are commonly used). Age specific fertility rate delineates age-wise population distribution or change. It is one of the most important measurements in fertility and used in the calculation of total fertility rate.

$$\text{Age Specific Fertility Rate } (ASFR_x) = \frac{B_X}{W_X} \times 1000$$

where, B_x = Births to women aged 'x'.
W_x = Average number of women aged 'x'.

(d) Total Fertility Rate (TFR)[8]: It is sum of the Age Specific Fertility Rates over the whole range of reproductive ages for a particular period (usually a year). It can be interpreted as the number of children a woman would have during her lifetime if she were to experience the fertility rates of the period at each age. It is an estimate of the number of children, which a cohort of 1000 women would produce, if they all went through their reproductive years exposed to the same age specific fertility rates that were in effect at particular time. It is computed by summing age specific fertility rate values for all ages and multiplied by the interval into which the ages are grouped *i.e.*, the magnitude.

$$\text{Total Fertility Rate} = 5 \text{ x} \sum_{X=15}^{49} ASFR$$

where '5' denotes the interval into which the ages are grouped *i.e.*, the magnitude, for example 15-19, 20-24, 25-29, 30-34, 35-39, 40-44, 45-49.

Total Fertility Rate (TFR) provides an overall summary of the fertility level unaffected by age structure. Although one of the most frequently quoted measures of fertility, the TFR sometimes requires a certain caution in interpretation. It is a hypothetical measure, not necessarily applicable to any true cohort, and may be dubious value when the quantum or level and timing or tempo of fertility are changing.

(e) Gross Reproduction Rate (GRR): It is the ratio of number of female children (potential future mothers) reaching childbearing age, to the number of mothers in reproductive age. It is the average number of daughters that would be born to a woman during her life time if she passed through the childbearing ages experiencing the average age specific fertility pattern of a given period (often a year). The rate is related to the TFR in the following manner: GRR= TFR × Proportion of Female births

Or,

Gross Reproduction Rate =

$$5 \times \left(\sum_{X=15}^{49} \text{ASFR}\right) \times \frac{\text{Female life births in a year}}{\text{Total (Male + Female) live births in that year}}$$

where '5' denotes for the magnitude of the age group interval.

It also reflects the projective reproductive performance of a population. The GRR is contrasted with Net Reproduction Rate, which takes account of mortality as well as fertility. Both are normally calculated solely for the female population.

(f) Completed Family Size (CFS) or Completed Fertility Rate (CFR): It is the cumulative fertility at the end of the reproductive ages. The term lifetime fertility is also encountered. It is the average number of children born to women, who have completed the childbearing period, *i.e.*, women who are 49 years and above. Otherwise, it is known as the mean number of children born per woman in a cohort of women who have reached the end of their childbearing years. It is an average childbearing experience, over a lifetime of all women in the population, and it is used for married women only.

(g) Mean Number of Children: It is calculated by dividing the total number of children surviving by the number of mothers.

(h) Child-Woman Ratio (General Fertility Ratio): It is the number of children aged 0-4 (occasionally 0 to 9) divided by the number of women in childbearing age (usually 15 to 49) and commonly expressed per 1000. In other words, it is the ratio of number of surviving children in the age 0-4 years to the women in their reproductive period, *i.e.*, 15 to 49 years.

Child-Woman Ratio (CWR) =

$$\frac{\text{Children of 0 - 4 years}}{\text{Women of age 15 – 49 years}} \times 1000$$

The ratio is used as a rough indicator of fertility when more detailed measures are not available. Since, it simply employs the most basic of census age data, the ratio is calculable for any area for which an age-sex structure exists. It is not an accurate measure of fertility in populations where the infant mortality and early childhood mortality are high.

(i) Mean Fertility: It is calculated by dividing the total number of live births by the number of mothers.

(j) Survival Rate: It is the ratio of surviving children to the live births. It indicates the chance of survival level of a population to a particular environment, which even implies its adaptability pattern.

Relative Range Method

In the present study, the Relative Range Method has been used to classify the income groups. According to this method,

$$\frac{\text{Highest Income of the Household} - \text{Lowest Income of the Household}}{\text{Number of Observations}}$$

Now this value becomes the scale for identifying economic classes in the community.

Statistical Tools

Some of the following statistical tools given below are used in the processing of first hand data. These are percentage, mean, standard deviation, standard error and 't' test.

1. Percentage: Individual absolute values are standardized per cent (100). It is calculated as,

$$\frac{\text{Individual Value}}{\text{Total Value}} \times 100$$

It is easy to calculate. It helps in understanding the representation of individual parameter from the total sample.

2. Arithmetic Mean: This is one of the most familiar measures of central tendency. It is calculated by dividing the total values of all observations by the number of observations. This is generally called the mean.

$$\text{Mean } (\overline{X}) = \frac{\text{Total of all Individual Values}}{\text{Number of Observations}}$$

Mean is easy to calculate. It is based on all the observations and least affected by sampling fluctuations but it is affected very much by extreme values.

3. Standard Deviation: It is the most commonly used measure of variation or dispersion. It takes into account all the values of a variable. Standard deviation is defined as the square root of the arithmetic mean of the squared deviations of the individual values from their arithmetic mean. It is also called as root mean square deviation from the arithmetic mean.

$$\text{Standard Deviation (SD)} = \sqrt{\frac{\text{Sum of squares of deviations of individual values from the arithmetic mean}}{\text{Sample Size (n)}}}$$

$$\text{For small samples, SD} = \sqrt{\frac{\Sigma(x\,j\;\overline{x})^2}{n-1}}$$

Standard Deviation (SD) is universally accepted as an adequate measure of variability. Though SD is based on all the values, it too can get seriously affected by extreme observations, primarily due to the distortion of mean.

4. Standard Error: The standard deviation of mean values is known as standard error. This is used to compare means with one another.

$$\text{Standard Error (SE)} = \frac{\text{Standard Deviation (SD)}}{\sqrt{\text{Sample Size (n)}}}$$

*5. **Student's 't' Test:*** Small samples do not follow normal distribution as large ones do. In case of small samples, Prof. W. S. Gossett in the pen name of student, developed 't' test. When samples are small and population variance is not known, 't' test is utilised. Student's 't' test or simply 't' test can be useful for testing differences between (*i*) two means of small independent samples, (*ii*) sample mean and population mean, and (*iii*) two proportions of small independent samples.

The ratio of the observed difference between two means (or proportions) of small samples to the standard error (SE) of difference is denoted by *t*. Probability of occurrence of any calculated value of t is determined by comparing it with the value given in the row of the table corresponding to the degree of freedom (df) derived from the number of observations in the sample under study. If the calculated value of *t* exceeds the tabulated value, it is said to be significant at a particular level of probability and null hypothesis (H_0) is rejected and alternate hypothesis is accepted. Assumptions made in the use of *t* test are: (*i*) samples are randomly selected, (*ii*) data utilized is quantitative, (*iii*) variables follow normal distribution, (*iv*) sample variances (SD^2 = variance) are mostly same in both the groups under study, and (*v*) samples are small, mostly lower than 30 or 100.

$$t = \frac{\text{Differences between means} = |\bar{x}_1 - \bar{x}_2|}{\text{Standard Error of } (\bar{x}_1 - \bar{x}_2)}$$

$$\text{Standard Error of } (\bar{x}_1 - \bar{x}_2) = \text{SE } (\bar{x}_1 - \bar{x}_2)$$

$$= \text{SD}\sqrt{1/n_2 + 1/n_2}$$

$$\text{Where SD} = \sqrt{SD^2} =$$

$$\sqrt{\frac{(n_1-1)\,SD_1^2+(n_2-1)\,SD_2^2}{n_1+n_2-2}}$$

SD_1^2 is the variance of the first sample,
SD_2^2 is the variance of the second sample,
SD^2 is the combined or pooled variance,
x_1 and x_2 are means of samples, and
n_1 and n_2 are sample sizes.

To sum up, it is understood that 'Demography' is a discipline in which the data are collected by field survey. Analysis is done on the basis of empirical evidences. Anthropological studies concentrate on the small populations in order to understand their cultural and biological adaptation. This, in fact, is possible through the first-hand information. The researcher collects data by using the interview tools like questionnaire and schedule. It is effective as part of in-depth research, if the quantitative information is supplemented by the qualitative information. Participant observation strengthens the process by engaging a researcher to take part and mingle with the people for drawing the best possible information about the aspects of life of the community. In order to understand the impact of the altitude on the demographic structure and fertility pattern, the interview schedules were used to collect the information from people inhabiting the high and low altitudes of the district Pithoragarh in Uttaranchal Himalayas. Married women, who were not divorced and had at least a child, were selected as the unit of study. They were asked questions related to the family, economy, occupation, reproductive life, etc. The genealogy method was used in comprehending the information on the generations of a family. The cross checking was done by involving other members including their respective husband in the household.

The fieldwork was carried out in between the years 1998 and 1999. Demographic data were collected from 262 households from 17 villages (7 villages from high altitude and 10 villages from low altitude). The sample size is 262 households that consist 110 from high altitude and 152 from low altitude. The average altitude of villages consulted at high altitude is 3,433 m and 1,861 m at low altitude. The demographic analysis is done from two dimensions. First, population composition includes age-sex composition, sex ratio, masculinity proportion, index of aging and dependency ratio. The other, fertility measures include pregnancy history, survival level and rates. The analysis also involves the human resources like education, occupation and economy and their mobilization in the Bhotia populations in high and low altitudes of Uttaranchal Himalayas. Percentage, mean, standard error, 't' test of significance are some of the statistical parameters used to measure variability and significance level among the Bhotia populations settled at high and low altitudes.

Notes

1. The high and low altitudes in the study refer to the spatial context of social ecology of Bhotias in Pithoragarh district of Kumaon Himalaya, Uttaranchal. The Bhotias are traditionally high land dwellers inhabiting in between the Middle and Greater Himalayas. Here, low means the settlement up to the height of 2,500 m and settlement above this is high. The value of 2,500 m is critical in the context of Bhotia regions because this is also the altitude, which divides the permanent settlement from semi-nomadic settlements. Moreover, this is also the lowermost limit of summer pastures or *Bugyals*, which are used for rearing of stocks during summer. Apart from this, the resource base, forest cover, economic life and activities of people change sharply. For example, up to the altitude of 2,50C m, snowfall during winter is a normal phenomenon, which makes it possible for the growth of alpine type of vegetation. Whereas, altitude below that have predominance of subtropical mixed forest cover.
2. Population or universe is well defined in the science of statistics. Though biological definition of this term 'population' is the totality of the individuals of a given species per given time and given area; population in 'statistics' always means the totality of the individual observations about which inferences are to be made. Observations can be on heights, weights, nutrients, etc. A sample is a small collection of observations from some larger aggregate or population (universe) about which we wish to have information (Rao, 1996:12-3).
3. 'Fully Married woman', whose husband was alive, had normal

married life, and was not divorced or become widow by the time of fieldwork.

4. It may be noted that in the following chapters, the terms such as respondent, ego, mother, woman, and wife have been used interchangeably.
5. The exact ages chosen as the bounds of these groups vary, depending on the minimum age at leaving school and retirement age, but 0-14, 15-64 and 65 and above are commonly used especially for international comparisons. In India old aged persons are considered those persons of aged 60 years and above (SRS 1996:18).
6. Age Pattern of Fertility is a term, used to express the way in which fertility varies with age. The fertility is restricted to the reproductive ages (for women roughly 15 to 50 years), and within this range it shows a characteristic pattern. An initial rise from low levels to a peak, usually in the 20s, is followed by a decline. This pattern varies depending on a number of factors such as the level of fecundity, the prevalence of marriage or other sexual unions, the degree of family limitation and so on.
7. In the present study, the fertility rates are calculated in reference to the married women. So here, the Age Specific Marital Fertility Rate has been taken into account. It is the number of live births (in a year) occurring to married women of a particular age or age group (five-year age groups from 15-19 to 45-49 are commonly used), normally expressed per 1000 women (or sometimes per woman). Since childbearing in many societies largely takes place within marriage these rates give a clear indication of changes in actual childbearing than the more commonly quoted ASFRs, which are also influenced by changes in marriage patterns.
8. Instead of TFR, the Total Marital Fertility Rate (TMFR) has been taken into account. It is the sum of Age Specific Marital Fertility Rates of a particular period (often a year) over the whole range of reproductive ages. It represents the number of children a woman would have if she experienced the average marital fertility at every age.

4

CONTEXTUALISING THE DEMOGRAPHIC STRUCTURE OF BHOTIAS

In social science research, the society is conceived as a natural system and human being as an object of observation. Demography belongs to that group of empirical studies whose data are produced by the observation and recording of events occurring to the human population. Demography is known to be a vast area of study, as it deals with providing information on all aspects of human being. The study of demographic structure of a population group constitutes a key to all population-related events, which not only feeds on quantitative but also qualitative information. The demographic composition describes the population situation at a particular point of time and place with the help of different variables, as these affect the population dynamics, which in turn are to determine the stability and sustainability of a population group. Demography as a discipline is concerned itself with the totality of people and their quantification in many ways. Thus, the main themes of demography are to determine the size, proportion, age distribution, sex composition, distribution by marital status, levels of education, etc., of the population as a whole. In turn these demographic attributes are the result of multiple factors. Variation in altitudes is one of them. Though an important one, yet so far it is the most neglected aspect in the demographic studies.

In recent times, the scholars have drawn their attention to

study the interrelationship between altitude and demography. It is particularly important in communities, which are placed in the margins of modernisation and development. The Bhotia tribe of Pithoragarh in Uttaranchal is one of them. In this Chapter, attempts have been made to study the demographic structure of high and low altitude Bhotia populations. The categorisation and analysis of high and low altitude population composition of Bhotia tribe have been done to comprehend and scientifically analyse the interrelationship between altitude and demographic structure. Important attributes of demographic structure such as age, sex, family size and type, marital status, etc., have been selected to study the variations. These variables are essential in demographic studies, as these are significantly associated with the other vital factors of population change.

- It is necessary to study age and sex composition in order to understand the dynamics of population, because in a peripheral and relatively stagnant society, like that of the Bhotias of Pithoragarh, age and sex selective migration results into predominance of economically dependent children and post productive[1] section and higher sex ratio in favour of females. Because of out-migration, the gender ratio reflects more number of females; but there are exceptions and it is necessary to prove the reasons of varying masculinity proportion.
- Similarly, index of ageing will be studied in order to understand the natural process of population growth due to differences in birth and death rates, which in fact indicates the proportion of aged sections in comparison to the child population.
- Dependency ratio will reflect the ability of working population to support the unproductive young children and post productive (old age and physically challenged population) section.
- Family structure will show the nature of support to newborn that is required for upbringing and rearing of young and post productive members of the family. It is

observed that the larger family has better support system and provides good care for younger and elderly people.

- Births out of matrimonial bonds are not just simple births, but they also receive legitimisation out of this. Marriage, therefore, is not a simple mundane ritual performed by the member of the society but it is a process of sharing and discharging social responsibility along with the claims of legitimacy. Therefore, marital status of individuals is vital to understand the involvement of couples in the sexual life and hence the reproduction is processed through legitimate and recognised means.

Age-Sex Structure

Age-sex structure of a population provides an important component for demographic analysis. It bears reflection of fertility, mortality and migration of the past and also influences the present and future birth, death and migration of a community (Bhasin and Bhasin, 1993:179). Populations with rapid growth rates have young populations with a high proportion of children. More slowly growing or stationary population have a smaller number of children with commensurately more adults and old persons (Pressat, 1972:33-7). Besides age and sex, the term population composition also refers to the distribution within a population of one or more traits or attributes such as education, income, marital status, etc., (Chachra and Bhasin, 1998:409). From the age-sex composition, planners and policy makers can have an idea about the manpower and labour force population, school age population, voting population, total dependent population including young and old section and proportion of masculinity. Therefore, age and sex compositions are two important demographic characteristics of a population. The age-sex structure of a population is well represented graphically by population pyramid (see Figures 4.2 to 4.4).

Table 4.1 and Appendix 4 provide information on the age and sex structure (in number and percentage) of Bhotia population at high and low altitudes in Kumaon Himalaya, Uttaranchal. Table 4.1 displays information about the infant (below one year of age), early childhood population (0-4 years), child population as such (0-14 years), the economically active population[2] (15-59 years), and old age population (60 years and above). Appendix 4 depicts the data regarding age and sex structure in detail starting from the age group below one year of age to the old age group in five-year grouping. At high altitude, there are 53.34 per cent males and 46.66 per cent females. However, these figures do not vary much in consideration to low altitude, *viz.*, 51.46 per cent males and 48.54 per cent females. In the total sample of Bhotia population, there are 52.24 per cent males and 47.76 per cent females. The economically active population (15-59 years) in high altitude is 62.59 per cent, while it is 62.64 per cent at low altitude. The old age population (60 years and above and along with the physically challenged population) constitutes 3.56 per cent at high altitude, which is much lower than the 6.75 per cent of population at the low altitude, and in the totality it constitutes 5.42 per cent (see also Figure 4.1).

Table 4.1: Age and Sex of Sample Bhotia Population by Major Age Groups

Age Group (in yr.)		*High Altitude*			*Low Altitude*			*Total*		
		Male	*Female*	*Total*	*Male*	*Female*	*Total*	*Male*	*Female*	*Total*
Below 1	No.	8	8	16	13	11	24	21	19	40
	%	1.14	1.14	2.28	1.31	1.11	2.42	1.24	1.12	2.36
0-4	No.	41	39	80	59	48	107	100	87	187
	%	5.83	5.55	11.38	5.94	4.83	10.78	5.90	5.13	11.03
0-14	No.	126	112	238	150	154	304	276	266	542
	%	17.92	15.93	33.85	15.11	15.51	30.61	16.27	15.68	31.96
15-59	No.	237	203	440	329	293	622	566	496	1062
	%	33.71	28.88	62.59	33.13	29.51	62.64	33.37	29.25	62.62
60+	No.	12	13	25	32	35	67	44	48	92
	%	1.71	1.85	3.56	3.22	3.52	6.75	2.59	2.83	5.42
All Ages	No.	375	328	703	511	482	993	886	810	1696
	%	53.34	46.66	100.00	51.46	48.54	100.00	52.24	47.76	100.00

Source: Primary Data.

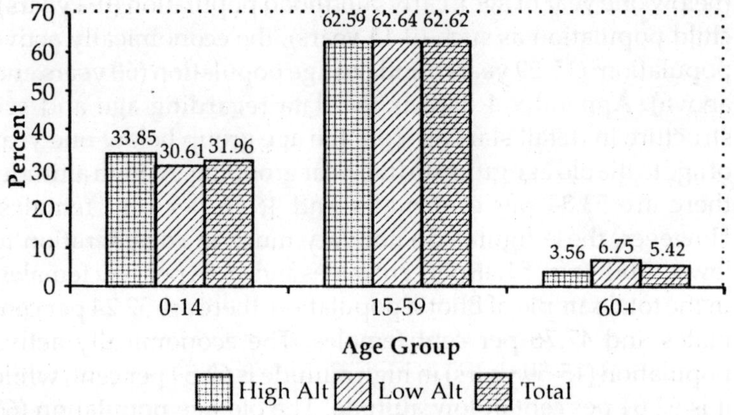

Fig. 4.1 : Age Structure among the sample Bhotia Tribe in Kumaon, Uttaranchal Himalaya

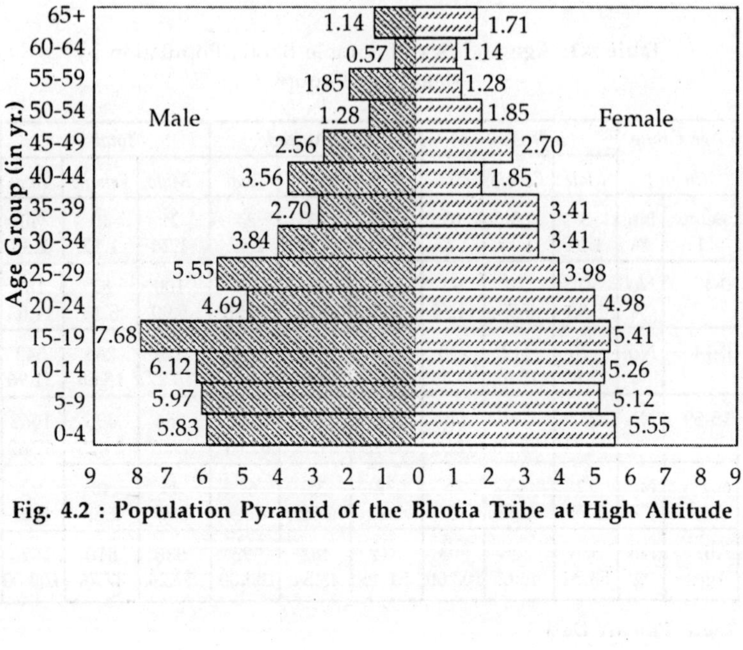

Fig. 4.2 : Population Pyramid of the Bhotia Tribe at High Altitude

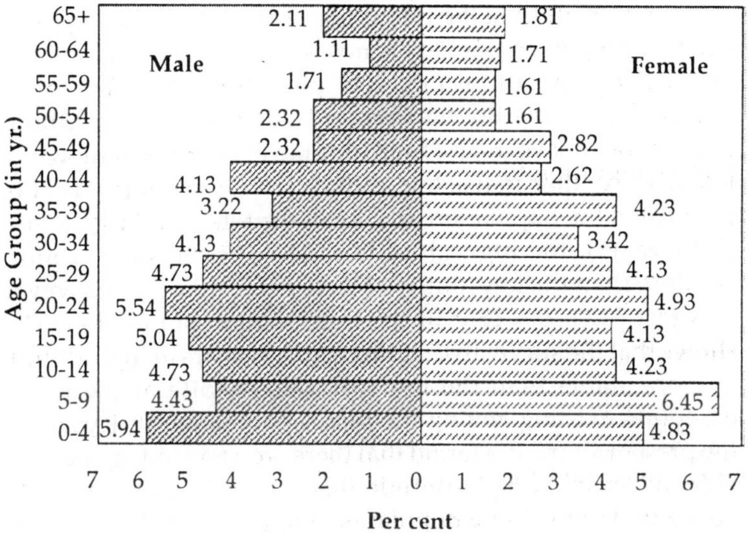

Fig. 4.3 : Population Pyramid of the Bhotia Tribe at Low Altitude

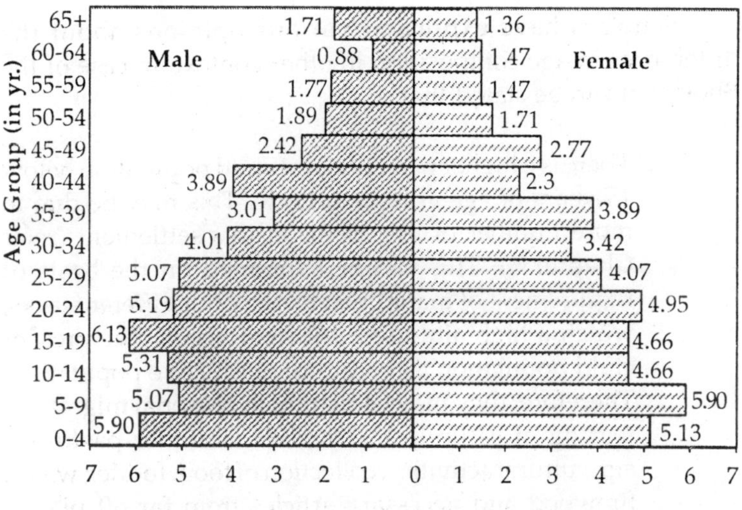

Fig. 4.4 : Population Pyramid of the sample Bhotia Tribe

In high altitude the infant population (below one year of age) is 2.28 per cent, which is not very different from the low altitude composition, i.e., 2.42 per cent. The total infant population in the Bhotia tribe is 2.36. The early childhood population (0-4 years) for high altitude is 11.38 per cent, which is just higher than that of low altitude (10.78 per cent). It is 11.03 per cent in the population. In case of the total child population (0-14 years), the high altitude (33.85 per cent) bears more children than the low altitude (30.61 per cent) does. However, it is just 31.96 per cent in the total sample population. This shows that the survival of children in 1-14 years in high altitude is more stable than the low altitude, despite at the minor exception existing among the infant population (0-1 year). In the present study, it is found that there are a few old age persons (3.56 per cent) in high altitude than in the low altitude (6.75 per cent). In the Bhotia population, there are only 5.42 per cent of the people over the age of 59 years. As such, there are no such major differences marked in the age structure of Bhotias at high and low altitudes.

Scholars have expressed various opinions about the differences in age composition in other context. In case of the Bhotias, it can be stated that—

1. There is a higher percentage of child population below 15 years of age at high altitude. This may be due to more number of live births at this settlement (refer Chapter 6). This can be explained on the basis of requirement of manpower to carry out different tasks, which a high altitude settlement needs. The present child population is the future productive population. Therefore, they may be helpful in seasonal migration, rearing of cattle in the *Bugyals* (summer pastures), agricultural activities, collection of food, fodder, water, firewood and necessary articles from far off places, guarding female folk, children and other dependent ones, more so for social and physical security.
2. As the natural forces continuously threaten the high altitude settlement, either through the selective

out-migration or the loss of children, it further reduces the high and low altitude differences among the economically active population, which existed at the level of child population.

3. The old age population is reduced at high altitude because of either early deaths or due to migration to other suitable places in search of better medical facilities and comfort. Loss of old age people and increase in the base population is a typical situation of underdeveloped societies. In this case, the precondition for higher birth ratio and low level of life expectancy is related to the high altitude settlement that is considered to be a manpower demanding habitation.

The present finding resembles the study conducted by Gupta (1980:103) among the Sherpas of Upper Kumbu at high altitude in Nepal and Kalimpong at the low altitude in the district Darjeeling of West Bengal. Balgir (1991:175-6) observes that in Western Himalayas there are more infants (0-4 years) among the Muslim Gujjars (18 per cent) of Himalayan region of Himachal Pradesh than that of Hindu Gujjars (10 per cent) of sub-Himalayan region. However, Balgir observes that the compositions of child population, economically active population and old age population of Himalayan Muslim Gujjars are 47.83 per cent, 47.95 per cent and 4.22 per cent, while the sub-Himalayan Hindu Gujjars show 32.78 per cent, 56.9 per cent and 10.32 per cent respectively. Another study from Western Himalayas among the Gaddis of Himachal Pradesh also shows that there are 41.5 per cent, 55.2 per cent and 3.3 per cent people in the age groups 0-14 years, 15-64 years and 65+ years respectively (Bhasin and Bhasin, 1993:181).

Similarly, the population distributions in Lachung village (altitude 2,300 m) and Lachen village (altitude 2,600 m) in Sikkim in Eastern Himalayas also indicate absence of significant differences in the child, reproductive, and old age populations. The study shows that they are 34.95 per cent, 54.12 per cent and 10.93 per cent in the Lachung village and 35.37 per cent, 54.27 per cent and 10.37 per cent respectively in Lachen village (Das *et al.*, 1982:157). In a view to this, the percentage of age composition among the War Khasis of Meghalaya in Eastern Himalayas depicts that there are 42.8 per cent, 49.5 per cent and 7.7 per cent populations among the same age groups (Khongsdier and Ghosh, 1994:196).

From Central Himalayas, it has been reported that among the Bhotias of Mana village (altitude 3,200m) in the district Chamoli in Garhwal Himalaya, the distribution of population groups is 34.19 per cent, 52.83 per cent and 12.98 per cent in child, reproductive, and old age categories respectively (Guha, 1997:65). Similarly, the study on Marcha Bhotia (Chachra and Bhasin, 1998:411) in Garhwal Himalaya, resembles the present finding with 31.87 per cent, 61.69 per cent and 6.24 per cent in the same age groups respectively. They show a series of data on Kumaoni populations including the Johari and Dharchula Bhotias. Their findings reveal that the age distribution of child, economically active and old age populations for Johari is 35.21 per cent, 59.93 per cent and 4.85 per cent; for Dharchula Bhotias it is 43.50 per cent, 51.65 per cent and 4.85 per cent; and for Kumaoni caste groups, it is 42.17 per cent, 53.87 per cent and 3.95 per cent respectively.

Sex Composition

The sex composition of a population generally influences the form and tempo of life in a community. The balance between sexes is an important aspect of population structure. Many economic and social relationships are closely related to the balance or disparity between the number of males and females. Sex composition is an important indicator of fertility trends, family structure, marriage patterns, and to know about the status of the women in the society and so on. Sex composition may be studied with reference to sex ratio. Sex ratio in a population is the number of females to the number of males. The ratio at each age is also a feature of considerable importance, as it varies considerably due to the impact of sex-selective mortality and migration. Since males tend to be more mobile than females, areas of in-migration usually have a lower sex ratio than areas of out-migration. Higher female mortality also leads to access of males at almost all ages.

According to Table 4.2 (see also Figure 4.5), the sex ratio is found to be 1000 for infants (below one year) at high altitude. The prevailing pattern that is found in the infant population considerably decreases thereafter. This pattern even remains unchanged for the economically active population (15-59 years). For the old age population, the sex ratio is quite high (1083), which means that there are more females than males. Considering all age groups together at high altitude, the sex ratio is 875, which is well below the figure at low altitude (943). This indicates that there is more number of females in comparison to males at low altitude. In low altitude the infant group and the early childhood, the sex ratio is 846 and 816 respectively; whereas, the overall sex ratio in the total child population is 1027. Furthermore, this ratio is significantly decreasing among the economically active population (891) and with a rise among the old age people (1094). As a whole, in the Bhotia population, the sex ratio is relatively higher at the old age population level (1091), compared to other age groups. The sex ratio, in totality, is 914 of the population.

Table 4.2: Sex Ratio of the Sample Bhotia Population

Altitude	*Age Group (in Years)*					
	Below 1	*0-4*	*0-14*	*15-59*	*60+*	*All Ages*
High	1000	951	889	857	1083	875
Low	846	816	1027	891	1094	943
Total	905	870	964	876	1091	914

There are numerous determining factors for variation in sex ratio. However, in case of the Bhotias, it is observed that—

1. At high altitude, there is an equilibrium of live births between sexes at the infancy; and then this gap is widened between sexes, which means the percentage of male children is more in comparison to the female children. As the girls are subject to improper care and

negligence, discrepancy results in the sex ratio. This is so, because the patriarchal nature of society considers the male children superior, and the future assets for parents. They would, in turn, be helpful to them during seasonal migration, agricultural activities, and rearing of cattle, goats and sheep.

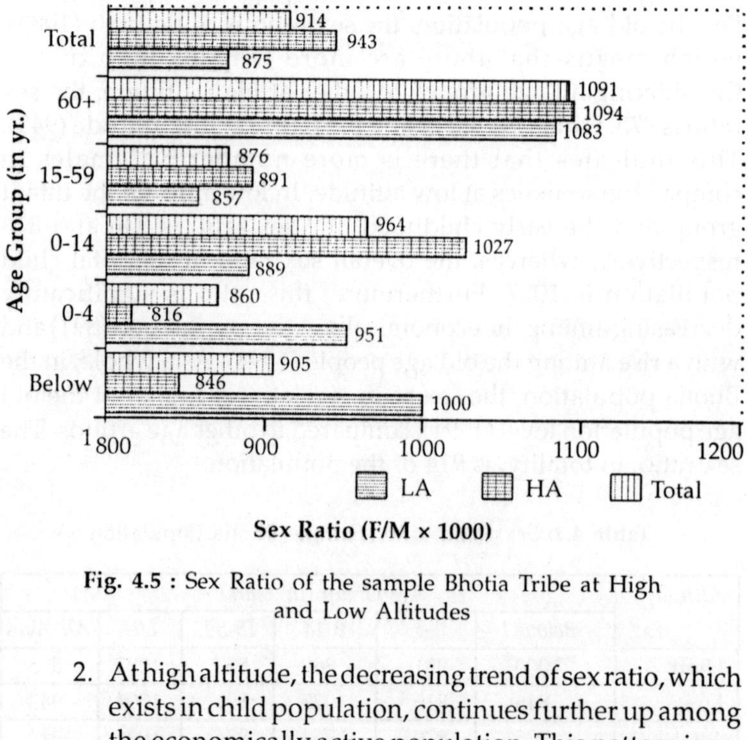

Fig. 4.5 : Sex Ratio of the sample Bhotia Tribe at High and Low Altitudes

2. At high altitude, the decreasing trend of sex ratio, which exists in child population, continues further up among the economically active population. This pattern is so, because it is the child of today that graduates into the economically active section in future. That means the child population is the future productive population.
3. At low altitude, the stage of infancy shows that there are more male births. In the later part of the childhood the sex ratio tilts in favour of girls. This is because the low altitude is conducive for the proper nourishment among the girls, particularly due to the availability of

medical facilities, awareness and education. Thus, it implies that proper attention is paid to both boys and girls equally at low altitude by the parents and elders. It is worth noticing here that sex discrimination is prevalent in societies. But the discrimination becomes a part of the structure where the challenges for survival are more and resource availability is uncertain, as is the case of high altitude settlement, where the economy is uncertain and facilities are rare. Therefore, the family prefers to devote their limited resources on the nourishment of male child. As opposed to this, the economic conditions are favourable in low altitude villages, where the girl child takes the advantage out of it. When resources are limited, the risks are more. Then male child becomes the choice, as is the case in high altitude. As opposed to this, when resources are available, though the discrimination continues, the girl child too receives her share of resources to meet her necessities.

4. At low altitude, the trend of sex composition was found to be the reverse of the high altitude situation among the child population. But later, it tilted in favour of males in the economically active population. This is, because of, more number of deaths among the female population, either due to pregnancy complication, frequent conception and childbirth or due to negligence. This process makes women subject to malnutrition, weakness and early loss of life. However, those who survive during their reproductive performance continue to survive further adjusting to the situation. This is quite evident from the population pyramid (see Figures 4.2 to 4.4).
5. At high and low altitudes, among the old age population, the women sections of the Bhotia tribe have better adaptive fitness than their male counterparts. The onset of ageing process is quite early for the male population. However, the prevalence of more old age population at low altitude implies theirs

access to better care and medical facilities in a system of settled life.

Worldwide data show that there is, on an overage, a surplus of females in the industrial nations (Davis and Oever, 1986:13-5). The sex ratio[3] among infants in the entire high altitude Tibetan and Sherpa populations in Nepal shows 847 females in 1000 males and 1120 females in 1000 males respectively (Weitz *et al.*, 1978:184-5),[3] which highlights a surplus of males in the Tibetan population and a surplus of females in Sherpa population. However, the sex composition of Tibetan population resembles the present findings at high altitude. Bangham and Sacherer (1980:325)[3] supports the findings of Weitz *et al.* (1978) on sex ratio at birth among Sherpas at moderate altitude (2,200-2,600 m) where 1087 females count for 1000 males.

In the Western Himalaya, Balgir (1991:175-7) points out that the sex ratio (F/M x 1000) among the Muslim Gujjar (976 females in 1000 males) in Himalayas is better than that of the Hindu Gujjars (690 females in 1000 males) in the sub-Himalayan region. The sex ratio at the 0-4 years is higher among the Muslim Gujjars (973 females per 1000 males) than the Hindu Gujjars (595 females per 1000 males). The sex ratio among the Gaddis in Himachal Pradesh is 870 (Bhasin and Bhasin, 1993:179-80), which resembles the findings of the present study among the high altitude Bhotias.

In the Eastern Himalaya, from the study conducted by Das *et al.* (1982:157) in Sikkim, it is calculated that the sex ratio is found higher in the village Lachen (1103) at high altitude than that of the village Lachung (951) in the low altitude. The figure of high altitude village does not resemble present finding among the high altitude Bhotias. The sex ratio at 0-4 years is higher in both the villages than the present findings. The sex ratio for the Idu Mishmis of Arunachal Pradesh is 933, 1006, and 973 among the children 0-4 years, children 0-14 years and overall populations respectively, while the figures for the Digaru Mishmis of the same state are 1136, 1019, and 950 (Pandey, 1991:65-9). Among the War Khasis in Meghalaya, there are more males, *i.e.*, 109 males per 100 females (Khongsdier and Ghosh, 1994:196), which resemble the present finding.

Studies conducted in the Central Himalayas by scholars (Guha, 1997; Dube and Singh, 1997; Chachra and Bhasin, 1998) show a similar kind of result. The village Mana, a high altitude village in the Garhwal Himalaya, exhibits the sex ratio of Bhotia population as 989 females in 1000 males (Guha, 1997:65). The sex ratio of Bhotias in Mana village in the child population (0-14 years), economically active population (15 to 59 years) and old age population (above 59 years) are 1253, 912 and 571 respectively. It is reported that the sex ratio of Marcha Bhotias in Garhwal Himalaya and Johar and Dharchula Bhotias in Kumaon Himalaya is 1005, 960 and 993 respectively for the three age groups (Chachra and Bhasin, 1998:409-10). It is also noticed that the sex ratio of Bhotias in Garhwal Himalaya is more or less equal to Kumaoni Bhotia (981) and Kumaoni caste groups (998). According to the Census of India 1961 and 1971 the sex ratio of Bhotias does not vary much, *i.e.*, 917 in 1961 and 912 in 1971 (cited: in Dube and Singh, 1997:283).

The sex ratio of the Bhotia tribe in the district Pithoragarh, Kumaon Himalaya, and Central Himalayas according to the Census 1981 is 976, 964 and 981 respectively. The sex ratio in the district Pithoragarh in 1991 was 985, which was significantly better than the overall Himalayan region (930 in 1991). The sex ratio of the Scheduled Tribes in India was 972 in 1991 and 978 in 2001. According to the Census 2001, in Uttaranchal, the sex ratio is 964 and for the district Pithoragarh, it is 1031 females for 1000 males.

Masculinity Proportion

Masculinity proportion is another measure of sex composition. It is the percentage of males in a population. The masculinity proportion is 53.34 per cent and 51.46 per cent at high and low altitudes respectively. The proportion remains 50 per cent for the infant population at high altitude, that increases among the child population (52.94 per cent) and economically active population (53.86 per cent). It decreases considerably among the old age population (48.00 per cent) at this altitude. Unlike the high altitude, at low altitude the masculinity proportion is found higher among the infant and early child population *viz.*, 54.17 per cent and 55.14 per cent respectively. This is 49.34 per cent among the total child population. However, among the economically active population, the proportion is 52.89 per cent, and it is 47.76 per cent among the old age population. However, in general at the population level, it can be mentioned that there is more male population than the female except among the old age people where males are 47.83 per cent (see Table 4.3 and Figure 4.6).

Table 4.3: Masculinity Proportion of the Sample Bhotia Population

Altitude	*Age Group (in Years)*					
	Below 1	*0-4*	*0-14*	*15-59*	*60+*	*All Ages*
High	50.00	51.25	52.94	53.86	48.00	53.34
Low	54.17	55.14	49.34	52.89	47.76	51.46
Total	52.50	53.48	50.92	53.30	47.83	52.24

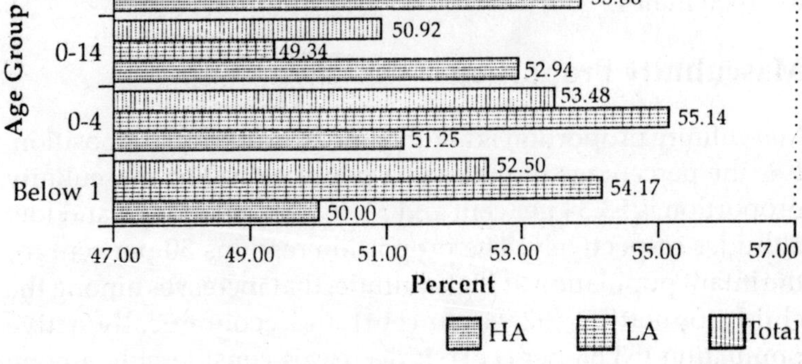

Fig. 4.6 : Masculinity Proportion of Bhotia Population at High and Low Altitudes

Plate 1: Panchachuli (approx. 6,500 m) as seen from Munsiyari: Famous for the Legend in Mahabharat; Pandavas used these five hilltops to cook their food on the way to heavens.

Plate 2: Aum Parvat (Mountain): The natural patterning of Aum by the ice on the Hilltop.

Plate 3: Head Quarter of Dharchula Tehsil (900 m) in the District Pithoragarh.

Plate 4: Munsiyari (2,050 m) during winter.

Plate 5: A Bhotia man in the traditional Rajput uniform.

Plate 6: A Johari Bhotia family of village Jalath (1,930 m) in Munsiyari Tehsil.

Plate 7: Byansi Bhotia of village Nabi (3,566 m) in Dharchula Tehsil: A couple in a dancing mood at an informal gathering.

Plate 8: The village Kuti: A high altitude village (3,871 m).

Plate 9: The village Darati in Munsiyari Tehsil: A low altitude village (1,810 m).

Plate 10: Khalia Top (approx. 4,200 m) on the way to Johar valley: Areas adjoining Summer pastures (Bugyals), which was scaled by the Author.

Plate 11: Step cultivation in Himalayas.

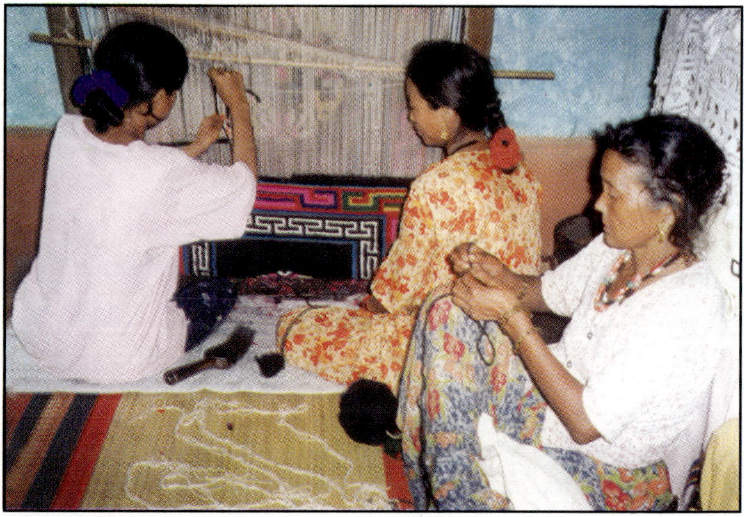

Plate 12: Female folk of Darma valley carrying out spinning and weaving activities.

Plate 13: Preparation of Chakti (country liquor).

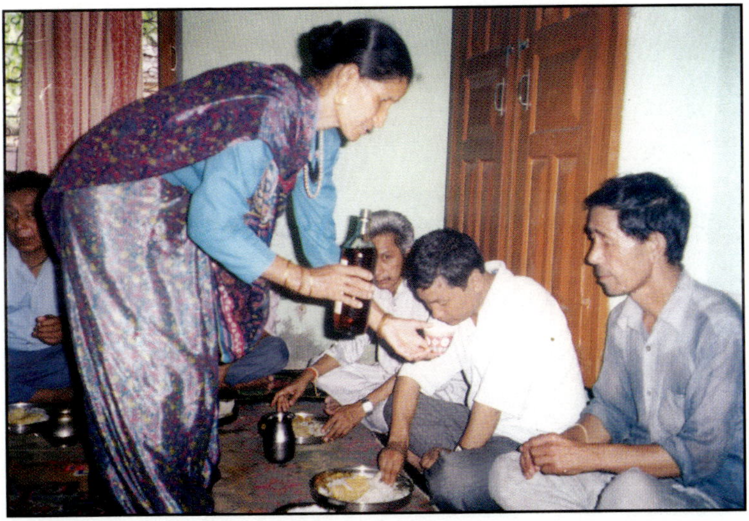

Plate 14: English wine being served in an occasion.

Plate 15: Rakshya Bandhan: A celebration by the young Bhotia girls.

Plate 16: Narayan Ashram in Chaudans valley.

Plate 17: Bhotia students with the teacher in Ashram Type school at Balwakot in Dharchula tehsil.

Plate 18: A Bhotia House of the village Himkhola (2,350 m) in Chaudans valley.

Plate 19: A locked Bhotia house in the Winter Habitat: Family left for Summer Habitation.

Plate 20: Bhotia women of village Kuti (3,871 m) in their traditional dress.

Plate 21: Bhotia women in *Saree* attending a function: Wearing of *Saree* is a common practice.

Plate 22: Young Bhotia Children.

Plate 23: A group of Bhotia boys and girls in a festive mood.

Plate 24: A widow from the village Sella (approx. 2,550 m) in Darma valley offers flower to her deceased husband's effigy at the first death anniversary. The effigy is made out of the items used by the deceased person.

Plate 29: Educated Johari Bhotia couple with their kids and domestic help.

Plate 30: Mules carrying gas cylinders to the village Pangu (2,240 m) in Chaudans valley: A way to save deforestation; some NGOs provide gas cylinders to the people in subsidized price.

Plate 31: Author (third from right) with the Bhotia people.

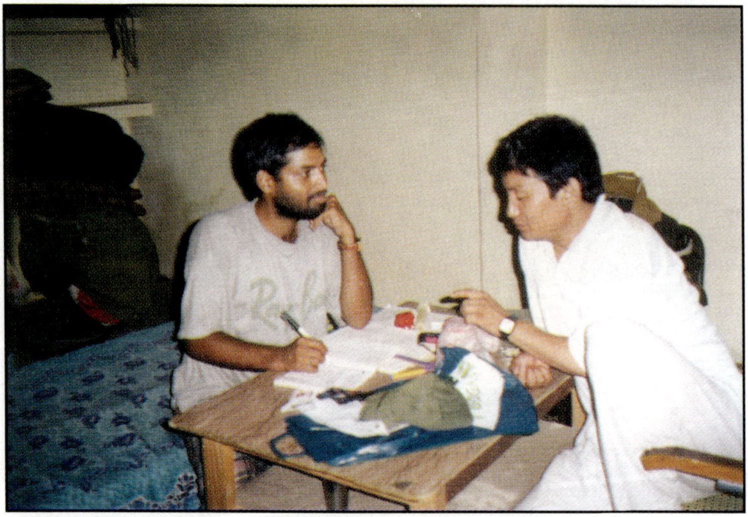

Plate 32: Author (left) interviewing Mr. Bhimraj Singh Nabiyal, Headman of village Nabi.

Moreover, in the present case it is observed that—

1. The Bhotia population irrespective of their altitudinal settlements shows a favourable degree of masculinity. The population tries to accommodate more males than the females. This is primarily due to the need of manpower in the population. The other reason may be related to the patriarchal framework of society, which always favours male domination.
2. The female sections of the society have been considered weaker ones. Other members in fact, decide their fate. Their birth and presence are always found declining. At high altitude, even though the proportion remains balanced, it is further minimised. At low altitude, the proportion begins with in favour of male sections. Whatever, the fact may be proper nourishment and caring for the females is not extended at par with that of the males; thus, blindfolding the gender in favour of males. However, masculinity is low among old age population.

From the studies in the Himalayas by various scholars (Das *et al.*, 1982; Balgir, 1991; Bhasin and Bhasin, 1993; Khongsdier and Ghosh, 1994; Chachra and Bhasin, 1998), it is observed that the proportion is in support of males (*i.e.* above 50 per cent), which is not an exception for the present finding too. Masculinity proportion of Gaddis in Western Himalayas is 53.48 per cent (Bhasin and Bhasin, 1993:181-2). The masculinity proportion of the Bhotias of Central Himalayas is 50.47 per cent and in the Kumaoni caste groups, it is found 50.04 per cent. For the Marcha Bhotia of Garhwal Himalaya and Johari and Dharchula Bhotias of Kumaon Himalaya, it is 49.87 per cent, 51.01 per cent and 50.15 per cent respectively. The findings of Chachra and Bhasin (1998:410) in the Johari and Dharchula Bhotias resemble the present study.

Index of Ageing

Index of ageing[4] is a measure describing the relative number of older people in the population. The index is low in those populations in which a high proportion of population is below 15 years. At high altitude, the index of ageing is 10.50, which is quite lower than that of the low altitude population with an index 22.04 (see Table 4.4).

Table 4.4: Index of Ageing for the Sample Bhotia Population

Altitude	*Index of Ageing*
High	10.50
Low	22.04
Total	16.97

The reasons behind these differences may be—

1. At high altitude, the index of ageing is quite low because of very thin concentration of old age population. The survival capacity is low among the old age population at high altitude as it puts the aged population at a constant threat of high altitudinal stress and strain.
2. The situation is quite better for the old age population at low altitude because of the conducive environment and other facilities prevalent at this settlement.
3. Moreover, the high altitude environment provides inadequate amount of Oxygen; therefore, the oxygenation process of the body gets reduced giving rise to the reduction of physiological activities among old age people, thus reducing life expectancy.

This can be corroborated by the study conducted in other parts of Himalayas. The index of ageing is reported to be 7.95 among the Gaddis of Himachal Pradesh of Western Himalayas (Bhasin and Bhasin, 1993:182). The index is 17.65 among the Bhotias in Mana village of Garhwal Himalaya in Central Himalayas (Guha, 1997:64-5). However, Chachra and Bhasin (1998:411) reported a much lower value among the Bhotias of Central Himalayas (7.09) and among the Kumaoni caste groups

Plate 25: A Bhotia woman delivering speech at 'Janjati Maha Sammilani' that held on 24th May 1998 at Pithoragarh.

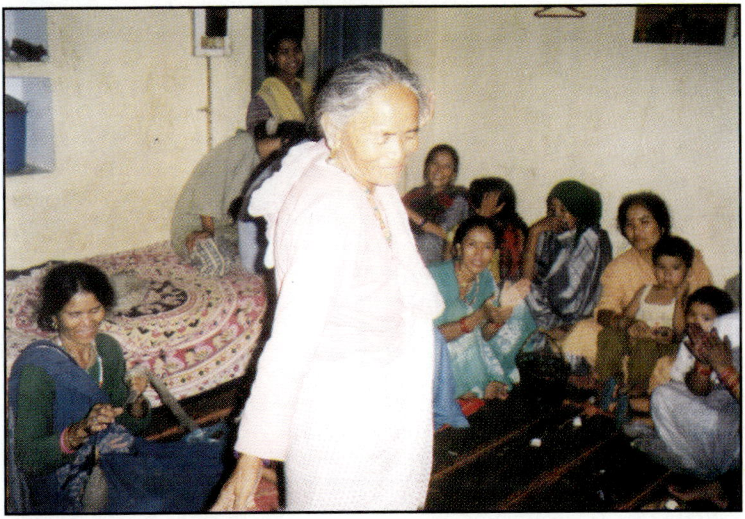

Plate 26: A Byansi Bhotia woman in a dancing mood.

Plate 27: Bhotia leaders at a Socio-cultural Gathering: Second from the left Mr. Jawahar Singh Nabiyal, Ex–Chairman, Dharchula Block.

Plate 28: An international bridge over the river Kali connecting Dharchula (India) and Darchula (Nepal).

(5.07), which are closer to the present findings regarding high altitude Bhotias.

Dependency Ratio

Dependency ratio is another way of looking at the age composition of a population. The young age dependency ratio is higher at high altitude (54.09) than at low altitude (48.87). However, the old-age dependency ratio is quite low at high altitude (5.68) than at low altitude (10.77). At the level of total dependency ratio, there is no such difference existing between two altitudes. However, in the total sample population, the young age dependency ratio and the old age dependency ratio are 51.04 and 8.66 respectively (see Table 4.5).

Table 4.5: Dependency Ratio of Sample Bhotia Population

Altitude	*Young Age Dependency Ratio*	*Old Age Dependency Ratio*	*Total Dependency Ratio*
High	54.09	5.68	59.77
Low	48.87	10.77	59.65
Total	51.04	8.66	59.70

To explain these changes one may argue that—

1. Higher dependency ratio is a hindrance for proper functional achievements. When too many burdens are accredited on the productive population, they stand unable to deliver their exercise along the line of requirement and need of the society.
2. Higher young age dependency ratio at high altitude because of the higher percentage of child population signifies higher fertility level. High altitude demands for more births, which may be due to higher child mortality (refer Chapter 6) or due to selective migration of the productive population.
3. Reduction in the old age dependency ratio at high altitude implies high altitude constraints among the old age people.

4. As far as the total dependency ratio is concerned, it is found that no difference exists between altitudes. Therefore, it can be said that even if the populations are settled at different altitudes, the similarities are shared between them because of their ethnic relationship and similar historical background.

In a study conducted among the Gujjars in the Western Himalaya, Balgir (1991:176) shows that the young age dependency ratio and the total dependency ratio among the Muslim Gujjars of Himalayan region outnumber the Hindu Gujjars of sub-Himalayan region. However, old age dependency ratio is reported higher among the Hindu Gujjars than among the Muslim Gujjars, which seem to be higher than the present finding except the old age dependency ratio among Muslim Gujjars in Himachal Pradesh. Bhasin and Bhasin (1993:181-2) report that the young age dependency ratio, old age dependency ratio and total dependency ratio among the Gaddis of Himachal Pradesh Himalayas are 75.18, 5.98 and 81.16 per cent respectively.

Between the Idu and Digaru Mishmis in Arunachal Pradesh, Pandey (1991:63-9) reports a much higher young age dependency ratio, old age dependency ratio and total dependency ratio than that of the present findings. In the Central Himalayas, the study of Guha (1997:65) shows higher values for young age dependency ratio, old age dependency ratio and total dependency ratio among the Mana Bhotias in Garhwal Himalaya, compared to the present findings. The old age dependency ratio has been found 4.21 per cent among the Bhotias of Central Himalayas (Chachra and Bhasin, 1998:411-2) and it resembles the present finding at high altitude. The corresponding figures for all India population are 73 and 5 respectively for young age dependency ratio and old age dependency ratio (Jones, 1974:110). Dependency ratios for the district Pithoragarh and India are presented in the Census of India (2001) are much higher than the present findings.

Family Structure

The size of the family is classified into four categories such as small (with members 1 to 3), medium (members from 4 to 6), large (7 to 9 members) and very large (10 and above). At high altitude, the average family size is found to be 3.00, 5.40, 8.15 and 11.40 individuals belonging to the family size categories such as small, medium, large and very large respectively. The average family size at high altitude is 6.39 individuals. Moreover, 5.54 per cent families bear 2.56 per cent of population, 59.09 per cent families bear 49.93 per cent of population, 30.91 per cent families bear 39.40 per cent of population and 4.55 per cent families bear 8.11 per cent of population in small, medium, large and very large family size categories respectively. At low altitude, the average family size is calculated to be 2.78, 5.77, 8.61 and 14.86 individuals belonging to the small, medium, large and very large family size categories respectively.

The average family size at low altitude is 6.53 individuals. Furthermore, 9.21 per cent families bear 3.93 per cent of population, 64.47 per cent families bear 57 per cent of population, 21.71 per cent families bear 28.6 per cent of population and 4.61 per cent families bear 10.47 per cent of population in small, medium, large and very large family size categories respectively.

At the population level, the average family size is 6.47 individuals. The average family size is calculated to be 2.85, 5.63, 8.37 and 13.42 individuals belonging to the small, medium, large and very large family size groups respectively. As far as the Bhotia population is concerned, only 7.63 per cent families bear 3.36 per cent population, 62.21 per cent families bear 54.07 per cent population, 25.57 per cent families bear 33.08 per cent population and 4.58 per cent families bear 9.49 per cent population in small, medium, large and very large family size categories (see Table 4.6).

However, the average family size is lower at high altitude (6.39 individuals per family) than at low altitude (6.53 individuals per family), with overall family size of 6.47 individuals per family. The average family size of medium (4-6 individuals), large (7-9 individuals) and very large (10 individuals and above) families have been found to be larger at low altitude. The study conducted among the Gujjars of Western Himalayas shows the average family size to be 7.09 and 8.22 for Hindu and Muslim Gujjars respectively (Balgir, 1991:177).

Table 4.6: Distribution and Average Family Size (AFS) of the Sample Bhotia Population

Family Category	*High Altitude Distribution of*			*Low Altitude Distribution of*			*Total Distribution of*		
	Family	*Popn.*	*AFS*	*Family*	*Popn.*	*AFS*	*Family*	*Popn.*	*AFS*
Small (1-3)	6 5.54	18 2.56	3.00	14 9.21	39 3.93	2.78	20 7.63	57 3.36	2.85
Medium (4-6)	65 59.09	351 49.93	5.40	98 64.47	566 57.00	5.77	163 62.21	917 54.07	5.63
Large (7-9)	34 30.91	277 39.40	8.15	33 21.71	284 28.60	8.61	67 25.57	561 33.08	8.37
Very Large (10+)	5 4.55	57 8.11	11.40	7 4.61	104 10.47	14.86	12 4.58	161 9.49	13.42
Total	110	703	6.39	152	993	6.53	262	1696	6.47

Where, Popn. stands for pupulation.

Table 4.7: Distribution of Family Type of the Sample Bhotia Population

Types of Family	*High Altitude*		*Low Altitude*		*Total*	
	No.	*%*	*No.*	*%*	*No.*	*%*
Nuclear	65	59.09	91	59.87	156	59.54
Joint	45	40.91	61	40.13	106	40.46
Total	110	100.00	152	100.00	262	100.00

At high and low altitudes the Bhotia people have more nuclear families than joint families. There are marginally more joint families at high altitude (40.91 per cent) than in low altitude (40.13 per cent). There are just a little more joint families at low altitude (59.87 per cent) in comparison to their strength in high altitude (59.09 per cent). Altogether, there are relatively more nuclear families (59.54 per cent) in comparison to the joint families (40.46 per cent) (see Table 4.7). Some of the important reasons that may explain these variations are—

1. The family size is larger at low altitude. This shows

that members of the family at low altitude remain together because of proper facilities and entitlement available for them. Furthermore, the high altitude environment is not conducive for old age people giving rise to reduction of family size.

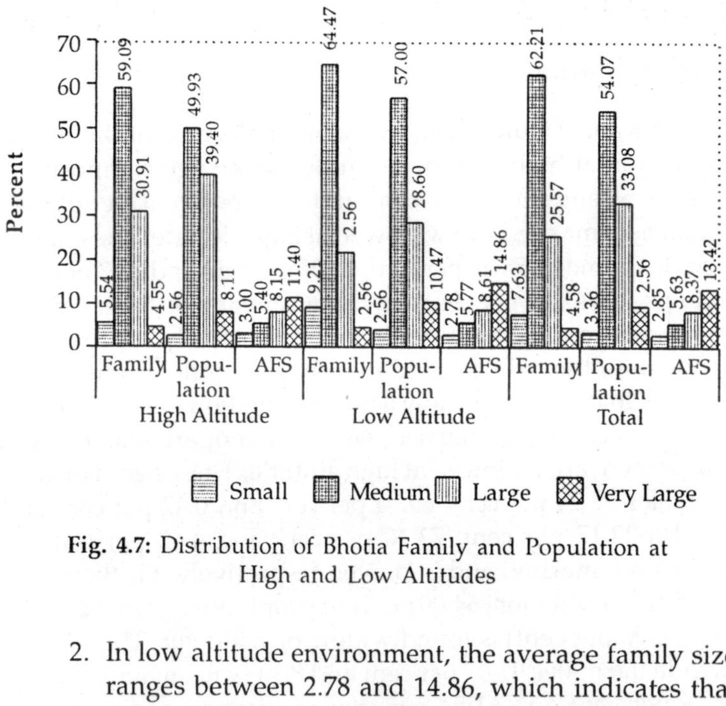

Fig. 4.7: Distribution of Bhotia Family and Population at High and Low Altitudes

2. In low altitude environment, the average family size ranges between 2.78 and 14.86, which indicates that the attitude of the people in some cases is extremely nuclear and self-centred, and in other cases devoted towards group, we-feeling and togetherness. This even implies a move towards modern concept of living. As people here are educationally better off and engaged in service sector (refer Chapter 5), the chance of out-migration is high. These, in fact, transcendence the idea of functional living, which keep them back to their place of origin at the time of ceremony, celebration and ritual in the family or village level.
3. Contrary to the low altitude settlement, the high altitude environment limits the family size by

constraints and pressure on individuals. Collective living and group formation is an outcome to the fact.

The present study finds similarities with the study conducted in the Western Himalayas (Bhasin and Bhasin, 1993). The study also shows that the Gaddis have more nuclear families which resembles the findings of the present study.

Marital Status

Table 4.8 and Figure 4.8 show the marital status of the Bhotia population at high and low altitudes. In all age composition, 53.49 per cent, 43.81 per cent and 2.70 per cent people are unmarried, married and widowed at high altitude. These again include the males 58.40 per cent, 40.07 per cent and 0.53 per cent and females 47.87 per cent, 46.95 per cent and 5.18 per cent, as unmarried, married and widowed respectively. In the child population, the case of child marriages is conspicuous by its absence. In the economically active population (15 to 59 years), 31.36 per cent are unmarried, 66.37 per cent are married and 2.27 per cent are widowed at high altitude. These again include the males 39.24 per cent, 60.34 per cent and 0.42 per cent and females 22.17 per cent, 73.40 per cent and 4.43 per cent, as unmarried, married and widowed respectively. Furthermore, in old age population, 64.00 per cent people are married and the rest (36.00 per cent) is found widow or widower. These again include the males 91.67 per cent and 8.33 per cent and females 38.46 per cent and 61.54 per cent as married and widowed respectively.

In low altitude, in all age composition, 49.14 per cent, 44.11 per cent and 6.75 per cent people are unmarried, married and widowed. These again include the males 53.62 per cent, 42.86 per cent and 3.52 per cent and females 44.40 per cent, 45.44 per cent and 10.17 per cent as unmarried, married and widowed respectively. Here also, no case of child marriage below 15 years is reported. In the economically active population (15 to 59 years), 29.58 per cent are unmarried, 65.43 per cent are married and 4.99 per cent are widowed at low altitude. These again include the males 37.69 per cent, 59.88 per cent and 2.43 per cent

Table 4.8: Marital Status of the Sample Bhotia Population

Age Group (in Yr.)		Male				Female				Total			
High Altitude													
		Unm.	*Mar.*	*Wid.*	*Total*	*Unm.*	*Mar.*	*Wid.*	*Total*	*Unm.*	*Mar.*	*Wid.*	*Total*
0-14	No.	126	—	—	126	112	—	—	112	238	—	—	238
	%	100.0			52.94	100.0			47.06	100.0			33.85
15-59[5]	No.	93	143	1	237	45	149	9	203	138	292	10	440
	%	39.24	60.34	0.42	53.99	22.17	73.40	4.43	46.24	31.36	66.37	2.27	62.59
60+	No.	—	11	1	12	—	5	8	13	—	16	9	25
	%		91.67	8.33	48.00		38.46	61.54	52.00		64.00	36.00	3.56
Total	No.	219	154	2	375	157	154	17	328	376	308	19	703
	%	58.40	40.07	0.53	53.34	47.87	46.95	5.18	46.66	53.49	43.81	2.70	100.0
Low Altitude													
Age Group (in Yr.)		Male				Female				Total			
		Unm.	*Mar.*	*Wid.*	*Total*	*Unm.*	*Mar.*	*Wid.*	*Total*	*Unm.*	*Mar.*	*Wid.*	*Total*
0-14	No.	150	—	—	150	154	—	—	154	304	—	—	304
	%	100.0			49.34	100.0			50.66	100.0			30.61
15-59[5]	No.	124	197	8	329	60	210	23	293	184	407	31	622
	%	37.69	59.88	2.43	52.89	20.48	71.67	7.85	47.11	29.58	65.43	4.99	62.64
60+	No.	—	22	10	32	—	9	26	35	—	31	36	67
	%		68.75	31.25	47.76		25.71	74.29	52.24		46.27	53.73	6.75
Total	No.	274	219	18	511	214	219	49	482	488	438	67	993
	%	53.62	42.86	3.52	51.46	44.40	45.44	10.17	48.54	49.14	44.11	6.75	100.0

Contd. **Table 4.8**

		Total											
Age Group		*Male*				*Female*				*Total*			
(in Yr.)		*Unm.*	*Mar.*	*Wid.*	*Total*	*Unm.*	*Mar.*	*Wid.*	*Total*	*Unm.*	*Mar.*	*Wid.*	*Total*
0-14	No.	276	—	—	276	266	—	—	266	542	—	—	542
	%	100.0			50.92	100.0			49.08	100.0			31.96
15-59[5]	No.	217	340	9	566	105	359	32	496	322	699	41	1062
	%	38.34	60.07	1.59	53.30	21.17	72.38	6.45	46.70	30.32	65.82	3.86	62.62
60+	No.	—	33	11	44	—	14	34	48	—	47	45	92
	%		75.00	25.00	47.83		29.17	70.83	52.17		51.09	48.91	5.42
Total	No.	493	373	20	886	371	373	66	810	864	746	86	1696
	%	55.64	42.10	2.26	52.24	45.80	46.05	8.15	47.76	50.94	43.99	5.07	100.0

and females 20.48 per cent, 71.67 per cent and 7.85 per cent, as unmarried, married and widowed respectively. Furthermore, in old age population, 46.27 per cent people are married and the rest (53.73 per cent) is found widowed. These again include the males 68.75 per cent and 31.25 per cent and females 25.71 per cent and 74.29 per cent as married and widowed respectively.

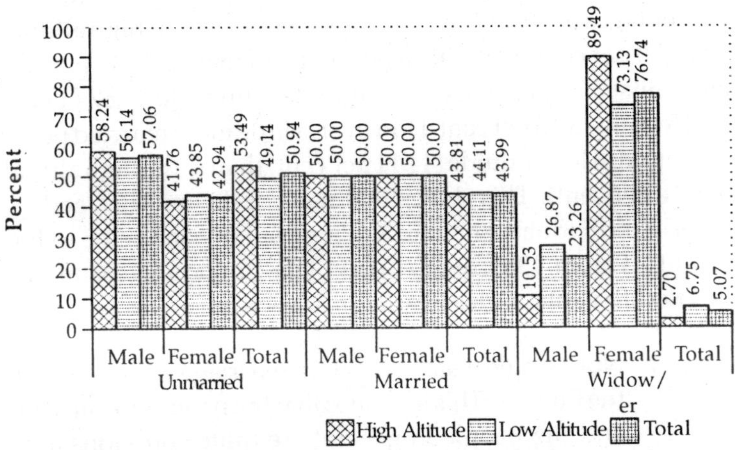

Fig. 4.8: Marital Status of the Sample Bhotia Tribe at High and Low Altitudes

In the Bhotia population, the all age composition, 50.94 per cent, 43.99 per cent and 5.07 per cent people are unmarried, married and widowed at low altitude. These again include the males 55.64 per cent, 42.10 per cent and 2.26 per cent and females 45.80 per cent, 46.05 per cent and 8.15 per cent as unmarried, married and widowed respectively. In the population, no case of child marriage below 15 years is reported. In the economically active population (15 to 59 years), 30.32 per cent are unmarried, 65.82 per cent are married and 3.86 per cent are widowed. These again include the males 38.34 per cent, 60.07 per cent and 1.59 per cent and females 21.17 per cent, 72.38 per cent and 6.45 per cent as unmarried, married and widowed respectively. Furthermore, in old age population, 51.09 per cent people are married and the rest (48.91 per cent) is found widowed. These again include the males 75.00 per cent and 25.00 per cent and females 29.17 per cent and 70.83 per cent are married and widowed respectively.

In the Bhotia population, there are more unmarried people at high altitude (53.49 per cent with male 58.25 per cent and female 41.75 per cent) than in the low altitude (49.14 per cent with male 56.15 per cent and female 43.85 per cent). The percentages of widowed are comparatively low at high altitude, *i.e.*, 2.70 per cent (male 10.53 per cent and female 89.47 per cent) as against 6.75 per cent at low altitude with male 26.87 per cent and female 73.13 per cent. However, a little more married people are found at low altitude (44.11 per cent) than in the high altitude (43.81 per cent). This shows that most of the middle aged and elderly individuals are married, a situation conducive to high fertility (Gupta, 1980:104-5). Some of the important reasons may be cited to explain these variations, such as—

1. Not a single instance of child marriage is found among the Bhotias. This indicates that the parents in particular and the people in general are quite conscious about the ill effects of child marriage.
2. As marriage leads to family and family is the basic social institution, which ascribes legality not only to the marital life between husband and wife but also suffices legitimacy to the upcoming infants. Therefore, this is the first important initiation of the reproductive life of a community.
3. At high or low altitude, almost equal percentage of people have married. This is because of the similarity found at both the altitudes in the age and sex distribution of people at economically productive stage. Marriage restriction prevails on the basis of settlements, and valley-level identity often takes a dominant place as far as the matrimonial alliance is concerned, thus allowing the traditional clan-based rules to operate. Social sanction restricts the people to opt polygamy.

4. From the Table 4.8, it is found that there are equal number of married males and females. It is evident that the Bhotia people prefer monogamy irrespective of high or low altitude settlement. This is an indicator of social stability and gender equality.
5. At high altitude, early male deaths give rise to higher percentage of widows than in low altitude. The death of elderly male members is due to the stress-strain factors of high altitude environment.

A similar kind of situation has been observed among the Gujjars in the Western Himalayas, where the widows outnumber the widowers showing thereby high mortality among the males (Balgir, 1991:178-9).

To sum up, it is found from the present study that the Bhotia people, settled at two different altitudes (high and low) in Kumaon Himalaya, display a quite interesting demographic characteristic. Age and sex structures of the Bhotias at high and low altitudes do not show much deviation, apart from the fact that there is quite a low concentration of the old age people at high altitude. The sex ratio, in general, is found quite low, *i.e.*, in favour of males in high altitude than in low altitude. The sex ratio is favourable for the female among the infant, early child and old age population except the total child and economically active population at high altitude. However, the sex ratio is favourable for female in the total child and old age population leaving the infant, early child and economically active population at low altitude. The masculinity proportion is higher at high altitude than at the low altitude. The index of ageing is quite low at high altitude, which signifies that there are less old age people at high altitude. The young age dependency ratio is found higher at high altitude. Unlike this, the old age dependency ratio is found quite low at high altitude than at low altitude. The average family size and percentage of nuclear family are found low at high altitude than at low altitude. Similarly, there is low percentage of married male persons and higher percentage of married female persons at high altitude. There is a higher percentage of widows than that of widowers at high altitude. The similar situation arises at the low altitude, but the percentage of widow and widower is quite higher at low altitude. In general, the percentage of unmarried people is higher at high altitude. Above all, there is no instance of marriage among the children below 15 years of age at both high and low altitudes.

Notes

1. Post Productive refers here to population age group at 60 years and above and those are physically challenged, exclusively dependent on the productive population for their survival.
2. The people of the age group 15 to 59 years who may be considered as economically active and also productive, working or resource-generating group.
3. In the western way of expressing the sex ratio is the 'number of males in 100 female population'. In this paper, their calculation has been converted to express the sex ratio in terms of number of females in 1000 male population.
4. It is calculated on the basis of formula described in the Chapter 3 of this book.
5. Though legally minimum age for girls and boys is 18 and 21 years respectively but during the survey it was noticed that young population above the age 15 years are also married. Therefore, they have been included in the married population. However, there was not a single case of child marriage noticed, *i.e.*, below 15 years at high and low altitudes.

5

EDUCATION AND ECONOMIC STRUCTURE

It is commonly believed that resources or resource base is important for all developmental activities. However, it is often seen that people have confusion or misunderstanding about the concept of resource. Scholars have defined resource in many ways. For the purpose of this research work, resource has been defined as 'Resources constitute all the attributes of our environment both material and metaphysical that can be used for meeting human demands which are economically feasible, culturally acceptable, technologically accessible and environmentally sustainable' (Butola, 1992:101). It means that mere availability of any substance is only a precondition for considering it as resource. To become a resource, the pattern and aspects of their mobilization are equally important. It is basically the nature of mobilization that separates the developed region from the backward. The developed countries have minimum gap between resource inventory and resource mobilization. While in the underdeveloped countries the gap is large. In Uttaranchal, particularly the Bhotia tribal community falls within the latter group. The Bhotias have too many handicaps in resource mobilization. Some of the most important ones are low level of education, low level of technology leading to non-specialization due to low division of labour and non-specialization of occupational structure, and low level of income. In the present chapter, the resources like education and economy of the Bhotia populations have been studied in the context of high and low altitude settlements.

Education

Human resource implies two important aspects of human being such as education and economy. These put them into a real path of development. Education is an important wealth for any society because it increases the level of information, and ultimately the knowledge received through formal and informal ways incorporates different dimensions to the human life. Advancement of a society can be estimated through its educational level. It designs the members to be reactive and sensitive in a particular manner through the strength of information and awareness. Information brings awareness and awareness brings knowledge to operate in a particular way. Education is the basic thing by which the level of information is elevated. The technological innovation is directly related to the educational status of members in a society. Therefore, education becomes the basic needs and it is the only and foremost-required wealth and welfare (Sen, 2001:128) for any society. The level of development is understood from its educational structure.

In case of the Bhotia tribal community, it is found that 83.5 per cent people are literate, which consists 91.9 per cent male and 74.1 per cent female with gender disparity level of 17.8 points. There is no much difference found in the educational level in between the high and low altitudes. In the low altitude, people are a bit more educated than their high altitude counterparts. In both the altitudes, the literacy rate among the males is higher than that of the females. The male literacy rate is 91.7 per cent and the female literacy rate is 71.7 per cent with a gap of 20 points at high altitude, and the total literacy rate is 82.5 per cent. The male literacy rate is 92.1 per cent and the female literacy rate is 75.7 per cent with a gap of 16.4 points at low altitude and the total literacy rate is 84.2 per cent. However, the percentage of female literates is more at low altitude than the high altitude environment (see Table 5.1).

The gender disparity increases with the increase in age group. There is a minimum gender disparity in the age group 6-14 years. At the high altitude, the disparity is just 0.3 point in this age group. At the low altitude, there is no disparity at all.

That means the boys and girls are at par as far as their education is concerned. The gender disparity is further elevated in the economically active population (15-59 years). Among the high altitude Bhotia people, the gender disparity in education is 25.1 points. The male literacy rate is 91.1 per cent and the female literacy rate is 66.0 per cent. The total literacy rate is 75.5 per cent in the economically active population. For the same age group, the gender disparity in education is 16.9 points at low altitude. The literacy rate for male is 93.0 per cent and female literacy rate is 76.1 per cent. The total literacy rate is 85.0 per cent in the economically active population at low altitude. In this age group (15 to 59 years), there is a difference of 10 points in the total literacy rate between high and low altitudes. In this case, there is also a higher percentage of literates for both male and female at low altitude. In the economically active population (15 to 59 years), the total literacy rate is 82.8 per cent with male 92.2 per cent and female 72.0 per cent. The gender disparity level is 20.2 points. Among the old age people, the gender disparity is lower (27.5 points) at high altitude than at low altitude (51.1 points). The total literacy rate is 44.0 per cent with male 58.3 per cent and female 30.8 per cent in high altitude. At low altitude, the total literacy rate is 35.8 per cent with male 62.5 per cent and female 11.4 per cent. The total literacy rate for the old age people is 38.0 per cent with male 61.4 per cent and female 16.7 per cent. The gender disparity is highest among the old age people (44.7 points) compared to other age groups (see Figures 5.1 to 5.4). In addition to this, there are a few cases of child illiteracy at high altitude (see Appendix 5).

Following are some of the observations that emerged from the study such as—

1. The gender discrepancy on educational status, which is found at high altitude, may be related to its rough and harsh climate. The people tend to give more attention to the nature for agriculture and allied occupations. The children are considered as helping hands for the parents and their attention is diverted towards earning and doing the seasonal work. The girl children are more subject to this. The seasonal migration also puts the people engaged to cover the

distance from the low altitude residence to the high altitude settlements and *vice versa*. The energy and time that are supposed to be invested in the learning process is rather utilized in seasonal and life activities that are peculiar them.

Table 5.1: Literacy Rate of Bhotia Population under Study

Age Group (Yr.)	*Gender*	*High Altitude*	*Low Altitude*	*Total*
6-14	Male	98.7	100.0	99.4
	Female	98.4	100.0	99.3
	Total	98.6	100.0	99.4
	Gender Disparity	0.3	0.0	0.1
15-59	Male	91.1	93.0	92.2
	Female	66.0	76.1	72.0
	Total	75.5	85.0	82.8
	Gender Disparity	25.1	16.9	20.2
60+	Male	58.3	62.5	61.4
	Female	30.8	11.4	16.7
	Total	44.0	35.8	38.0
	Gender Disparity	27.5	51.1	44.7
Total	Male	91.7	92.1	91.9
	Female	71.7	75.7	74.1
	Total	82.5	84.2	83.5
	Gender Disparity	20.0	16.4	17.8

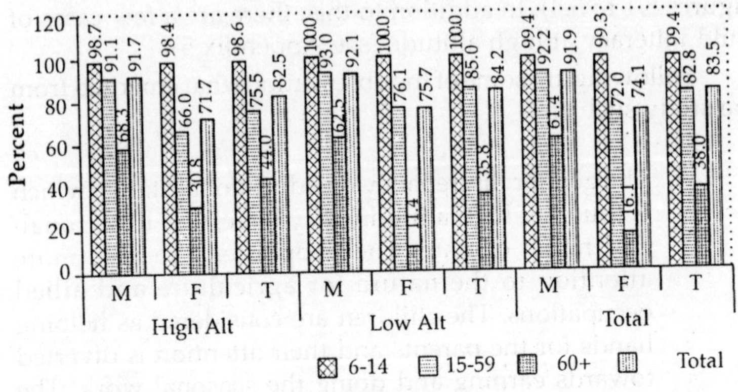

Fig. 5.1: Literacy Rate of Sample Bhotia Population in High and Low Altitudes

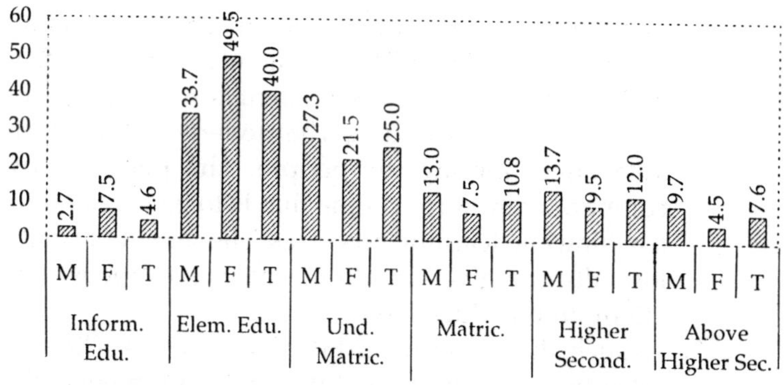

Fig. 5.2: Education Structure of Sample Bhotia Population at High Altitude

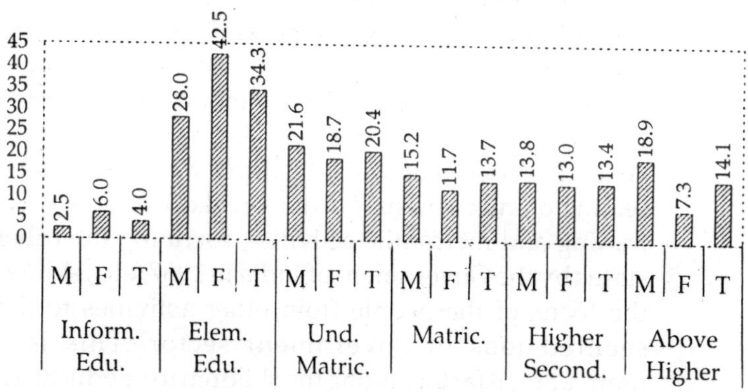

Fig. 5.3: Education Structure of Sample Bhotia Population at Low Altitude

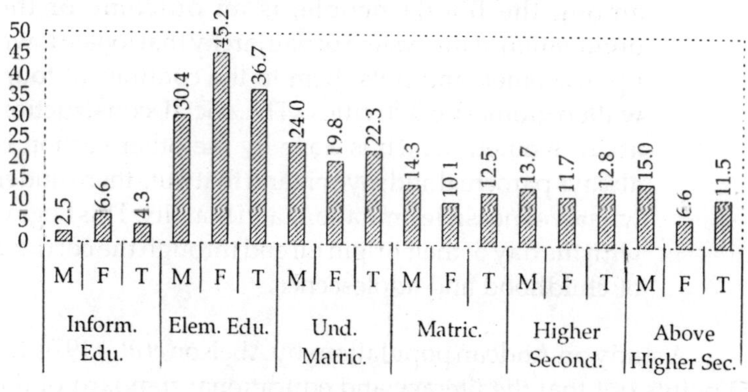

Fig. 5.4: Education Structure of Bhotia Tribe under Study

2. The nature of low altitude settlements of the Bhotia people is supportive. The availability of facilities here makes the life easier that is different from the struggling kind of life at high altitude. The modern facilities bring awareness among the people. The people have comparatively surplus time that is to be invested for teaching and learning processes. The settled life in the low altitude gives children a chance to focus their attention on education.
3. As such, there is no much difference in terms of literacy rates between the two-altitudinal settlements. The people have a long historical background from a pure nomadic and transhumance activities to partly settled life. Their exposure and awareness are synchronized through the interaction with the people in the plains and trans-Himalayan territories as they were connecting two frontiers during these trading years. The Indo-Sino war (1962) and subsequently the sealing of international border, breakdown of age old trading and mercantile activities, ascribing the tribal status by the Government of India in 1967, etc., shifted the focus of the people from other activities to the secured jobs in government sector. This is a motivational factor among the children to be educated.
4. The gender disparity in education, which is observed among the Bhotia people, is an outcome of the domination of the system of patriarchy that looks down upon women and puts them to the confines of four-walled domestic activities. The social construction about women, which is done by the other section is always parochial and myopic and that puts them under whatever possible limitations and scarcity. This begins with the day of their origin till end through the corridor of childhood and adolescence.

A study on Andean populations by Abelson *et al.*, (1974:12-5) points out that the literacy and educational standard of the people is higher at low altitude than those born at high altitude and this finding no doubt resembles the present study. Among the Gaddis in Himachal Pradesh Himalayas, it is reported that there are quite a number of illiterates where females have more representation. The percentage of male and female illiterates is 66.7 and 87.8 respectively and the percentage of male and female literates is 34.3 and 12.2 respectively (Bhasin and Bhasin, 1993:187-8). The literacy rate among the Bhotias of Central Himalayas is reported to be 66.29 with male 77.98 per cent and female 54.38 per cent (Chachra and Bhasin, 1998:412-4) and it is much higher than Kumaoni caste groups (58.95 per cent) with male 75.4 per cent and female 42.48 per cent. Furthermore, the present finding resembles the Census figures (2001) at national level. It is even better than the state of Uttaranchal. The district Pithoragarh is even better than that of the Kumaon region in the state of Uttaranchal and India as such. In respect of the educational status, the present finding is above them (see Appendix 5).

Occupation Structure

The availability of natural resources, the level of educational attainment, strength of the economy, normative behaviour and socio-psychological adjustment of the people determine the occupation structure of a society (Datta and Sinha, 1997:55-7). Occupation of an individual is decided by one's ability and constraint. Occupation implies to earn the livelihood. Prosperity of a society and level of technological innovation are decided by the kind of occupations held by its members. The level of educational attainment of the people determines the level of technological innovation. Therefore, both education and occupation determine the level of societal development. In a tribal society like the Bhotias, occupations are primarily carried out according to the nature of their settlements to the Himalayan environment; secondarily, their traditional and historical approach is considered to be a dominant factor besides the environment of the Bhotia people that designs their occupation structure. Appendix 6 displays the occupation structure of the Bhotia tribe at high and low altitudes of Kumaon Himalaya.

Agriculture is the mainstay of people at high altitude. Almost 32.1 per cent people have been engaged in the agricultural activities. It is found that participation of women in agricultural activities is high. Other than the agriculture, people have involvement in doing business (14.4 per cent) and employment in service sector (14.7 per cent). The participation of women in these sectors is very much discouraging. Spinning and weaving and household activities are the tasks for women. Likewise, 18.3 per cent women have been involved in the household works. About 10.2 per cent women take part in the traditional spinning and weaving. Almost 3.6 per cent people have been associated with animal husbandry and herding. However, there are also people belonging to labour class (3.6 per cent). It is noticed that almost 3 per cent people are unemployed at high altitude (See Appendix 6).

Contrary to the facts at high altitude, service sector accommodates higher percentage of people (22.5) than that of agriculture (21.1) at low altitude. Doing business is also a major option for people here (15 per cent). In agriculture, there is predominance of women (22.5 per cent) than what is observed in the service sector (6.2 per cent). Spinning and weaving (15.4 per cent) and household activities (18.8 per cent) have been taken more seriously by the women. Furthermore, like the high altitude, there is some incidence of labour class (3.3 per cent) and unemployed people (2.5 per cent) in this settlement.

Considering the Bhotia tribe as a whole, it is observed that 25.6 per cent of people have agriculture as their primary occupation followed by the service sector (19.3 per cent) and business (14.7 per cent). Women (26.9 per cent) have major share in agricultural activities. In comparison to male folk, a very low percentage of women take part in both business and service sectors. It is a matter of fact that the spinning and weaving and household activities are taken over by women (see Appendix 6 and Figures 5.5 to 5.7). Following are some of the reasons—

1. The occupational differentiation, which exists among people in the high and low altitude settlements primarily connotes that the people have major

agricultural holdings at high altitude. Leading the transhumance life and being traders for centuries, their accumulation of major holdings is confined to the high altitude areas. The lower altitude settlements are comparatively new—a post-war development. In-migration from plains has made the low altitude Bhotias hackneyed for which they are landless. As a matter of fact, majority of land holdings is found with the non-Bhotias at low altitude.

2. Due to the availability of education and modern facilities, people look into occupations other than agriculture that profits them more. Employment in service sector is taken as a defence mechanism to sustain their livelihood at lower altitudes. Not having the agricultural land has again shifted the attention of people to other sectors. Seasonal migration is considered to be a non-profitable and time-consuming laborious activity. Instead of consuming time and energy in these, people are more focused and ambitious to shift the traditional occupation from agriculture and trading to service and business sectors.
3. The women sections in the Bhotia society basically control spinning and weaving industry. However, the traditional involvement of people in the handicraft industry is comparatively decreased. It is found that women at low altitude are more associated with spinning and weaving as they have more time to spend for. There is no particular time for the spinning and weaving, rather, it is a leisurely affair. However, the expertise and specialization on the craft mechanism is monotonous and traditional in pattern that needs refinement and revision in the making of new designs. This may attract the attention of customers, which is nothing but creating a market for their products.
4. The growth of labour class and unemployed sections in the Bhotia society is a post-development scenario. Educational attainment, not getting a job in the service sector due to competition, the youths do not revert to

their traditional occupations, and all these lead to unemployment as a by-product. Labourers are basically the landless people who depend on working in the agricultural land of others on daily wages. They were traditionally involved in trading activities. The shift in occupation and lack of ownership on landholding led them to be the perpetual labour class people.

Considering the type of employment in Andean populations, a higher proportion of people at high altitude gets employment in manual work compared to those at low altitude (Abelson *et al.*, 1974:12-5). Among the Kumaoni populations, Chachra and Bhasin (1998:414-5) report that the principal occupation of people appears to be service (38 per cent) followed by agriculture (13.8 per cent), which is very close to the pattern found at low altitude in the present study. They are of the opinion that in the hill region, small land holdings, hard terrain, adverse weather conditions and poor irrigation facilities have made agriculture unviable, causing the local population to look for other alternatives.

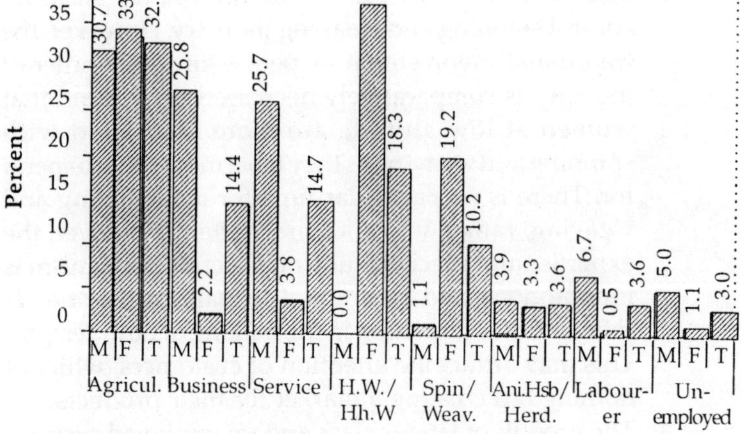

Fig. 5.5: Occupation Structure of Sample Bhotia Population at High Altitude

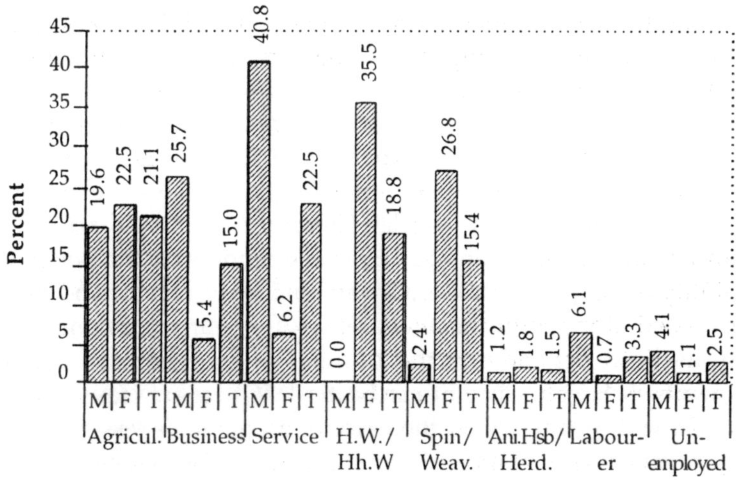

Fig. 5.6: Occupation Structure of Sample Bhotia Population at Low Altitude

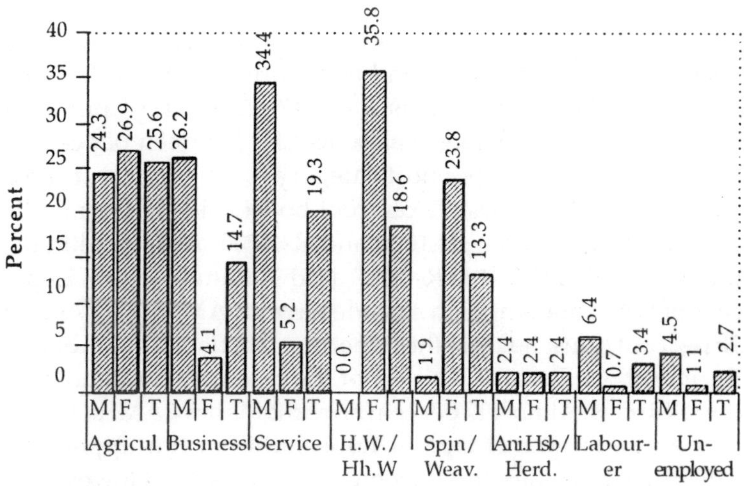

Fig. 5.7: Occupation Structure of Bhotia Tribe under Study

Income

Income is a basic requirement for any individual. Income is generated through employment. Employment of a person depends on his ability to earn the livelihood. Ability is basically the status of knowing things that involves specialization. Specialization is derived out of experience and exposure to the world of wisdom and craftsmanship. Income generation in the tribal society primarily depends on its adaptation to the environment. The nature of environment decides the level of income generation of people. Therefore, economic activities and income generation sources are dependent on the personal ability of people and the environment into which the society is exposed along with the availability of resources. Income of a household depends on the number of economically active members. Surplus income can be made if there area few burden and the dependency on the earning members is less. Surplus generation is a matter of question in a subsistence kind of tribal economy. In this section, the average monthly income (AMI) of the Bhotia households is taken in order to understand if any dichotomy exists between the high and low altitude settlements.

Table 5.2 presents the Average Monthly Income (AMI) of Bhotia households at high and low altitudes. The AMI of the Bhotia tribal population is Rs.2342. Almost 13 per cent households have AMI just below Rs.750. Fourteen per cent of households in the uppermost category have monthly income above Rs.4000. The rest 73 per cent households in the middle have income between Rs.1000 and Rs.4000. At high altitude, the AMI is Rs.2124. It is Rs.2487 at low altitude. Just 7.27 per cent of households at high altitude have an AMI of Rs.879, and 10 per cent households in the uppermost sections have monthly income above Rs.4000. This is not the case with households at low altitudes. Almost 17 per cent households have AMI of Rs.700 and an equal percentage of households in the uppermost categories have monthly income above Rs.4000. However, at low altitude, the income of households is uniformly distributed. At high altitude, the income of households is higher and pronounced in the middle than at the two extreme poles, which are presented in the disparity graphs (see Figures 5.8 to 5.10).

Table 5.2: Average Monthly Income (AMI) of Bhotia Households under Study

Sl. No.	*Income Category (in Rs.)*	*High Altitude*		*Low Altitude*		*Total*	
		No. %age of Family	*AMI (in Rs.)*	*No. %age of Family*	*AMI (in Rs.)*	*No. %age of Family*	*AMI (in Rs.)*
1.	Below 1000	8 7.27	879	26 17.11	700	34 12.98	736
2.	1000-1499	33 30.00	1274	16 10.53	1150	49 18.70	1235
3.	1500-1999	22 20.00	1658	18 11.83	1613	40 15.27	1633
4.	2000-2499	13 11.82	2246	15 9.87	2189	28 10.69	2215
5.	2500-2999	10 9.09	2729	16 10.53	2659	26 9.92	2679
6.	3000-3499	4 3.64	3117	24 15.79	3169	28 10.69	3163
7.	3500-3999	9 8.18	3622	12 7.89	3613	21 8.02	3617
8.	4000-4499	3 2.73	4267	11 7.24	4134	14 5.34	4160
9.	4500-4999	2 1.82	4600	6 3.95	4567	8 3.05	4575
10.	5000 and above	6 5.45	5575	8 5.26	5613	14 5.34	5600
11.	Total	110 100.0	2124	152 100.0	2487	262 10.00	2342

Some of the observations are given below—

1. At high altitude settlement, there is a concentration of households in the middle-income groups (Rs.1500-3999). This is because, in this kind of settlement, the natural constraints restrict the opportunities for enlarging the resource basket. Therefore, high-income generation is difficult and cost intensive. At the other

extreme of social ladder, there are low-income groups. It is observed that at high altitude the minimum level of subsistence is essential, below which it is difficult for households to sustain.

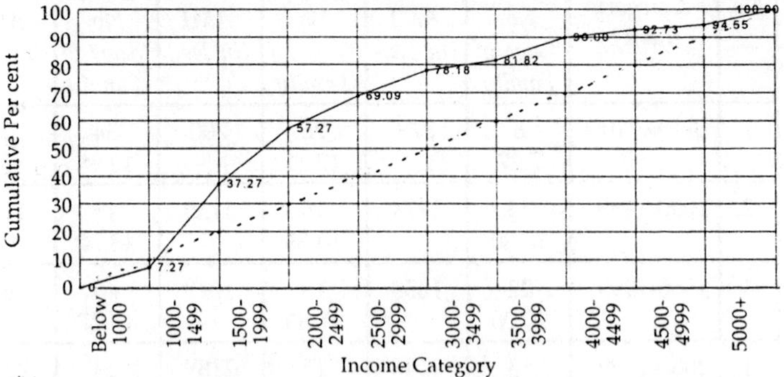

Fig. 5.8: Disparity Graph Showing Average Monthly Income of Sample Bhotia Population at High Altitude

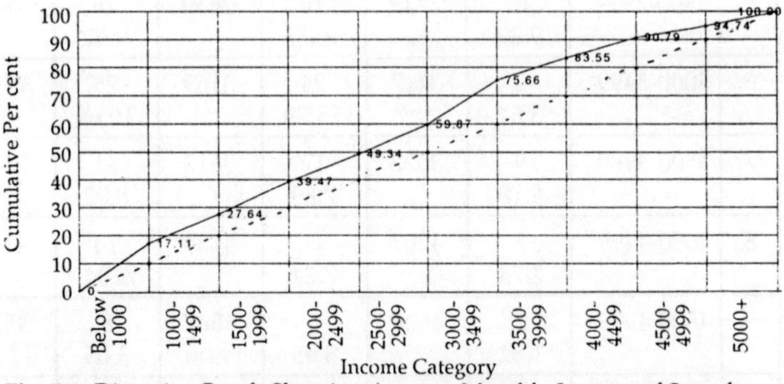

Fig. 5.9: Disparity Graph Showing Average Monthly Income of Sample Bhotia Population at Low Altitude

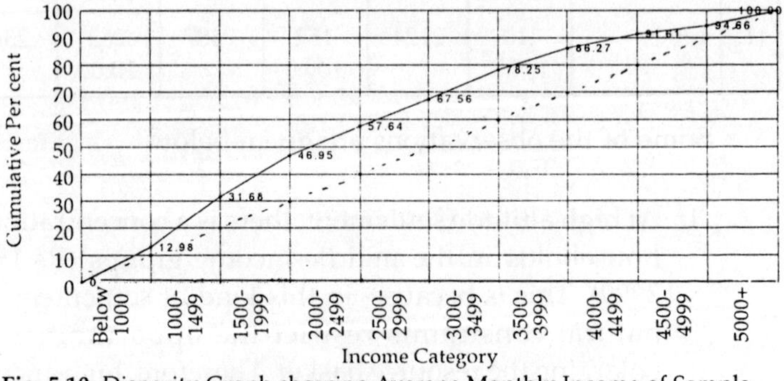

Fig. 5.10: Disparity Graph showing Average Monthly Income of Sample Bhotia Tribe under Study

2. As opposed to this, at low altitude, there is relatively a greater proportion of people at the lower level of income distribution because of the ever-shrinking low resource basket, but there is as increasing alternative economic opportunity to economic diversification.
3. Broadly, it can be observed from the disparity graphs that the differentiation and concentration of resource baskets, however, indicate the nascent state of it, and the overall picture confirms a typical mode of production. Though the Bhotias have displayed remarkable achievements in the field of employment and income generation, the overall ethos continues to be predominantly tribal. This does not exclude the tendencies towards differentiations, which is evident from the graph of low altitude (see Figure 5.9).

To conclude, it is mentioned that resources constitute the entire attributes of our environment. Human resources include all aspects of human beings, which make them proliferate with material avenues in terms of quantitative and qualitative dimensions that nourish and enrich the life. For example, education is an important wealth for any society. Other important resources could be the ability to generate livelihood in terms of occupational strength and income generation. Education, occupation and income generation form a trinity to a real path of development. In the Bhotia community, almost 83.5 per cent of people are literate, which consist 91.9 per cent male and 74.1 per cent female. The gender disparity in education is almost 17.8 points. However, there is no much difference in the educational level between the high and low altitude Bhotias. In the occupation structure, agriculture is the mainstay for people at high altitude. The people at low altitude are much more exposed to and influenced by the dominant culture that put them into education and employment in service sector. This is even an alternative to their helplessness among the low altitude Bhotias. There is a shift in the attitude and outlook among the members of new generation. In the income front, there is disparity among the members at high and low altitudes. The average monthly income is little less at high altitude. This indicates that the resource availability and its exploitation are limited. Contrary to this, the low altitude is much more open to the alternative avenues.

6

FERTILITY PATTERN AND INNER DYNAMICS OF HIGH ALTITUDE SOCIAL ECOLOGY

Fertility is the childbearing performance of individuals, couples, groups, or populations. It is in contrast to fecundity, the physiological capacity to reproduce, which may or may not lead to actual fertility. Fertility is a concept, which encompasses a complex time-dependent process covering events ranging from exposure to intercourse and child bearing to the formation and dissolution of unions (Bhasin and Bhasin, 1993:191-2). The study of fertility has received considerable attention in recent years, particularly in developing countries because of its relationship with and important bearing on the family building process. It is a complex system representing a set of different reproduction strategies. Though reproduction is a biological phenomenon, social norms and practices can influence levels in fertility. Sometimes, the term natality is used to refer to the most general analyses of childbearing, though this usage is becoming less common. The term fertility is commonly used to cover all aspects of reproduction (Pressat, 1985:81-2). Measures of fertility normally refer only to live births. Several different qualifiers are applied to fertility to specify more exactly the focus of analysis. By convention, most measures of fertility are related to mothers.[1] In some cases, they are limited to examining the way in which mothers give birth to daughters (female fertility), a definition which is most common in studies of the replacement of generations.

An appropriate reproductive performance is one of the prime requirements and indicators of environmental adaptation. Moreover, the ability of a population to adapt to its environment depends on its fertility and population growth (Parkash and Malik, 1990:175). Fertility is a demographic measure of adaptation, which could partially be examined (Baker and Dutt, 1972:355-6). Some studies have measured fertility of high altitude natives under the assumption that populations adapted to high altitude have depressing effect on fecundity, which appears to be the major component of reduced fertility at high altitude. Therefore, in this chapter an attempt has been made to study the fertility pattern of the Bhotia populations adapted to high and low altitudes in Kumaon Himalaya, Uttaranchal.

Biological Events

Some biological events bring a person (applicable to both male and female) close to the reproduction activities. Onset of puberty or the adolescence is considered as the marker of reproductive activities. For women, the menarche, *i.e.*, the first menstruation in women's life, marks the potential beginning of the physiological level of reproduction. It is the first sign of women's attainment of reproductive age. But full fecundity is not established until some period. The menstruation process continues among the women till they attain the age of cessation, *i.e.*, the menopause, when the female fecundity approaches zero. However, the occurrence and completion of this periodic cycle are greatly affected by the environmental and social factors. For example, poor economic strength of the society and malnutrition even delay the process of menarche to occur. The environmental factors also affect these events. For example, the average age at menarche in the cold climate is reported to be 15.8 years. The high altitude environment is even responsible for delaying the menarche to occur and early approach of the menopause. The lack of proper amount of Oxygen is responsible for this. Therefore, there is a reduction in the reproductive time span in the life of women.

Menarche usually takes place in the early or mid teens. The mean age at menarche is near 13 years in modern developed countries and slightly higher in poor and malnourished populations. Over the years, the age at onset of menarche has come down (Tanner *et al.*, 1965:3-5). The mean age at menopause of most populations for which measurements exist falls between ages 45 and 50 years, but the age of menopause of individual woman ranges from less than 40 to near 60 years (Beard, 1976: 3-4). In the Bhotia society, the mean age at menarche is 13.4 years and the mean age at menopause is 44.5 years. This indicates that the duration of reproductive cycle continues for about 31.1 years. In the high altitude settlement, the mean age at menarche is 13.5 years and the mean age at menopause is 44.4 years, which indicate the duration of reproductive cycle is about 30.9 years. However, at low altitude, the mean age at menarche is 13.3 years and the mean age at menopause is 44.6 years with the duration of reproductive cycle of 31.3 years (see Table 6.1).

Table 6.1: Comparative Account of the Mean Value of Biosocial Events of Women in Himalayas

Himalayan Range	*Western Himalayas*		*Kumaon Himalaya (Central Himalayas)*		
Population	Bod		Bhotia		
Religion	Buddhism		Hinduism		
Himalayan State	Himachal Pradesh		Uttaranchal		
Biosocial Events/Altitude (Mean age in Year)	High Alt. (Mean ± SD)	Low Alt. (Mean ± SD)	High Alt. (Mean ± S.E.)	Low Alt. (Mean ± S.E.)	Total (Mean ± S.E.)
Menarche	16.11±0.98	14.75±1.13	13.47±0.09	13.28±0.08	13.36 ± 0.06
Menopause	47.43±1.95	47.53±1.68	44.36±0.28	44.56±0.30	44.48 ± 0.21
Reproductive Span	31.32	32.78	30.93	31.29	31.12
First Marriage	20.33±3.48	20.63±3.98	19.85±0.25	19.28±0.20	19.52 ± 0.16
Gap between Menarche and Marriage	4.22	5.88	6.37	6.00	6.16
First Childbirth	22.72±3.95	22.67±3.87	21.46±0.27	21.06±0.22	21.23 ± 0.17
Gap between Marriage and First Childbirth	2.39	2.04	1.62	1.78	1.71
Last Child Birth	—	—	29.373 ± 0.511	27.829± 0.429	28.48 ± 0.33
Gap between First and Last Child Birth	—	—	7.91	6.77	7.25
Author	Parkash, 1990		**Present Study**		

Between the altitudes, in these respects, there is a minor difference. Even if there is no major difference, however, there is a reduction in reproductive life cycles of women at high altitude than at low altitude. This itself proves the fact that the high altitude environment is conducive for reduced reproductive life span. The environment, being tough and harsh along with the lack of proper nutrition and Oxygen concentration, gives bottleneck effect to the reproductive events to be fully operative. However, the low altitude environment is population friendly along with the availability of substantive resources.

Among the Bhotias of Nepal, it is found that the mean age at menarche is higher at high altitude (16.7±1.4 years) than at low altitude (16.2±1.7 years) (Laurenson *et al.*, 1985:66). Parkash (1990:65-9) also reports that the high altitude environment delays in the onset of menarche among the Bods of Himachal Pradesh in Western Himalayas. The mean age at menarche is found 16.1±0.98 years at high altitude and 14.8±1.13 years at low altitude among the Bods. According to him, there is reduction of reproductive span at high altitude (31.3 years) than at low altitude (32.8 years) among the Bod women (see Table 6.1). High altitude is found to delay menarche (Valsik, 1965:75-6). Hypoxia and hypothyroidism too, may operate to retard menarche as part of its general effect on the pattern of growth and development at high altitude (Frisancho and Baker, 1970:279-82). Furthermore, Harrison *et al.*, (1969:147) argues that altitude has certain apparent effect on the course of reproductive development in Ethiopia.

The study conducted in Andes, among the high and low altitude Bolivian women in south America (Dutt, 1980:107) shows that there is no marked difference observed as far as the mean age at menarche is concerned. The occurrence of menarche among the Japanese women living at Bolivian high altitude (La Paz) is 13.5±1.1 years and at low altitude (Santa Cruz), it is 14.4±1.8 years (Kashiwazaki *et al.*, 1988:836). The average age at menarche reported in the Sherpa population at high altitude Himalayas (Weitz *et al.*, 1978:187) is considerably higher than that of the high altitude Andean women (Cruz-Coke *et al.*, 1966:426-8). Among the Sherpas at moderate altitude (2,200-

2,600 m), it is estimated to be 16.3±2.3 years (Bangham and Sacherer, 1980:324). Weitz *et al.*, (1978:185) mention that the onset of menarche among the Sherpa women at high altitude is 16.8±2.0 years, which in fact has been reported to be higher than the women at low altitude (15.9±2.4 years), that is again supported by Bangham and Sacherer (1980:323-5). However, Beall (1983:367) reports that the median age at menarche among Upper Chumik females in Nepal (a high altitude population) is 16.2±1.1 years.

Paul (1997:56) reports that the mean age at menarche among the Central Himalayan populations is 13.01 years for the Marcha Bhotia in Garhwal Himalaya, 12.84 years and 13.03 years respectively in Dharchula and Johari Bhotias in Kumaon Himalaya, 12.98 years for the Bhotias and 13.03 years for the Kumaoni caste groups. It is reported that the Gaddis of Himachal Pradesh in Western Himalayas show the onset of menarche at 14.01 years (Bhasin and Bhasin, 1993:183-4).

Parkash (1990:65-71) has reported that the mean age at menopause among the high altitude Bods is 47.43±1.95 years, which is just marginally lower than that of the low altitude Bods (47.53±1.68 years) (see Table 6.1). The estimated median age at menopause among the Upper Chumik females in Nepal (a high altitude population) is 46.8±1.1 years (Beall, 1983:367). The mean age at menopause among the Manipuri Meitei women (44.95 years) is reported lower than the Pangal Muslims in Manipur in Eastern Himalayas (Choudhury and Devi, 1997:53). The mean age at menopause among the Gaddi women in Himachal Pradesh has been reported 44.41 years (Bhasin and Bhasin 1993:183), which resembles the present finding. Paul (1997:57-9) reports that the mean age at menopause among the Central Himalayan populations is 45 years, 44.83 years, 45.45 years, 45.23 years and 44.7 years for the Marcha Bhotias in Garhwal Himalaya, the Dharchula Bhotias and Johari Bhotias in Kumaon Himalaya, the Bhotias and the Kumaoni caste groups respectively in Uttaranchal.

Social Events

Marriage is the legal union of persons of opposite sex, the legality is being established by civil, religious or other means according to the custom and laws of each society. Menarche is the beginning of physiological ability of women for reproduction. But marriage brings the real reproductive abilities to be performed between the husband and wife. So, marriage is the actual initiation of the fertility process. Many demographic measures and research strategies have been based on the assumption that marriage is a necessary and sufficient condition for childbearing. In all societies, first marriage is a highly age-specific phenomenon, concentrated largely in the early adult years between 15 and 30 years. Because of this concentration, demographers pay great attention to differentials or changes in the mean age at first marriage. The marriage pattern in the Bhotia society is mostly monogamous.[2] In the recording of demographic events, it is found that marriage in the Bhotia society plays an important role in bringing out legitimate intimacy between a man and a woman and subsequently giving birth to offspring who even gets social identity and reckoning from parenthood. No intra-village marriage ceremony takes place because it is considered that fellow villagers belong to a single clan structure. Rather, inter-village marriage alliance is preferred one.

The mean age at marriage among the Bhotia women is 19.5 years. The mean age at marriage is found to be 19.8 years and 19.3 years at high and low altitudes respectively. Though, there is a difference in the mean age at marriage in between two altitudes, but it is quite negligible. The delay in marriage could be related to the delay in onset of menarche among girls at high altitude. This event even delays the birth of first child among women at high altitude. The settlement at high altitude is dispersed type; it is difficult for parents to search a boy for their daughter. The marriage obligation and fulfilment of required economic strength even delays the marriage process to occur. However, the communication and negotiation is rather easy at low altitude. At this habitation, the difficulty faced by parents to arrange a boy for the daughter is minimized.

A study conducted by Laurenson *et al.*, (1985:66) among the Bhotias in Nepal shows higher mean age at marriage at high altitude (24.1±8.6 years) than at low altitude (19.6±5.5 years).

Parkash (1990:65-71) reports that there is only a marginal difference in mean age at marriage between high altitude Bods (20.328±3.482 years) and low altitude Bods (20.629±3.984 years) of Himachal Pradesh in Western Himalayas (see Table 6.1).

Another study on high altitude suggests that the mean age at marriage is relatively higher at high altitude (19.57±0.44 years) than the low altitude (19.09±0.57 years) among the populations in Tambo valley in Andes (Abelson *et al.* 1974:16), which in fact resembles the present findings. Dutt (1980:106) reports that the mean age at marriage among the Bolivian women in Andean altitudes in South America ranges between 30.0 years and 34.4 years. The mean age at marriage among the Japanese women living at Bolivian high and low altitudes is reported to be 24.8±2.9 and 22.9±3.5 years respectively (Kashiwazaki *et al.*, 1988:836). The mean age at first marriage among the Sherpa women in Khumbu is reported to be 24.6 years, but the mean age at first pregnancy among the same women is 23.7 years, suggesting that the relatively late marriage has little effect on fertility (Weitz *et al.*, 1978:191-3). The Sherpas attach little or no stigma to premarital sex (Furer-Haimendorf, 1964:6).

It has been observed from the studies on Western Himalayas among the Gaddis (Bhasin and Bhasin, 1993:183) that the mean age at marriage among females and males was 18.22 and 24.47 years respectively. Balgir reports that the mean age at marriage for females is about 17 years in the Gujjar populations. In the Eastern Himalayas, the mean age at marriage of Manipuri women is reported to be 19.09 years and 16.40 years of the Meitei and Pangal Muslim populations respectively (Choudhury and Devi, 1997:55-6). The studies from Central Himalayan populations show that the mean age at marriage is 16.73 years, 16.39 years, 15.36 years, 16.01 years and 15.87 years among the women of Marcha Bhotias in Garhwal Himalaya, Dharchula Bhotias and Johari Bhotias in Kumaon Himalaya, Bhotias and the Kumaoni caste groups respectively in Uttaranchal (Paul, 1997:60-2). According to the Census (1981), the age at marriage in India for females was 18.3 years and for the Central Himalayas, it was 18.2 years. The mean age at marriage (Census 1991) of currently married women in the district Pithoragarh, Kerala and India in general is 17.2 years, 19.8 years and 17.7 years respectively.

The mean age at first childbirth among the women at high altitude is 21.5 years; whereas, it is 21.1 years at low altitude. The gap between the marriage and first childbirth is 1.6 years and 1.8 years at high and low altitudes respectively. The difference in the gap may be related to the proper birth placement among women at low altitude. At high altitude the gap is shortened because there is no recreation and entertainment facility; therefore, sex gets an important place in the life and this brings women at the greater risk of child birth. This fact is further evidenced by the mean age at last childbirth, which is higher at high altitude (29.4 years) than at low altitude (27.8 years). However, the mean age at last childbirth among the Bhotia women is 28.5 years. The gap between the first and last childbirth is more at high altitude (7.9 years) than at low altitude (6.8 years). It is 7.2 years among women at the population level. This indicates that the women have more awareness at low altitude about how to place the order of births. Therefore, it seems that these sections of women have better understood the positive aspect of smaller family size than their high altitude counterparts (see Table 6.1).

Parkash (1990:62-5) has reported that there is a minor difference at the age at first childbirth of mothers between high altitude Bods (22.716±3.954 years) and the low altitude Bods (22.667±3.869 years) in Himachal Pradesh (see Table 6.1). Abelson *et al.*, (1974:16) reveal that the mean age at first childbirth of high altitude born women (20.25±0.39 years) is more than the low altitude born women (19.09±0.48 years) in Tambo valley in Andes. In another study, the mean age of women at first childbirth among the Sherpas in Khumbu of Nepal is 23.6 years (Weitz *et al.*, 1978:187). Similarly, Bangham and Sacherer (1980:324) report that the mean age at first childbirth among the Sherpa women in Nepal is 22.2 years. Again, Bangham and Sacherer (1980:327-8) conclude that the Sherpas at high altitude have first childbirth 1.5 to 2 years earlier than those at moderate altitude. However, among the Bhotias of Nepal, it has been reported that the mean age at first childbirth is later at high altitude (26.2±5.9 years) than at low altitude (21.9±2.9 years) (Laurenson *et al.*, 1985:66). Among the Japanese migrant women to Balivia in Andean altitude, the mean age at first pregnancy is reported to be higher at La Paz high altitude (25.3±3.2) than at Santa Cruz low altitude (23.2±4.1) (Kashiwazaki *et al.*, 1988:836). The findings of the study by Dutt (1980:107) show that the mean age at first pregnancy of women at Bolivian altitudes occurs slightly earlier among women at low altitude than that of high altitudes in South America. Furthermore, some researchers conclude that the mean age at first live birth does not vary remarkably with altitude (Abelson *et al.*, 1974:, Dutt, 1980:106).

From the Western Himalayas, it has been reported that among the Gaddis of Himachal Pradesh the mean age at child bearing is 29.61 years (Bhasin and Bhasin, 1993:195). Choudhury and Devi (1997:54-6) report from the Eastern Himalayas that the mean age of mothers at first delivery is higher among the Meiteis (22.03 years) than among the Pangal Muslims (18.01 years) in Manipur. From the Central Himalayas, it has been observed that the mean age at child bearing in the Bhotia tribe of Uttaranchal is found to be 27 years and it is 30 years among the Marcha Bhotias of Garhwal Himalaya and 24 years among the Dharchula Bhotias of Kumaon Himalaya. The Kumaoni caste groups display the mean age at child bearing 25 years, which is higher than that of Dharchula Bhotias (Chachra and Bhasin, 1998:422).

Pregnancy History

Pregnancy history is a type of life history, which records details of all the pregnancies of a woman including the date at which each began and ended and the outcome. This provides data on every aspect of a woman's childbearing experience. The appendices 7, 8 and 9 provide information about the reproductive history of high altitude, low altitude and the Bhotia tribal women respectively. It is found that 20 to 25 per cent of the pregnancies are concentrated among the women in the age group of 35-39 years. It is 20.1 per cent at high altitude and 24.1

per cent at low altitude. Above 50 per cent of pregnancies are found in the age group of 30-44 years. At high altitude there is a smooth elevation in the pregnancy record of middle-aged women and not being squeezed at the two extreme age groups. However, at low altitude it increases sharply and gets the spurt among the women at 35-39 years and immediately it falls (age group 40-44 years) and again rises (age group 45-49 years), making the configuration zigzag and being squeezed at the two extreme age groups (see Figure 6.1). It indicates that the long-term adaptation with the high altitude environment has helped the women to be potentially active and bearer of the pregnancies without interference of the physical and social environment. Contrary to this, the low altitude environment is quite open and receptive, where there is a chance of external interference (*i.e.*, the knowledge from the nurses and other medical staff, influence of mass media, etc.) in the reproductive activities of women.

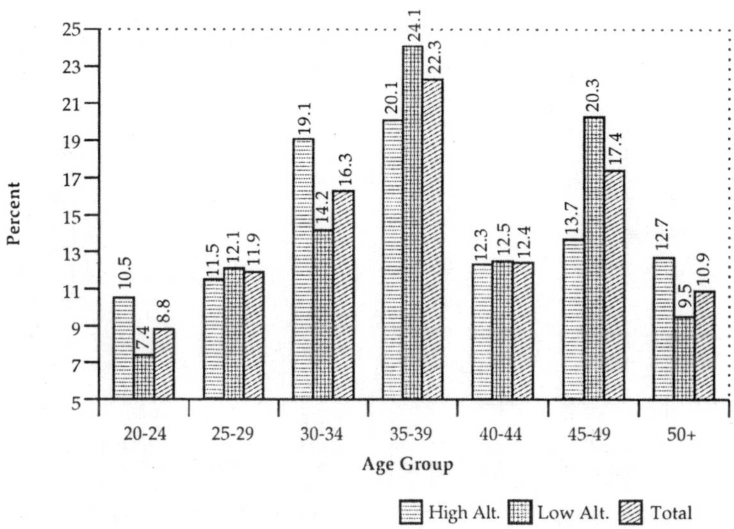

Fig. 6.1: Pregnancies among the Sample Bhotia Women at High and Low Altitudes

At high altitude 95.6 per cent pregnancies have led to live births and the rest is foetal death[3] either in the form of abortion or stillbirth. At low altitude, almost 95.1 per cent pregnancies are the successful ones, which have led to live births. In the level of women of Bhotia tribe, 95.3 per cent pregnancies are live births. In this respect, it can be inferred that at high altitude women are slightly better adapted than their low altitude counterparts. At high altitude the foetal deaths are found to be highest (44.4 per cent) among the women in their post-reproductive phase of life. Some significant proportion of foetal deaths has also been observed among the women in the age group 25-29 years (22.2 per cent) and 30-34 years (11.1 per cent). Contrary to the fact of age selective foetal deaths at high altitude, these occurred almost to the women in all age groups at low altitude. The maximum number of foetal deaths (26.9 per cent) is observed in the age group 35-39 years (see Figure 6.2). This can be correlated with the maximum number of pregnancies, which have also occurred to women in this age group. Therefore, more number of pregnancies is associated with more number of foetal deaths. At the level of population, the deaths are affiliated most to the post-reproductive age group, followed by the age group 35-39 years and below (see also Appendices 7 to 9).

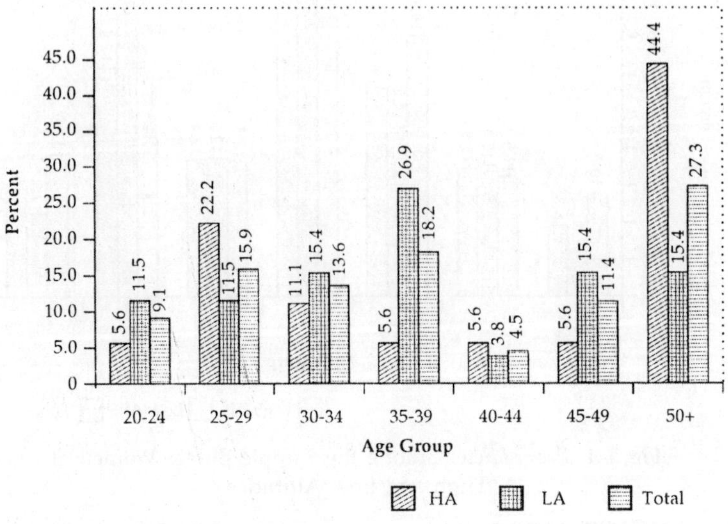

Fig. 6.2: Embryonic Loss among the Sample Bhotia Women at High and Low Altitude

Survival Rate of Children

The survival rate of the children is almost 89 per cent in the Bhotia population. There is no difference between the two altitudes in this respect. When it is looked at from the gender level survival, the rate is lower for females (85.3 per cent) than males (91.7 per cent) at high altitude. It is other way round at low altitude. The survival rate for females is higher (89.7 per cent) than the males (87.6 per cent) at low altitude (see Table 6.2). Survival rate of children born to mothers at high altitude is highest in the age group 20-24 years (97.6 per cent). Then the ratio decreases in the subsequent age groups and becomes minimum in the age group 45-49 years. It is found that the high altitude environment supports the male survival. Among the women of early age groups, the survival rate of male children is 100 per cent, though it is subsequently reduced. The reason may be the natural selection, as the high altitude needs male sections for being effective requirement in the fulfilment of basic necessities, which have to be arranged from the nature through agricultural activities, collection of food, fodder and firewood, rearing of animal wealth, protection for the younger and weaker sections and many other things in this direction (see Figure 6.3).

Table 6.2: Survival Rate of Children to the Bhotia Women under Study

Age Group of	*High Altitude*			*Low Altitude*			*Total*		
Mothers (in Yr.)	*M*	*F*	*T*	*M*	*F*	*T*	*M*	*F*	*T*
20-24	100.0	95.5	97.6	100.0	100.0	100.0	100.0	97.6	98.7
25-29	100.0	75.0	88.4	96.9	100.0	98.4	98.2	89.8	94.2
30-34	91.3	93.3	92.1	85.7	91.7	88.7	88.9	92.4	90.5
35-39	92.5	82.9	87.7	93.4	86.4	90.0	93.1	85.0	89.1
40-44	86.2	85.0	85.7	84.6	92.3	87.7	85.3	89.1	86.8
45-49	85.2	75.0	80.0	79.5	84.7	82.5	81.7	81.6	81.6
50+	90.5	91.3	90.9	73.9	82.6	78.3	81.8	86.9	84.4
Total	91.7	85.3	88.7	87.6	89.7	88.6	89.5	87.8	88.7

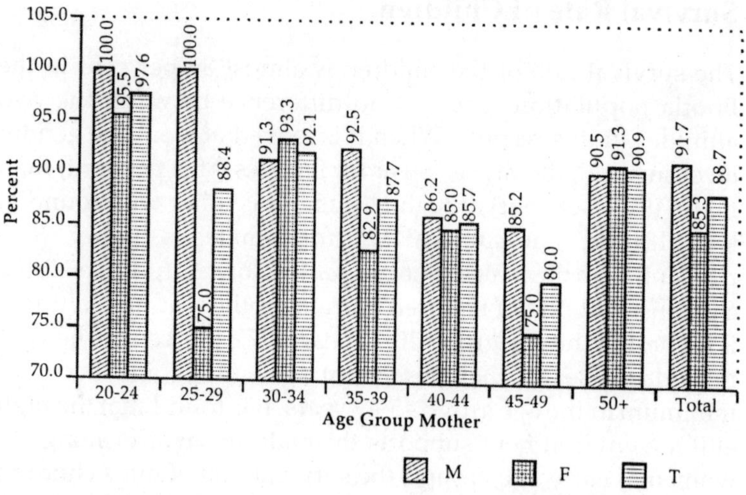

Fig. 6.3: Survival Rate of Children at High Altitude

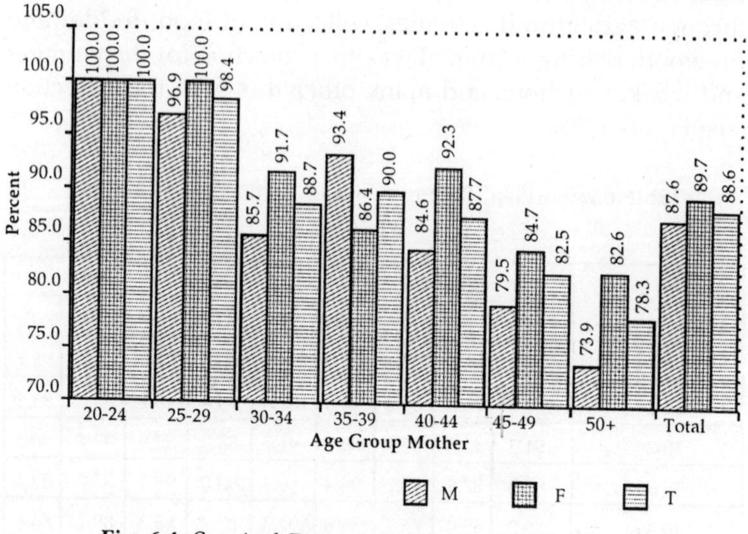

Fig. 6.4: Survival Rate of Children at Low Altitude

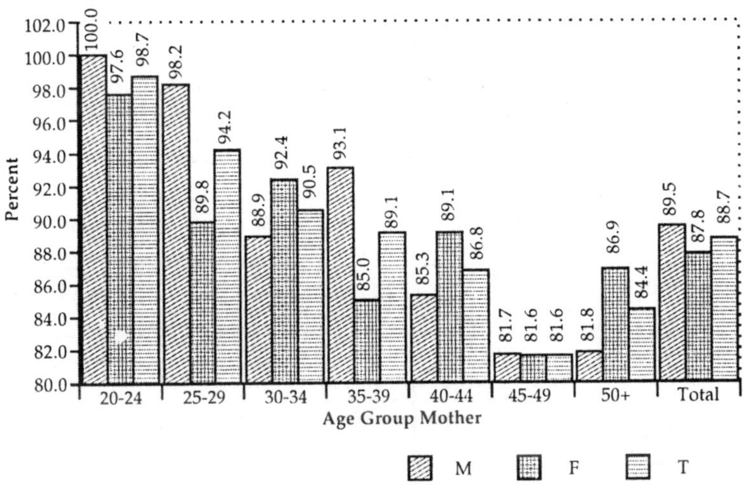

Fig. 6.5: Survival Rate of Children in the Bhotia Tribe under study

Against this trend, the low altitude supports female children more on their survival process. The survival ratio of the children among the women in 20-24 years is 100 per cent. The gender level discrepancy occurs in favour of females in the subsequent age groups. The difference on survival of sexes varies a bit (2.1 points). Therefore, it signifies that the low altitude environment shows gender neutrality as far as the survival of children is concerned. It even encourages the female children more in the socio-cultural selection. Exposure of people to the outside world, influence of mass media and educational and cultural achievement suffice to the fact (see Figure 6.4). It being a tribal community which is situated far off from the mainstream with minimum resources and avenues, the survival ratio in totality is much behind the cent per cent level. Overall, the survival ratio is found to be in favour of males. This indicates the dominance of patriarchal pattern of society that supports for the better nourishment of male sections in comparison to the female ones (see Figure 6.5).

Mean Value Analysis

Table 6.3 shows the mean and standard error of reproductive parameters of the Bhotia Women of Kumaon Himalaya, Uttaranchal.

Table 6.3: Mean and Standard Error of Reproductive Parameters of the Bhotia Women under study

Reproductive Parameters	*High Altitude (Mean ± S.E.)*	*Low Altitude (Mean ± S.E.)*	*Total (Mean ± S.E.)*	*t-value*	*Degree of Freedom*	*Remark**
Pregnancy	3.71 ± 0.45	3.47 ± 0.43	3.57 ± 0.43	0.384	12	Not Significant
Live birth	3.55 ± 0.43	3.30 ± 0.41	3.40 ± 0.40	0.418	12	Not Significant
Foetal Deaths	0.16 ± 0.09	0.17 ± 0.04	0.17 ± 0.06	0.097	12	Not Significant
Stillbirth (Mean)	0.064	0.066	0.065			
Abortion (Mean)	0.100	0.105	0.103			
Deceased Children	0.40 ± 0.12	0.38 ± 0.14	0.39 ± 0.12	0.106	11	Not Significant
Surviving Children	3.15 ± 0.33	2.93 ± 0.29	3.02 ± 0.29	0.497	12	Not Significant

* Not Significant at the level of 5% probability.

Pregnancy

The mean number of pregnancies or conceptions per woman is higher at high altitude (3.71±0.45) than at low altitude (3.47±0.43). The difference marked between high and low altitudes is found statistically insignificant (t=0.384, d.f.=12, not significant at 5 per cent level of probability) and it is 3.57±0.43 for the Bhotia population. The mean number of pregnancies is highest (5.09) among the women in the age group 45-49 years, as these sections have been reaching their final stage of childbearing and no differences are found between the two altitudes (5.09 at high and 5.10 at low altitudes), which reflects the fact that they bear common characteristic in this aspect. It is reported that the mean number of pregnancies per woman among the Japanese communities living in Bolivia (in Andes) in South America is lower at La Paz high altitude (3.1±2.1) than at Santa Cruz low altitude (4.5±2.5) (Kashiwazaki *et al.*, 1988:836), which is just the reverse of the present finding. Studies from the Eastern Himalayas show that the mean number of pregnancies is found quite lower among the Khamtis of Himalayan region of Arunachal Pradesh *i.e.* 3.67±0.09 (Chowdhury *et al.*, 1991:6-9) than that reported among the Khamtis in Assam, *i.e.*, 5.11±0.34 (Barua *et al.*, 1994:139).

Live birth

In the present study, it has been observed that the mean number of live births per Bhotia woman is higher at high altitude (3.55±0.43) than at low altitude (3.30±0.41). This difference is statistically not significant (t=0.418 and d.f.=12) at 5 per cent level of probability. The mean live birth is 3.40±0.40 for the Bhotia population. Gupta (1980:111) reports similar kind of findings where the mean live births per woman is higher at high altitude (4.74) than at low altitude (3.91) among the Sherpa women in Eastern Himalayas.

Another study (Dutt, 1980:107) reports that the mean number of live births ranges from four births to five births per woman in Bolivia (South America). However, the Bolivian women residing at high altitude had significantly fewer living children than the women residing at low altitude. Mirrakhimov (1978:311) observes a very small difference at high altitude in the USSR (5.0 compared with 5.4) and the fertility is found high among the women of Eastern Pamir. The mean number of live births is found low among the Japanese women living at Bolivian (Andean) La Paz high altitude (2.3±1.6) than at low altitude Santa Cruz (3.5±2.1) in South America (Kashiwazaki, *et al.*, 1988:836).

A number of works that have been reported from the Eastern Himalayas (Das *et al.*, 1982; Bhasin and Kshatriya, 1990; Choudhury *et al.*, 1991; Barua *et al.*, 1994; Khongsdier and Ghosh, 1994), show that in Sikkim the Brahman population has as many seven live births per woman in comparison to the Bhutias of Sikkim (5.41±0.29) (Bhasin and Kshatriya, 1990:271). The Khamtis of Arunachal Pradesh have three to four live births per woman (Chowdhury *et al.*, 1991:6-9), which in fact resembles the present finding. Sengupta and Gogoi (1997:339-40) report that Hindu Oraon women have an average 6.13 live births per woman, which is higher than that of the Christian Oraon, *i.e.*, 5.54 per woman in the tea garden of Assam. A study from the Western Himalayas reports that the Gaddis of Himalayan zone have more mean live births per woman (4.8) than that of the Gaddis of inner-Himalayan zone (4.5) in Himachal Pradesh (Bhasin and Bhasin, 1993:202). Garg *et al.*, (1981:367-9) report that the mean live births per woman is 6.40 among the Boksas of Uttaranchal in Central Himalayas (see Appendix 11).

Foetal Death

It is observed in the present study that the mean number of foetal deaths per woman is lower at high altitude (0.16±0.09) than at low altitude (0.17±0.04). The difference between high and low altitudes is statistically not significant (t=0.097 and d.f.=12) at 5 per cent level of probability. It is 0.17±0.06 the Bhotia population. Likewise, the mean number of abortions and stillbirths per woman is lower at high altitude (0.064 and 0.100 respectively) than at low altitude (0.066 and 0.105) and these are 0.065 and 0.103 respectively in the Bhotia population. In the studies of Cruz-Coke (1967), Hoff (1968) and Buck *et al.*, (1968), it is understood that a very low incidence of abortions is reported among the high Andean populations. The rate of abortion is particularly lower at high altitude than that of low altitude (Ablson *et al.*, 1974:13). Harrison *et al.*, (1969:60-6) have also found a very low rate of spontaneous abortion at high altitude than at low altitude in Ethiopia (1/173 pregnancies compared to 21/232). The mean number of abortions is found lower among Japanese women at high altitude La Paz (0.7±0.9) than the low altitude Santa Cruz in Bolivian Andes (Kashiwazaki *et al.*, 1988:836). All the above-mentioned reports extend support to the present finding.

Deceased Children

The present finding shows that the mean number of deceased children per woman is little more at high altitude (0.40±0.12) than at low altitude (0.38±0.14), which is not statistically significant (t=0.106 and d.f.=11) at 5 per cent level of probability and it is 0.39±0.12 in the Bhotia population. The increased childhood mortality has been observed among the offspring of high altitude Bolivian women (Dutt, 1980:109-10). Higher percentage of mortality has been observed among the Sherpas of Upper Khumbu in Nepal compared to the low altitude Sherpas of Kalimpong in Darjeeling District of West Bengal and the difference is insignificant (Gupta, 1980:112-3).

Surviving Children

The mean number of surviving children per woman in the present study is 3.02±0.29 and it is higher at high altitude (3.15±0.33) than at low altitude (2.93±0.29). The difference between high and low altitude is statistically not significant (t=0.497 and d.f.=12) at 5 per cent level of probability. From the Eastern Himalayas, it has been reported that the mean number of surviving children per Sherpa woman is lower at high altitude Upper Khumbu (2.49) than at the low altitude Kalimpong (3.88) (Gupta, 1980:108). Das *et al.*, (1982:159) report from Sikkim Himalayas that the mean number of surviving children per woman is lower in the high altitude Lachen village (2.65) than at low altitude Lachung village (3.70), which do not resemble the present pattern of findings. Among the War Khasis of Meghalaya, it is reported that the mean number of surviving children is 4.18 children per woman (Khongsdier and Ghosh, 1994:198). It is interesting to note here that the mean number of surviving children per woman among the Bhotias of Mana (a high altitude village) from Garhwal Himalaya is 2.77±0.16 (Guha, 1997:66).

Fertility Measures

Table 6.4 describes the comparative account of fertility measures at high and low altitudes in Western and Eastern Himalayas and the present study in Kumaon Himalaya under Central Himalayas.

Crude Birth Rate

In the Bhotia population, the Crude Birth Rate (CBR) has been found lower at high altitude (22.78) than at low altitude (24.17) and it is 23.58 in the total Bhotia population. It shows that there are 23 births per 1000 population at high altitude and 24 births

Table 6.4: Comparative Account of Fertility Measures in Central, Western and Eastern Himalayas

Parameter	*Western Himalayas*		*Eastern Himalayas*		*Kumaon Himalaya (Central Himalayas)*		
Population	*Bod*		*Sherpa*		*Bhotia*		
Religion	*Buddhism*		*Buddhism*		*Hinduism*		
Himalayan State/ Country	*Himachal Pradesh*		*High Alt.: Upper Khumbu (Nepal) Low Alt.: Kalimpong (Darjeeling)*		*Uttaranchal*		
Fertility Measures	*High Alt.*	*Low Alt.*	*High Alt.*	*Low Alt.*	*High Alt.*	*Low Alt.*	*Total*
Crude Birth Rate (CBR)	42.76	35.66	—	—	22.78	24.17	23.58
General Fertility Rate (GFR)	141.69	114.28	—	—	141.41	134.75	137.50
Total Fertility Rate (TFR)	5.51	4.49	5.09	6.62	3.45	4.05	3.80
Gross Reproduction Rate (GRR)	2.76	2.23	—	—	1.73	1.49	1.61
Completed Fertility Rate (CFR)	6.27	4.92	4.53	7.44	4.00	4.18	4.09
Mean Number of Children per Mother	4.11	3.63	2.49	3.88	3.15	2.93	3.02
Child Woman Ratio* (CWR)	38.69	33.06	60.34	50.44	44.20	41.00	42.31
Age Specific Fertility Rate (Total)	1102.43	897.08	—	—	691.30	808.8	765.0
Author(s)	Parkash and Malik, 1990		Gupta, 1978, 1980		**Present Study**		

* Children of age 0-4 years to the Women in their reproductive period in 100 female populations.

per 1000 Bhotia population at low altitude. As far as this fertility indicator is concerned, the difference between high and low altitudes is negligible. It has been reported from Western Himalayas that the CBR was higher at high altitude (42.76) than at the low altitude (35.66) among the Bods of Himachal Pradesh

(Parkash and Malik, 1990:176). The CBR (31 to 33 per 1000) of Sherpas at high altitude (Weitz *et al* 1978:191) is considerably low compared to what is reported at high altitudes in South America (between 48 and 56 per 1000) (Baker and Dutt, 1972:365). The CBR among Sherpas in Nepal at moderate altitude (2,200-2600 m) is 55 births per 1000 population (Bangham and Sacherer, 1980:325). Among the Gaddis of Himachal Pradesh Himalayas, it is reported to be 28.4 births per 1000 population (Bhasin and Bhasin, 1993:190). The study on Central Himalayan populations (Chachra and Bhasin, 1998a:192) has reported that the CBR of Bhotias of Uttaranchal is 23.54, which includes 35.98, 24.16 and 15.64 among the Marcha Bhotias, Dharchula Bhotias and Johari Bhotias respectively, which are again more or less similar to that of Kumaoni caste groups, *i.e.*, 26.23. The CBRs among Idu Mishmis and Digaru Mishmis are 51.13 and 45.91 respectively (Pandey 1991:102).

General Fertility Rate

The General Fertility Rate (GFR) in the present study has been found higher at high altitude (141.41) than at low altitude (134.75) and it is 137.5 for the total Bhotia population. It indicates that there are 141 live births at high altitude and 135 live births at low altitude to 1000 Bhotia women of childbearing age, which depicts the fact that high fertility is associated with the high altitude women than their low altitude counterparts. Parkash and Malik (1990:179) report that the GFR is higher at high altitude (141.69) than at low altitude (114.28) among the Bods of Himachal Pradesh in Western Himalayas, which resemble the present finding. Among the Gaddis of Himachal Himalayas, it is reported that the GFR is 110.5 (Bhasin and Bhasin, 1993:193). The GFR among the Central Himalayan populations is reported as 95.23 in Dharchula Bhotias and 56.49 in Johari Bhotias of Kumaon Himalaya, 86.48 in Bhotias of Central Himalayas and 108.87 in Kumaoni caste groups (Chachra and Bhasin, 1998a:418).

Total Fertility Rate

In the present study, the Total Fertility Rate (TFR) has been observed to be low at high altitude (3.45) than at low altitude

(4.05) and it is 3.80 for the total Bhotia population. It can be inferred that 3.5 and 4 children per woman would have been born during her lifetime at high and low altitudes respectively, if she were to experience the childbearing (the age specific fertility rates of the period) at each age. Similar kind of findings have been reported among the Sherpas of Upper Khumbu in Nepal (high altitude) and Kalimpong (low altitude) in Darjeeling District of West Bengal from the Eastern Himalayas (Gupta, 1980:112), which reveal that the TFR is lower at high altitude (5.09) than at low altitude (6.62). In a study on Western Himalayan altitudes among the Bods (Parkash and Malik, 1990:176), it has been seen that the TFR is higher at high altitude (5.51) than at low altitude (4.49). Das *et al.*, (1982:159) have reported from the Eastern Himalayas (Sikkim) that the TFR is found lower in a high altitude Lachen village, *i.e.*, 3.79 than in a low altitude Lachung village, *i.e.*, 4.66. The TFR among the Gaddis of Himachal Pradesh Himalayas is 3.5 (Bhasin and Bhasin, 1993:199). The TFR is reported to be 6.11 among the War Khasis (Khongsdier and Ghosh, 1994:199). In the Dalu population in Meghalaya, it is reported 6.09 (Patra and Kapoor, 1996:276-7) in the Eastern Himalayas. The TFR among the Bhotias of Mana village in Garhwal Himalaya is reported to be very low, *i.e.*, 1.77 (Guha, 1997:67). Chachra and Bhasin (1998a:420) have reported that the TFR in Central Himalayan populations is found to be 4.20 among the Marcha Bhotias in the Garhwal Himalayas, 1.93 and 2.68 among the Johari and Dharchula Bhotias respectively in the Kumaon Himalaya, 2.75 among the Bhotias in the Central Himalayas and 3.08 among the Kumaon caste groups.

Gross Reproduction Rate

The Gross Reproduction Rate (GRR) in the present study has been found higher at high altitude (1.73) than that of low altitude (1.49) and it is 1.61 for the total Bhotia population. It means that 1.7 and 1.5 daughters would have been born to a high altitude Bhotia woman and a low altitude Bhotia woman respectively during their life time, if they passed through the childbearing ages experiencing the average age specific fertility pattern in the year of data collection. Similarly, there has been a report from the Western Himalayas on the high and low altitude Bods

(Parkash and Malik, 1990:176), which suggests that GRR is higher at high altitude (2.76) than at low altitude (2.23). The GRR among the Central Himalayan populations is reported (Chachra and Bhasin, 1998a:420) to be 2.04 in Marcha Bhotias of Garhwal Himalaya, 0.94 and 1.31 in Johari and Dharchula Bhotias respectively, 1.31 in Bhotias of Central Himalayas and 1.5 in Kumaon caste groups.

Completed Fertility Rate

Table 6.5 describes the chronology of studies on altitude and fertility in different Himalayan populations those are reported

Table 6.5: Completed Fertility Rates Reported in Different Himalayan Populations

Himalayan Region	*Order*	*Population*	*State/Country*	*Altitude*	*Completed Fertility Rate (CFR)*	*Author (s)*
Nepal Himalayas	1	Sherpa	Khumbu, Nepal	High	4.8	Weitz *et al.*, 1978
Eastern Himalayas	2	Sherpa	Khumbu, Nepal	High	4.5	Gupta, 1980
			Kalimpong, Darjeeling	Low	7.4	
Nepal Himalayas	3	Sherpa	Khumbu, Eastern Nepal	Moderate (2,200-2,600m)	7.8	Bangham and Sacherer, 1980
	4	Tibetan Speaking	Limi, North-west Nepal	High	6.3	Goldstein *et al.*, 1981
Western Himalayas	5	Ladhaki	Jammu and Kashmir	High	6.6	Goldstein *et al.*, 1983
Nepal Himalayas	6	Bhotia Speaking	Central Nepal	High	3.2	Laurenson, *et al.*, 1985
				Low	4.9	
Western Himalayas	7	Bod	Himachal Pradesh	High	6.27	Parkash and Malik, 1990
				Low	4.92	
Kumaon (Central Himalayas)	8	Bhotia	Uttaranchal	High	4.00	**Present Study**
				Low	4.18	

by different scholars. From the above table, it has been observed that the completed fertility rate (CFR)/completed family size (CFS) is the most commonest parameter used by the researchers to study the nexus between altitude and fertility. Completed fertility rate is the cumulative fertility at the end of reproductive age of women. It is the lifetime fertility of women. In the present study, among the Bhotias, the CFR has been found low at high altitude (4.00) than at low altitude (4.18) and it is 4.09 in the total Bhotia population. On an average, there are four children at high altitude and 4.18 children at low altitude per woman above 49 years of age. There is no much difference existing between the two altitudes. However, the depressing effect of high altitude on fertility cannot be overruled.

Among the Sherpas, it has been reported (Gupta, 1980:109) that the CFR is low at high altitude (4.53) than at low altitude (7.44). Whereas, the CFR is reported to be higher at high altitude (6.27) than at low altitude (4.92) among the Bods of Himachal Pradesh (Parkash and Malik, 1990:176). The above findings of Gupta (1980:109) resemble the findings of Weitz *et al.*, (1978:190) among the Sherpas in Nepal (*i.e.*, 4.8). Again, Bangham and Sacherer (1980:325-6) report that the CFR is 7.79 among the Sherpa women at moderate altitude in Nepal. Laurenson *et al.*, (1985:66) report that among the Bhotia speaking people in Nepal the CFR is lower at high altitude (3.2) than at low altitude (4.9), which resembles the present findings. The CFR has been reported to be 3.80 in the high altitude Lachen village and 6.91 in the low altitude Lachung village in Sikkim (Das *et al.*, 1982:159).

A number of contradictory findings show that among the Tibetan-speaking people in Tsang village in Limi in Northwest Nepal (a high altitude village), the CFR is 6.3 (Goldstein, 1981:25-7). Similarly, his (Goldstein *et al.*, 1983) study in Kyilung village of Ladhaki speaking people in Kashmir, India (a high altitude village) advocates higher CFR (6.6). The value of CFR (*i.e.*, 8.29) among the low altitude Andean women studied by Abelson *et al.*, (1974:17) is higher than that reported for high Andean population by Hoff (1968) and Cruz-Coke (1967).

Macfarlane (1976:120-5) has found that the CFR is 5.5 among the Gurungs, a Mongoloid hill tribe in Nepal. Guha

(1997:67) reports that the mean children of woman aged 45 years and above is 1.95 among the Bhotias in Mana village in Garhwal Himalaya. Among the War Khasis in Meghalaya, it is reported to be 6.30 (Khongsdier and Ghosh, 1994:198). The CFR for Meiteis and Pangal Muslims is reported 6.16 and 7.84 respectively in Manipur (Choudhury and Devi, 1997:55-8). The CFR of Idu and Digaru Mishmis is reported 7.21 and 5.84 respectively in Arunachal Pradesh (Pandey, 1991:102-3).

Child-Woman Ratio

The child-woman ratio (CWR) (C_{0-4} to 1000 women of childbearing age) has been found higher at high altitude (442.0) than at low altitude (410.0) and it is 423.1 in the Bhotia population. This reflects that there are 442 children (0-4 years) and 410 children (0-4 years) surviving per 1000 Bhotia women at high and low altitudes respectively. A similar kind of pattern in the child-woman ratio has also been reported among the high and low altitude Bods of Himachal Pradesh in the Western Himalayas (Parkash and Malik, 1990:176) and among the Sherpas of Upper Khumbu in Nepal and Kalimpong in Darjeeling District of West Bengal (Gupta, 1978 and 1980). Some of the earlier researchers have reported that a lower CWR exists among the high altitude natives (Stycos, 1963 and 1965; Heer, 1967 and 1969; Heer and Turner, 1965; Baker and Dutt, 1972; Dutt, 1976; Basu and Mukhopadhyay, 1980). It is noted that the CWR is not an accurate measure of fertility in populations where the infant and early childhood mortalities are high (Whitehead, 1968; Bradshaw, 1969; Baker ,1972; Dutt, 1976).

From the Eastern Himalayas, it has been reported that the CWR in the high altitude Lachen village (416.7) is higher than the low altitude Lachung village (380.3) in Sikkim (Das *et al.*, 1982:157); and it is 966.66 and 965.75 among the Idu Digaru Mushmis respectively (Pandey, 1991:102-3) in Arunachal Pradesh. In Western Himalayas, the CWR has been reported to be 583.70 among the Gaddis of Himachal Pradesh (C_{04} to 1000 women) (Bhasin and Bhasin, 1993:195-6). However, in the Central Himalayas, it has been reported that the CWR is 548.93 among the Bhotia population (Chachra and Bhasin, 1998a: 422-3), which shows a close resemblance to the present findings.

The CWRs among the Marcha Bhotias of Garhwal Himalaya and Johari Bhotias of Kumaon Himalaya show lower values than the present findings. The CWR is reported quite low among the Bhotias of Mana village (a high altitude village) in Garhwal Himalaya (Guha, 1997:67).

Age Specific Fertility Rate

The study among the Bhotias in Kumaon Himalaya shows that the age specific fertility rate (ASFR) is maximum in the age group 20-24 years in high altitude (391.3) and low altitude (400.0). Thereafter, ASFR decreases consistently from the lowest age group up to the age group of 30-34 years in the high altitude (100.00) and 35-39 years in the low altitude (62.50). The sum total of ASFR is found lower at high altitude (691.3) than at low altitude (808.8). In the total Bhotia population, ASFR ranges between 395.35 in age group 20-24 years and 38.46 in the age group 35-39 years (see Table 6.6). In the Himachal Pradesh Himalayas, the study (Parkash and Malik, 1990:178) among the Bods shows that the sum total of ASFR is higher at high altitude (1102.43) than at low altitude (897.08) (see Table 6.4). The rate is maximum in the age group of 25-29 years (242.36) at high altitude, whereas the rate is maximum in the age group of 20-24 years (231.58) at low altitude among the Bod Women.

Table 6.6: Age Specific Fertility Rates of Sample Bhotia Women

Age Group (in Yr.)	*No. of Women*			*Number of Live-births in Last One Year*									*Age Specific Fertility Rates*		
				Male			*Female*			*Total*					
	HA	*LA*	*Tot.*	*HA*	*LA*	*Tot.*	*HA*	*LA*	*Tot.*	*HA*	*LA*	*Tot.*	*HA*	*LA*	*Tot.*
20-24	23	20	43	5	4	9	4	4	8	9	8	17	391.3	400.0	395.4
25-29	15	27	42	1	4	5	2	3	5	3	7	10	200.0	259.3	238.1
30-34	20	23	43	1	2	3	1	—	1	2	2	4	100.0	87.0	93.0
35-39	20	32	52	—	2	2	—	—	—	—	2	2	—	62.5	38.5
40-44	10	18	28	—	—	—	—	—	—	—	—	—	—	—	—
45-49	11	21	32	—	—	—	—	—	—	—	—	—	—	—	—
Total	99	141	240	7	12	19	7	7	14	14	19	33	691.3	808.8	765.0

Table 6.7 shows a comparative account of age specific fertility rates (ASFRs) of Himalayan populations that are reported by different authors (Pandey, 1991; Bhasin and Bhasin, 1993; Khongsdier and Ghosh, 1994; Chachra and Bhasin, 1998a). From the table, it is revealed that the maximum fertility is being displayed by the women in the age group of 20-24 years except the War Khasis (Khongsdier and Ghosh, 1994:199) and the Bhotias of Uttaranchal (Chachra and Bhasin, 1998a:421), where the maximum fertility level lies among the women in the age group of 25-29 years. The present study resembles the pattern of previously reported populations and shows a little higher fertility in the age group of 20-24 years than that in others. However, Pandey (1991:106-11) reports comparatively higher ASFRs in the Idu and Digaru Mishmis in Arunachal Pradesh in the Eastern Himalayas.

Fertility and Mortality Nexus

Researchers, so far in demography have demonstrated considerable interest in the analysis of relationship between fertility and infant (and child) mortality. It has been observed that the mortality decline not only precedes the fertility decline in the so-called demographic tradition, but the former is at least a contributory cause of the latter (Patnaik, 1985:41). It is generally argued that when mortality rate is high, fertility level also goes up as parents desire that their children should survive and when greater number die, they produce more to ensure the survival of some (Singh, 1986:9-11). In this context, an attempt has been made to verify the hypothesis that infant (and child) mortality affects fertility of couples by analysing its impact on the mean fertility in the Bhotia populations at high and low altitudes in Kumaon Himalaya, Uttaranchal.

From the Table 6.8, it is understood that there is a positive correlation between fertility and mortality. It is clearly observable at the level of low altitude and the total Bhotia populations. At high altitude, the fertility and mortality nexus is uneven. The mean mortality is 0.27 among the women of 25-29

Table 6.7: Reported Age Specific Fertility Rates in Different Himalayan Populations

Himalayan Region	*State*	*Population Group*	*Age Group of Women (in Years)*							*Author(s)*
			15-19	*20-24*	*25-29*	*30-34*	*35-39*	*40-44*	*45-49*	
Eastern	Arunachal Pradesh	Idu	400.0	640.0	333.0	170.0	250.0	120.0	—	Pandey, 1991
		Digaru	600.0	307.0	400.0	111.0	136.0	55.0	—	
	Meghalaya	War Khasi	44.0	136.0	139.0	121.0	86.0	61.0	24.0	Khongsdier and Ghosh, 1994
Western	Himachal Pradesh	Gaddi	32.3	197.1	118.4	147.4	159.1	24.1	16.1	Bhasin and Bhasin, 1993
Central	Uttaranchal	Bhotia Tribe	12.7	166.7	171.9	160.7	38.5	—	—	Chachra and Bhasin, 1998a
		Marcha Bhotia (Garhwal)	—	117.6	260.9	307.7	153.8	—	—	
		Dharchula Bhotia (Kumaon)	58.8	235.3	166.7	76.9	—	—	—	
		Johar Bhotia (Kumaon)	—	150.0	103.4	133.3	—	—	—	
		Kumaoni Caste Group	54.1	272.7	155.2	94.1	41.1	—	—	
		Bhotia Tribe (Kumaon Himalaya)	—	395.4	238.1	93.0	38.5	—	—	**Present Study**

years, whereas their mean fertility is 2.87. The mean mortality is 0.09 among the women in the age group of 45-49 years, whose mean fertility is 5.00, which is highest among other age groups. The mean mortality is highest among the women above 49 years, who display fertility lower than the women in 45-49 years. Therefore, it can be concluded that even if their correlation is found positive at low altitude and total population levels, it is not uniform at high altitude. This, in fact, may be assigned to the typical high altitude character because the adaptive mechanism acts as a barrier between the two aspects. However, the low altitude in this respect resembles other reported works. Due to the lack of adequate data from other high altitude areas, it is not possible to give a clear-cut pattern of relationship between them (see Figures 6.6 to 6.8).

Table 6.8: Age Specific Mean Fertility and Mortality among the Sample Mothers

Age Group (in Yr.)	*High Alt.*		*Low Alt.*		*Total*	
	Mean Fertility	*Mean Mortality*	*Mean Fertility*	*Mean Mortality*	*Mean Fertility*	*Mean Mortality*
20-24	1.83	0.04	1.80	0.15	1.81	0.09
25-29	2.87	0.27	2.26	0.11	2.48	0.17
30-34	3.80	0.10	3.09	0.17	3.42	0.14
35-39	4.05	0.05	3.75	0.22	3.87	0.15
40-44	4.90	0.10	3.61	0.06	4.07	0.07
45-49	5.00	0.09	4.90	0.19	4.94	0.16
50+	4.00	0.73	4.18	0.36	4.09	0.55
Total	3.55	0.16	3.30	0.17	3.40	0.17

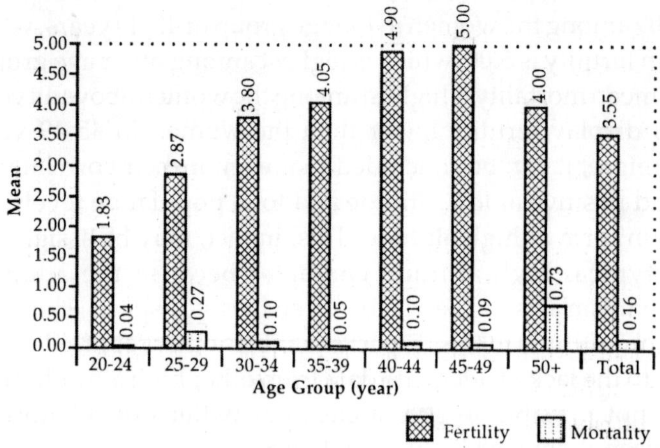

Fig. 6.6: Age Specific Mean Fertility and Mortality among the Sample Bhotia Mothers at High Altitude

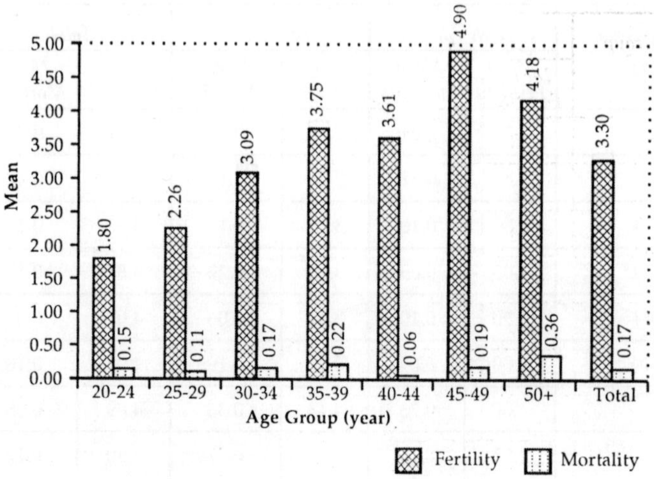

Fig. 6.7: Age Specific Mean Fertility and Mortality among the Sample Bhotia Mothers at Low Altitude

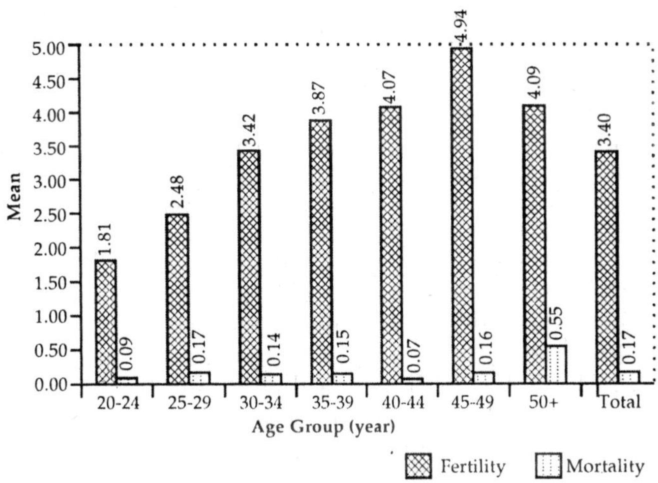

Fig. 6.8: Age Specific Mean Fertility and Mortality among the Bhotia Mothers under Study

It is reported that there is positive correlation between fertility and infant mortality. However, the higher fertility of women married at a young age is partly attributed to their attempts to replace the dead children (Srinivasan, 1991:51-6). The study of Kanungo (1987:121) in cities of Bhubaneswar and Cuttack reports that the highest percentage of child loss is found to be among the women who have had 10 and more than 10 children respectively. If parents do have a well-defined and limited demand for surviving children (and if they have clear demand at all, it must be for surviving children), then the level of child mortality should be positively associated with achieved fertility, defined in terms of the number of live births (Basu, 1991:88-97). In theory, he points out that the parental demand for the number of live births can rise with child mortality for two reasons, such as (*a*) as a response to actual child loss experience—that is known in the literature as the replacement effect; and (*b*) as a response to anticipated child loss that is known in the literature as the insurance effect. However, according to Driver (1963:27-31), when the fertility rate is more, the mortality rate is also more. His study shows that the percentage of child loss rises regularly from 26.6 per cent among couples having one child to 39.6 per cent among couples having seven children.

In lieu of the conclusion, it is understood that fertility covers the events ranging from exposure to intercourse and childbearing to the formation and dissolution of unions. It is actually the number of live births to a woman, as measures of fertility normally refer only to live births. By convention, most of the measures of fertility are related to mothers only. Menarche, the first menstruation in women's life marks the potential beginning of the reproduction. The menstruation process continues among the women till they attain the age of cessation, *i.e.*, the menopause, where the female fecundity approaches zero. Many socio-environmental factors delay the menarche. The high altitude environment is even responsible for the delay and early cessation of menstruation, thereby reducing the reproductive life of women. In the high altitude settlement, the mean age at menarche is 13.5 years and the mean age at menopause is 44.4 years, which indicate that the duration of reproductive cycle is about 30.9 years. However, at low altitude, the mean age at menarche is 13.3 years and the mean age at menopause is 44.6 years with 31.3 years duration of reproductive cycle. Even if there are no major differences, there is a reduction in reproductive life cycles of women at high altitude compared to those in low altitude. The mean age at marriage among the Bhotia women is 19.5 years. The mean age at marriage is 19.8 years and 19.3 years at high and low altitudes respectively. Though there is a difference in the mean age at marriage between two altitudes, however, it is found quite negligible.

It is found that 20 to 25 per cent of the pregnancies are concentrated among the women in the age group of 35-39 years. It is 20.1 per cent at high altitude and 24.1 per cent at low altitude. Above 50 per cent of pregnancies are accumulated in the age group of 30-44 years. At high altitude, the foetal deaths are found highest (44.4 per cent) among the women in their post-reproductive phase of life. Contrary to the fact of the age selective foetal deaths at high altitude, these occurred almost to the women in all age groups at low altitude. The maximum number of foetal deaths (26.9 per cent) is observed in the age group of 35-39 years. The survival rate of the children is almost 89 per cent in the Bhotia population. There is no difference between the two altitudes in this respect. When it is looked from the gender level survival, the rate is lower for the female (85.3 per cent) than the male (91.7 per cent) at high altitude. It is other way round at low altitude. The mean number of pregnancies, live births, surviving children and deceased children are higher at high altitude, while the mean number of foetal deaths is fractionally higher at low altitude. In the fertility measures, the CBR, ASFR, TFR, and CFR are reduced at high altitude. However, the GFR, GRR and CWR are higher at high altitude. This kind of uneven pattern puts question mark on the depressing effect of high altitude on fertility. Furthermore, higher mortality is not always associated with higher fertility at high altitude. But at low altitude, higher mortality level is associated with higher level of fertility.

Notes

1. In theory, there is no reason why fertility rates expressed with reference to the father should not be calculated. In practice, difficulty in determining paternity and less restrictive biological limits on the age range of male fertility makes measures problematic, and so they are rarely calculated.
2. However, there are exceptional kind of marriages such as polyandrous (a woman marries several men at a time) or polygynous (a man marries several women at a time) or marriage between persons of same sex (for example in Sudan society, among the Trobriand Islanders, etc.) or a marriage between a ghost and a person and so on. Therefore, it is difficult to arrive at a universal definition of marriage to accommodate all kinds of marital situations. Among the Bhotias, the marriages generally are monogamous where one man marries a woman at a time. In the present study, those women are chosen up who had monogamous marriages and were continuing the marital life without formal or informal breaks at the time of fieldwork (refer Chapter 3).
3. Foetal mortality is a term used to cover all stillbirths, miscarriages and abortions. Strictly speaking, foetal mortality does not include the termination of life at very early stages of pregnancy, which might more accurately be termed as embryonic mortality. An alternative terminology, recommended by World Health Organisation, is to group

all these as foetal deaths, and distinguishing early, intermediate and late mortality according to the duration of pregnancy. A distinction is made between spontaneous abortions or miscarriages, which are deaths before 18 weeks of pregnancy, and stillbirth, which are deaths after that duration when the foetus is assumed to be capable of independent life outside the uterus. However, in the present study, it is found that all the abortions are spontaneous ones.

7

FERTILITY DETERMINANTS, TRANSCENDENCE AND IMMANENCE

Human fertility is influenced by a host of biological, sociological and economic factors. The number of children produced by a group of women will depend upon their age, marriage duration, economic resources, educational facilities, housing conditions, etc. It may also depend upon the environment where they live. Reproduction is a regular process. It is possible to compile a much shorter list of variables that have a direct and inevitable effect on fertility. Inevitable effect is that the change in one of these variables may translate a change in fertility. These variables are known as the proximate determinants of fertility. Davis and Blake (1956:211-2) have suggested that fertility can directly be influenced by eleven proximate determinants. However, these proximate determinants are in turn influenced by various economic, social, cultural and environmental factors. In this chapter, a number of factors responsible for the differential fertility such as, mother's age at menarche and marriage, mother's education and occupation, income of the household, type of family, and the use of family planning methods have been taken into account among the high and low altitude Bhotia tribe of Kumaon Hills, Uttaranchal to understand the cumulative effect of these determinants on fertility pattern of the Bhotia women.

Menarche and Fertility

Menarche is an important physiological phenomenon in the

women's life. It is an event after which the women become biologically active to take part in the fertility performance. Table 7.1 shows the mother's age at menarche and the mean fertility level of Bhotia women at high and low altitudes of Kumaon Hills, Uttaranchal. It is a matter of contention that the length of the reproductive cycle of women increases when the event of menarche occurs early and the complete cessation of this event, *i.e.*, menopause is delayed. The hypothesis can be formulated that the early occurrence of menarche leads to increase in fertility as this enlarges the reproductive life of women. However, in the present study, it is found that the women who menstruated at their 12th year of life have fertility 2.80, which is much lower than those who menstruated later at high altitude. This is true for women at low altitude (3.12) and in the Bhotia population (3.02). The fertility is increased in case of women who menstruated at the 13th, 14th and 15th years in both high and low altitudes. This pattern remains same for women in the Bhotia population level. However, at both high and low altitudes, the fertility is constantly increased with the late onset of menarche.

Table 7.1: Mother's Age at Menarche and Mean Fertility of the Sample bhotia Women

Altitude	*Mean Fertility*	*Mother's Age (in yr.) at Menarche*				
		12	*13*	*14*	*15*	*Total*
High*	No. of Mothers	15	44	35	16	110
	Live births	42	154	130	64	390
	Mean Fertility	2.80	3.50	3.71	4.00	3.55
Low*	No. of Mothers	34	61	38	19	152
	Live births	106	197	128	71	502
	Mean Fertility	3.12	3.23	3.37	3.74	3.30
Total	No. of Mothers	49	105	73	35	262
	Live births	148	351	258	135	892
	Mean Fertility	3.02	3.34	3.53	3.86	3.40

* t = 0.853, d.f. = 6, Not significant at 5 per cent level of probability.

From the present findings, it can be argued that—

1. Onset of menarche is an important biological phenomenon in the reproductive life of women, but it is the actual sexual discourse, which leads to the stage of conception and subsequently birth of a child. Therefore, no matter when do women start menstruation, it is their sexual life, which brings them into fertility along with their physiological capacity to conceive *i.e.*, the fecundity. From the table it is understood that the fertility constantly increased along with the increase in age at menarche. It implies that the early maturity among girls is not being subject to early marriage. Therefore, the relationship between menarche and fertility is ambiguous.
2. So far as the comparison between the pattern of menarche and fertility is concerned among the women at high altitude and low altitudes, it is found that the difference between them in respect of altitudes is statistically not significant at the level of 5 per cent probability (t = 0.853, d.f. = 6). This is very much so despite the fact that there are different Bhotia populations on the basis of their settlements (high and low), but the populations bear ethnic and genetic similarity. Therefore, they do not display significant differences in this respect.

Adequate data are not available for studying the association between the age at menarche and fertility. The study on Gaddis of Chamba of Himachal Pradesh Himalayas (Bhasin and Bhasin, 1993:202) does not show uniformity in the association between the age at menarche of mothers and their mean fertility level. The study on urban women in Cuttack and Bhubaneswar cities reveals that the fertility rate gradually decreases with the increase in age at menarche, but the increase is not significant (Kanungo, 1982:142-5).

Marriage and Fertility

Marriage in the society is a basic and most fundamental institution, which brings family into existence. Marriage is the legal approval for sexual life of a man with a woman and the children born to the woman under such circumstances are legitimate offspring of the husband and wife. The age of woman at marriage is of considerable importance in determining the fertility performance, as the woman is socially acknowledged to take part in reproduction only after marriage. If someone marries at a lower age then the reproductive life span is more in comparison to late marriages. The chances of having more number of children are enhanced when women go for early marriage. The effect of lessening of reproductive life span on fertility is due to the increase in age at marriage.

The study among the high and low altitude Bhotia populations here reveals that the mean fertility decreases with the increase in mother's age at marriage (see Table 7.2). The mean fertility figures of the high altitude women are found 4.45, 3.55, 3.03 and 3.17 and for the low altitude women these are 4.08, 3.39, 2.58 and 2.14 respectively for those women whose age is in the range of 15-17 years, 18-20 years, 21-23 years and 24-26 years. However, the difference between the high and low altitudes in this respect is not found to be statistically significant (t = 0.450, d.f. = 6 at 5 per cent level of probability).

Table 7.2: Mother's Age at Marriage and Mean Fertility of the Sample Bhotia Women

Altitude	*Parameter*	*Mother's Age (in yr.) at Marriage*				
		15-17	*18-20*	*21-23*	*24-26*	*Total*
High*	No. of Mothers	20	51	27	12	110
	Live births	89	181	82	38	390
	Mean Fertility	4.45	3.55	3.03	3.17	3.55
Low *	No. of Mothers	38	69	38	7	152
	Live births	155	234	98	15	502
	Mean Fertility	4.08	3.39	2.58	2.14	3.30
Total	No. of Mothers	58	120	65	19	262
	Live births	244	415	180	53	892
	Mean Fertility	4.21	3.46	2.77	2.79	3.40

* t = 0.450, d.f. = 6, Not significant at 5 per cent level of probability.

Following readings can be made for the difference, which exist between the high and low altitude women, such as—

1. In general, the high altitude environment provides a favourable condition for women to beget more children than their low altitude counterparts, as their long association with high altitude environment is the key factor for better adaptability irrespective of similarity in the age at marriage.
2. In high altitude environment, agriculture is the main occupation. Both male and female folk contribute their labour for agricultural activities. At this altitude, the women have higher fertility because of the reason that their male partners as such remain with them which brings higher frequency of sexual intercourse, and this is one of the major sources of entertainment for couples at this altitude.
3. At low altitude, the economic activities are of relatively more diversed than in high altitude. The traditional occupation is shifted to other kinds, primarily due to the profit orientation. This leads the men to migrate outside their cultural territory for livelihood. This brings reduction in the frequency of sexual intercourse hence there is reduction of fertility among the low altitude women, even if the women of high and low altitudes have got married at the same age.

Some of the studies conducted by the scholars can be cited here. It has been reported that the age at first marriage among the Sherpa women is 26.6 years (in an average after eight years of menarche) and live births vary from five to seven. The fertility of Sherpa and Tibetan women living at high altitude over 3,400 m in Nepal is relatively lower than the low altitude peasant population. This may be associated with the retarded age at menarche and traditional delay of marriage, and above all, religious practices promote male and female celibacy (Weitz *et al.*, 1978:191-3).

The fertility study by different scholars in different places of India also shows negative correlation between female age at marriage and fertility performance (Majumdar, 1960; Driver, 1963; Agarwala, 1977; Kanungo, 1982). In all studies, it has been found that higher the age at marriage, lower the fertility is (Choudhury, 1984; Pandey and Talwar, 1987; Bhasin and Bhasin, 1993; Chachra and Bhasin, 1998a). The woman's age at marriage has been reported to be having significant effect on fertility among the Gaddis of Himachal Pradesh Himalayas (Bhasin and Bhasin, 1993:202). The mean fertility values have been found 5.1, 4.8, 3.8 and 3.0 among the women if their age at marriage is in the range of 15-19 years, 20-24 years, 25-29 years, and 30-34 years respectively. This even indicates a negative correlation between the mother's age at marriage and fertility pattern.

A study conducted by Chachra and Bhasin (1998a:426-7) in the Central Himalayan populations reveals that the average number of children ever born per ever married woman is greater when the woman marries at a younger age, and the average number of children ever born per ever married woman decreases as her age at marriage increases. Woman's age at marriage affects her fertility performance, since marriage marks the beginning of the reproductive life of a couple. Average number of children is 4.53, 2.8 and 1.87 among the Kumaoni caste groups, and 4.21, 2.70 and 2.92 among the Bhotias of Central Himalayas, per ever married woman, if their age at marriage is below 18 years, 18-21 years and 21 years and above respectively. Pandey and Talwar (1987:304-5) report that in rural Uttar Pradesh, the fertility of women who marry at an earlier age is more.

Family Type and Fertility

Table 7.3 shows the type of family and mean fertility of the Bhotia women at high and low altitudes of Kumaon Hills, Uttaranchal. It has been observed that the fertility is higher in case of women belonging to the nuclear family at high and low altitudes. The mean fertility rates are found 3.98 and 2.91 at high altitude and 3.48 and 3.03 at low altitude respectively in the family types such as nuclear and joint families respectively. The mean fertility among the women in the Bhotia population is 3.69 and 2.98 in the nuclear and joint families. The difference between the mean fertilities in two altitudes is statistically not significant (t = 0.423 and d.f = 2).

Table 7.3: Type of Family and Mean Fertility of the Sample Bhotia Women

Altitude	*Parameter*	*Type of Family*		
		Nuclear	*Joint*	*Total*
High*	No. of Mothers	65	45	110
	Live births	259	131	390
	Mean Fertility	3.98	2.91	3.55
Low*	No. of Mothers	91	61	152
	Live births	317	185	502
	Mean Fertility	3.48	3.03	3.30
Total	No. of Mothers	156	106	262
	Live births	576	316	892
	Mean Fertility	3.69	2.98	3.40

* t = 0.423, d.f. = 2, Not significant at 5 per cent level of probability.

Some of the reasons can be cited here, such as—

1. There is a shortage of manpower in the nuclear family among the tribals, especially the Bhotias. To fulfil the basic needs, to substitute working hands and also to take care of the parents in case they fall sick, etc., they go for more number of children in the nuclear family.
2. Higher mean fertility is observed among the high altitude women belonging to the nuclear family than among the women in the nuclear families at low altitude. This is also because of the reason that high altitude needs more manpower to overcome the tedious and difficult tasks. Starting from cattle, sheep and goat rearing, wool collection, firewood and fodder collection from the forest, fetching water from streams or river and also for agricultural activities, etc., they

need more manpower. The general attitude among the people here is that more hands can reduce the workload among them.

3. The degree of feeling of togetherness is comparatively higher at high altitude as this environment requires a collective approach among the members in the joint family to mitigate and surpass their problems. Therefore, nobody is given a chance to think of helplessness. Thus, this reduces the fertility level among the women at high altitude belonging to joint families in comparison to their low altitude counterparts.
4. The suggestions and advices of the elderly people given to the married couples are not found in case of the nuclear family in order to restrict their number of children. The husband and wife become adamant in their sexual relations and do not think of future placement of the conception and family size, which in turn brings higher fertility among them in the nuclear family.
5. The fear of sickness and old-age support is not found among the married couples in joint family. Joint family itself provides the moral support to the members. Therefore, this feeling encourages the married couples to reduce the fertility in the joint family environment.

Several studies conducted in India in different regions at different points of time by researchers have come out with the common findings that the joint family registers lower fertility in comparison to nuclear family (Davis, 1964; Davis and Black, 1956; Nag, 1965; Bhasin and Bhasin, 1993). The study conducted by Bhasin and Bhasin (1993:196-7) among the Gaddis from Western Himalayas in Himachal Pradesh, on the number of children ever born according to the family type, has come out with a common finding that the joint family registers lower fertility (4.8) in comparison to the nuclear family (5.2). The reason could be scarcity of labour, increase in demand for working hands, etc. Similarly, the study in cities of Bhubaneswar and Cuttack shows that the nuclear families have on an average, higher fertility than that of joint families (Kanungo, 1982:145-7).

Education and Fertility

In a developing nation like India where population growth is obstructing economic development and welfare, one of the controversial topics is the relationship between education and fertility. It is believed in western world that fertility declines have been caused, at least in part, by advances in education for the general population (Stycos, 1963:257-9). The standard of education of people shows prosperity of a country. Education enables people for better occupation and better economic condition. It also changes the outlook of people. Moreover, it changes the attitude towards the family size. So, education is very closely related with the fertility pattern.

In high and low altitudes, the illiterate mothers have higher fertility (4.44 and 4.08 respectively) than their literate counterparts (2.80 and 2.94 respectively). The general trend, which has been observed from the table (see Table 7.4) that higher is the mother's education, the lower is their fertility level. It is noticed that mean fertility rate is higher among the high altitude women (3.55) than the low altitude women (3.30) and it is 3.40 among the women in the population. This pattern is same for the high altitude illiterate women (4.44) compared to their low altitude counterparts (4.08). But, the mean fertility is lower in case of high altitude literate women (2.80) than that of low altitude literate women (2.94). In the population level, it is 4.27 and 2.89 for the illiterate and literate women respectively. A break up of educational standard of women at high and low altitudes shows that the mean fertility is higher among the women having formal and elementary educational qualification than among the matriculates and above. However, the difference between the high and low altitudes is statistically not significant ($t = 0.244$ and $d.f = 2$).

Table 7.4: Mother's Education and Mean Fertility of the Sample Bhotia Women

Altitude	*Mean*	*Mother's Educational Status*								
		*Illiterate**	*Literate*							*Total*
			Inf. Edu.	*Ele. Edu.*	*Und. Mat*	*Matri.*	*High. Sec.*	*Above High. Sec.*	*Total Literate**	
High*	No. of Mothers	50	10	26	12	2	6	4	60	110
	Live births	222	39	79	31	6	7	6	168	390
	Mean Fertility	4.44	3.90	3.04	2.58	3.00	1.17	1.50	2.80	3.55
Low*	No. of Mothers	48	14	34	19	9	18	10	104	152
	Live births	196	54	130	46	21	37	18	306	502
	Mean Fertility	4.08	3.86	3.82	2.42	2.33	2.06	1.80	2.94	3.30
Total	No. of Mothers	98	24	60	31	11	24	14	164	262
	Live births	418	93	209	77	27	44	24	474	892
	Mean Fertility	4.27	3.88	3.48	2.48	2.45	1.83	1.71	2.89	3.40

* t = 0.244, d.f. = 2, Not significant at 5 per cent level of probability. Informal Education (Inf. Edu.) means the educational attainment without attending the school or any institution; Ele. Edu. = Elementary Education *i.e.*, Up to Class VIII; Und. Mat.= Under Matriculation; Mat.= Matriculation; High Sec.= Higher Secondary; Above Higher Secondary = It includes Graduation, Post Graduation and Professional Courses like Medical, Engineering, Computer Education etc.

The probable reasons are such as—

1. There are more illiterate mothers at high altitude (45.45 per cent) than at low altitude (31.58 per cent). That means illiteracy among mothers is rampant at high altitude. Thus, it could mean that there is a degree of ignorance in case of mothers at high altitude. Therefore, higher fertility level is found in high altitude mothers than in low altitude.

2. Even if there is higher per cent of literate mothers in low altitude (68.42 per cent) than in high altitude (54.55), the fertility level is noticed higher in case of low altitude women (2.94) than among the high altitude women (2.80). This is so because at low altitude, women and their children have access to modern health facilities. Thus, the survival rate of the newly born ones is higher. Thus fertility is more among the literate women at low altitude than among their literate counterparts at high altitude.
3. There is reduction of fertility level among the high altitude literate women compared to their low altitude counterparts. This can be analysed from two angles: Firstly, entry of women to the educational system is a new phenomenon. The women who are in the educational system may shift their attention from domestic as well as farming and agricultural activities to the learning process. This diverts their familial activity to the process of inculcating modern ideas. Secondly, the high altitude literate women reduces the marital reproductive life by engaging themselves in education and learning process, which may be responsible for the reduction of fertility among the high altitude literate women than among the low altitude ones.

According to Chachra and Bhasin (1998a:424-5) among the populations studied in Central Himalayas, all population groups show that the illiterate woman tends to have a higher average number of children ever born per ever married woman than the literate woman. In addition, the less educated woman has higher average number of children ever born per ever-married woman than the more educated one has. The Gaddis of Himachal Pradesh Himalayas (Bhasin and Bhasin, 1993:199-201) show that higher mean number of children among the illiterate women (5.4), followed by primary educated (4.8), middle school educated, and the least among the high school educated women (3.3). Similarly, the study of Kanungo (1982) in Orissa indicates that the inverse relationship between education of mother and her fertility is common to the women of twin cities like Bhubaneswar and Cuttack. While education is negatively related to the fertility level, it is not clear, why it is so. The measurement of this effect is difficult, but it is certain that education changes parents' perception in bringing fertility within the sphere of conscious choice (Kanungo, 1982:156-9).

Occupation and Fertility

Table 7.5 shows the mother's occupation and mean fertility of the Bhotia women at high and low altitudes of Kumaon Hills, Uttaranchal. The female participation in the labour force has often been considered an important indicator that influences their fertility. The present study points out that the lowest mean

Table 7.5: Mother's Occupation and Mean Fertility of the Sample Bhotia Women

Altitude	*Parameter*	*Mother's Occupation*				
		Agricul-ture	*Spinning/ Weaving*	*House Wife/Hh. Work*	*Service*	*Total*
High*	No. of Mothers	42	14	51	3	110
	Live births	181	60	144	5	390
	Mean Fertility	4.31	4.29	2.82	1.67	3.55
Low*	No. of Mothers	41	32	73	6	152
	Live births	164	104	219	15	502
	Mean Fertility	4.00	3.25	3.00	2.50	3.30
Total	No. of Mothers	83	46	124	9	262
	Live births	345	164	363	20	892
	Mean Fertility	4.16	3.57	2.93	2.22	3.40

* t = 0.342, d.f. = 6, Not significant at 5 per cent level of probability.

fertility has been observed among the women holding services at high altitude (1.67) and low altitude (2.5), followed by the women as housewife and busy in household work (2.82 at high altitude and 3.00 at low altitude). The highest fertility has been observed among the women busy in agriculture (4.31 at high altitude and 4.00 at low altitude), followed by the women in spinning and weaving (4.29 at high altitude and 3.25 at low altitude). However, in respect of the differential fertility on primary occupations of the Bhotia women, the difference between high and low altitude is statistically not significant (t = 0.342 and d.f. = 6).

The probable reasons are such as—

1. Agriculture is the primary occupation at high altitude. As agricultural activities require more manpower, and therefore, it encourages women to go for higher fertility level than any other kind of occupation.
2. The women who are busy in spinning and weaving activities also need more hands to cooperate them in this occupation, and therefore, there is a desire for higher fertility level. After the agricultural activity is over, people also concentrate on spinning and weaving. The animals like goat and sheep have been useful for the major transportation of commodity and usable articles. Other than this, the high altitude environment provides *Bugyals* (summer pastures) for the animals. The wool cutting at high altitude is accompanied by drawing woollen threads out of the raw wool. The tendencies among the people to finish up the raw wool into usable garments or mats, which are to be sold when they come down to the low altitude settlements during winter, highly penetrated into the domain of their working culture, even to work when they are at the leisure hours. At high altitude, agriculture, spinning and weaving attract more manpower. Thus, the fertility among the women is higher at high altitude. However, higher fertility pattern has been observed among the women in these occupational categories irrespective of altitudes.
3. Those women who remain busy in the household work or as housewife are at the risk of higher frequency of sexual intercourse as they spend more time with their

respective husbands at home than the women holding any other occupations. The low altitude provides wider scope for the indoor works, as there is a minimum outdoor occupational activity. There is, moreover, little or no scope for people to be involved in agricultural or allied activities at low altitude. Even if these women are subject to higher frequency of sexual intercourse it is the collective decision in the family for placing a child.

4. The modern occupations like service, whether private or government, are directly related to the level of education, experience and training. The reduction of fertility level among the employed women is because of their higher awareness level as a result of higher education. They remain busy in personal career oriented development rather than giving time to childbearing. These women generally want to remain free from family burden along with their individualistic attitude.

However, even if there is a level of difference noticed among the women at high and low altitudes. The difference is not statistically significant. The study of Chachra and Bhasin (1998a:426) on the Central Himalayan populations reports that those women who are occupied in the services have the least average number of children born per ever married woman (2.57), whereas those involved in agriculture have an average higher number of children born per ever married woman (4.03). The study on the Gaddis of Himachal Himalayas (Bhasin and Bhasin 1993:197-9) shows that the mean number of children per mother is highest among the women in occupation such as agriculture (5.5) followed by animal husbandry (5.3), labourer (5.2), and least among the service holders (3.9). These values are quite higher compared to the present findings among the Bhotias.

Saxena (1965:25) reports that among the different occupational groups in rural Uttar Pradesh, the highest fertility rate is found among the agriculturists, and it gradually decreases among the labourers, then artisans and petty businessmen, and it is lowest among the service holders. Similarly, Pandey and Talwar (1987:306) in a study in rural Uttar Pradesh, found agricultural labourers that have the highest fertility, whereas the service holders have the lowest fertility. The study of Kanungo (1982:165) suggests in this connection that an inverse relation between the rise of livelihood-occupation and fertility. The fertility among the business persons and service holders is higher than that of the unskilled workers in the urban settlements of Cuttack and Bhubaneswar. The above findings support the earlier finding made by Davis (1951:49-53) that the fertility is higher in the households of agricultural labourers and artisans than in those of the traders, professionals and non-agricultural labourers. However, it has been observed that the lower occupational groups, on an average, have higher live births. The children of wealthier families have a higher rate of survival, whereas among the children of lower occupational groups, more children die at the stage of infancy. So, the women of lower and poorer groups tend to bear more children to supplement the loss (Davis, 1964:1946-7).

Income and Fertility

Income is definitely one of the important factors, which regulates the life pattern of people. Every underdeveloped or economically backward country is characterized by high fertility (UN, 1998:6-7). The present study among the Bhotias indicates that at high and low altitudes and also in case of the total Bhotia population, the fertility and household income has an inverse relationship. In the present study, the relative range method has been followed to classify the income groups. According to this method,

$$\frac{\text{Highest income of the Household} - \text{Lowest income of the Household}}{\text{Number of Observations}}$$

Now this value becomes the scale for identifying the classes. However, in order to restrict the range of classes, the adjustment to the scale has been done by multiplying a constant. In high altitude, the highest income of the household is Rs.6,000 and lowest income is Rs.600. Thus, 6000–600/110=49.09, 49.09×3=147.27≈147. In low altitude, the highest income of the household is Rs.7,000 and lowest income is Rs.400. Thus, 7000-400/152=43.42, 43.42×3=130.26≈130. Here, 3 is taken as constant.

Table 7.6: Monthly Income of the Household and Mean Fertility of the Sample Bhotia Women

Altitude	*Parameter*	*Monthly Income (Rs.) of the Household*				
		Very Low Income Group	*Low Income Group*	*Middle Income Group*	*High Income Group*	*Total*
High*	No. of Mothers	77	13	8	12	110
	Live births	295	46	14	35	390
	Mean Fertility	3.83	3.54	1.75	2.92	3.55
Low*	No. of Mothers	83	41	10	18	152
	Live births	307	134	21	40	502
	Mean Fertility	3.70	3.27	2.10	2.22	3.30
Total	No. of Mothers	160	54	18	30	262
	Live births	602	180	35	75	892
	Mean Fertility	3.76	3.33	1.94	2.50	3.40

* t = 0.340, d.f. = 6, Not significant at 5 per cent level of probability.

In both high and low altitudes, it is found by the relative range method that there are four economic classes in the Bhotia tribe on the basis of the monthly income of households. These classes are such as the Very Low Income Group, Low Income Group, Middle Income Group and High Income Group. In high altitude, the range of the household income for the Very Low Income Group is between Rs.600 and Rs.2,400, while it is Rs.2,600–3,200 for Low Income Group, Rs.3,500–3,700 for Middle Income Group and Rs.3,900–6,000 for High Income Group. In low altitude, the range of the household income for the Very Low Income Group is between Rs.400 and Rs.2,500, while the range for Low Income Group is Rs.2,700–3,650, Middle Income Group Rs.3,800–4,000 and High Income Group Rs.4,200–7,000.

The trend shows that there is an inverse relationship with income and fertility in the Low Income Group. But, the Middle Income Group (1.75 at high altitude and 2.1 at low altitude) becomes a kind of watershed between the Low Income Group (3.54 at high altitude and 3.27 at low altitude) and High Income Group (2.92 at high altitude and 2.22 at low altitude). Women belonging to High Income Group show increase in fertility from that of the Middle Income Group. This can be attributed to better nutrition, awareness and availability of medical facilities in the High Income Group (see Table 7.6). The reasons can be cited here such as—

1. On the basis of the above findings, it can be inferred that income levels have statistically no significant impact on the fertility levels in high and low altitudes. It may be because in an area, subject to large-scale out migration and lack of adequate medical facilities, the number of births to cope up with the dwindling population is more significant than anything else. In such a situation, the number of children born to female is directly proportional to the number of working hands available after certain age. Moreover, illiteracy and prevalence of cultural preferences to children do display significant role in fertility determination than income or status of the household.
2. Similarly, higher the income level of household, lower is the fertility level among the women as such in both high and low altitudes. High income leads to higher level of access to modern facilities such as TV, modern education, etc. These facilities have rather allowed them to infer wider worldviews other than their limited cultural interpretations to their life and behaviour.
3. Agriculture or allied traditional occupations are no more profit oriented. It is basically of subsistence type. Households with lower level of income refer to their dependence on traditional occupations. As traditional occupations need more manpower, the women who remain busy in these occupations have higher fertility as well as they have lower level of monthly income.

4. Higher income of the households indicates that the family has either modern employment or has preponderance in agricultural wealth like land and animal. Agriculturally powerful families do not invest their labour, but hire the labour from other households. Therefore, in both the cases, it does not require the household to raise the level of manpower. Thus, the fertility is reduced among the women belonging to higher economic stratum.

The study (Chachra and Bhasin, 1998a:425-6) on Central Himalayan populations shows that when the income level increases then the average number of children ever born per ever married woman decreases. Again, the study among the Gaddis of Himachal Pradesh Himalayas (Bhasin and Bhasin, 1993:202) reveals a similar kind of opinion that the mean fertility decreases with the increase of annual income of the family. However, the survey of Aggarwala (1977:85-9) reports that there is no reflection of such regular gradations and indicates that the people in the highest income categories also have high fertility.

Family Planning and Fertility

Birth control or family planning is a conscious attempt of couples or individuals to space births as well as to prevent them. Direct evidence of increased use of contraception to achieve family limitation is not generally available for historical or the pre-literate populations. However, the Bhotia tribal community with their long historical traditions of being traders, which in several ways emancipated them and nourished their worldviews that put them in the civic paths, adhered to the modern views regarding conscious efforts to space and prevent the births. However, the use of family planning methods is a new phenomenon to the Indian societies; this is true for the Bhotia tribal society also, and it is one of the most important national programmes to keep the population growth under control.

Table 7.7: Use of Family Planning Methods and Mean Fertility of the Sample Bhotia Women

Altitude	*Parameter*	*Family Planning Methods*		
		User	*Nonuser*	*Total*
High*	No. of Mothers	50	60	110
	Live births	125	265	390
	Mean Fertility	2.50	4.42	3.55
Low*	No. of Mothers	63	89	152
	Live births	166	336	502
	Mean Fertility	2.63	3.78	3.30
Total	No. of Mothers	113	149	262
	Live births	291	601	892
	Mean Fertility	2.58	4.03	3.40

* t = 0.222, d.f. = 2, Not significant at 5 per cent level of probability.

As far as the family planning is concerned, as many as 45.45 per cent of women at high altitude and 41.45 per cent of women at low altitude and 43.13 per cent of women in the Bhotia population have been reported to be the users of family planning methods. It has been noticed that high fertility has been recorded among the non-user women in comparison to the women who have been using the family planning methods (such as, 2.50 and 4.42 at high altitude, 2.63 and 3.78 at low altitude and 2.58 and 4.03 in the population level among the users and non-users respectively). Another important characteristic feature observed regarding this is that the younger women (between 20 and 39 years) have preferred the family planning process more than the elderly women (40 years and above) at high and low altitudes. Moreover, the difference that exists between high and low altitudes regarding the fertility differentiation is not statistically significant (t = 0.222 and d.f. = 2) at 5 per cent level of probability (see Table 7.7).

Study related to the use of contraceptives in the family planning process, done among the Andean countries (Abelson *et al.*, 1974:18) reveals that more than 50 per cent of women at low altitude have some knowledge of these methods, compared to less than 30 per cent of them at high altitude. However, Chachra and Bhasin (1998b:448-9) report that hill region has a higher percentage of couples using contraceptives than the plains have. India is the first country to launch an official programme of family planning, as part of its development strategy. The programme was launched as early as in 1952, as part of the First Five Year Plan. The family planning programme is viewed not only as a welfare measure for promoting the health of the mother and preventing unwanted births, but also as a demographic intervention for controlling the population growth rate (Srinivasan, 1991:65-8). Similarly, again Srinivasan (1991:73-5) reports that the acceptance and use of contraception by women of younger ages can be expected to have a greater impact on fertility, which of course resembles the present findings. Furthermore, according to Srinivasan *et al.* (1984:294-6), motivation to control fertility results from the difference between potential family size and desired family size. On the average, families in Uttar Pradesh would like to have 4.8 children while in Kerala families want only 3.9 children. Their results point to the predominant role of motivation and implicitly, modernization in promoting use of contraception.

It is understood that the relationship and association between the menarche and fertility is completely ambiguous in nature. Delay in the mean age at marriage brings down the fertility level. This pattern of association is similar to both the altitudes. Nuclear family set up has displayed higher fertility among the women where the pattern is uniform for both the altitudes. Illiterate mothers have higher fertility. Higher level of education is associated with lower fertility level. This is common to both the altitudes. The women who carry out agricultural or spinning and weaving activities have displayed higher fertility than the housewives and service holders. This pattern is similar for both the settlements. The women of Low Income Group have higher fertility than the High Income Group. But it is the women of Middle Income Group who display lowest fertility than both the extreme categories. Family planning method is used to control the natural fertility.

Therefore, the women who use family planning methods show lower fertility level. In all the cases, the pattern is uniform for both the altitudes. However, the mean fertility levels in respective aspects and categories differ, but the difference between the two altitudes (high and low) is statistically not significant at the 5 per cent level of probability. Though statistically this relationship has not been proved significant, it is very much so, because the populations at high and low altitude settlements bear ethnic and genetic similarity. Therefore, they do not display significant differences in these respects. Yet the validity of theory remains intact meaning thereby, at high altitude the risk of preserving life is far more difficult in comparison to low altitudes. The low altitude is relatively better off in terms of medical facilities, transport, accessibility, etc. These factors considerably reduce the risk of life and survival. However, in the initial stage of development as is the case of Bhotias in Pithoragarh District, these have not become pronounced. It is expected that by the passage of time, the process of spatial differentiation between high and low altitudes will also be reflected through the fertility behaviour. The study is quite indicative of the trends.

8

CRITICAL ENSEMBLE

The interaction of human beings with their environment is the domain of social ecology. The interaction is unavoidable so much so that life activities are drawn upon dependence on one another. For all living creatures, the environment determines their behavioural aspects. The human-environment nexus is superior to all other creatures. Human beings can modify the environment and accommodate themselves with the help of their cultural domain. As culture is the human creation, it is certainly a reaction to the environmental conditioning. As environment changes from macro level to micro level, likewise we do not find any single environment accommodating all human beings. As environment creates response on human beings, they build counter-response on environment through the adaptive process. Adaptive process is composed of a series of action-oriented phenomena in order to sustain and carry forward the race not letting the environment to demolish their efforts. Environmental adaptation by human beings is cultural in nature; and culture is the sum total of what human beings have. Therefore, the material accumulation in an environment is derived out of the need, which is brought out to nurture and nourish the race in a better manner. However, the material accumulation is a cognitive phenomenon, as mental blocks fulfil the need. Thus, social ecology is the interrelationship between mind, matter and environment, which form a trinity and channelise all possible interrelationships among them.

High altitude ecology poses a severe challenge for human adaptation. The availability of the most vital nutrient includes oxygen that is reduced at high altitude. The stress at high altitude includes hypoxia, high solar radiation, severe cold, aridity, rough terrain, limited nutritional base, high wind, etc. These physical elements collectively determine the impact of environment on individuals and populations. There is no such pinpoint definition or answer to exactly demarcate the 'high' altitude from the 'low'. However, most individuals experience some high altitude effects at altitudes of 2,500 m and above. For the purpose of describing the effects of altitude, the '2,500 m contour line' has been taken as a general divider between 'high' areas of land as opposed to 'low'.

A good deal of research works report that high altitude environment acts as a cursive agent to dismantle the demographic structure, more so to the fertility pattern of populations in the form of shortening the reproductive life of women and increasing the possibility of mortality at infancy and childhood. However, some others put forward their propositions that a long-term association and acquaintance increase the level of adaptive mechanism, so that smooth survival is an outcome for populations at high altitude. Looking at the pros and cons of both the schools of thought, I have attempted in this book to do away with the academic confusion over high altitude *vis a vis* demographic structure.

Anthropologists have always tried to explore information studying small societies especially peasant and tribal cultures dependent on nature and exhibited a greater interest in ecological questions. The internal dynamics of a population are in a way, part and parcel of the environment. The internal dynamism of a population is related to the level of outcome, in terms of fertility. The burden of fertility lies with the mothers or women sections. Their counterparts initiate the whole reproductive activities but it is the women section who carry it forward. In all societies, reproduction is covert with social significance that is culturally sterilized. Any negative occurrence on women is a negation to the whole procreation and reproduction process. Rather, it is an attempt to harm at whole humanity and race. Thus, women are centrally placed in the trinity of biology of reproduction, culture and environment.

Demography is the empirical, statistical and mathematical analysis of human populations. Analysis of events is contextualised with socio-cultural, historical and environmental aspects of the population. The special emphasis is laid upon the relative measurement of size, composition and distribution of population through space and time. With the development of technological innovation, the fertility behaviour is controlled. All population groups have some sort of checks and balances to its fertility behaviour. It does not remain as a normal biological process, but it is affected by different variables like social, cultural and economic determinants and particularly family planning or effectiveness of contraception. In this book, transcendence and immanence of fertility is compared and comprehended from both the angles such as the socio-cultural determinants and the environmental conditions within the domain of high and low altitude settlements.

The first kind of research work on high altitude goes to Monge's effort (1942) in observing difficulties in reproduction experienced by Spanish women at Andean high altitudes. Taking a clue from his work, many scholars have drawn light on other populations adapted to different high altitude zones. Some of the prominent scholars are Cruz-Coke *et al.*, 1966; Hoff, 1968; Baker, 1969 and 1978; Baker and Dutt, 1972; Abelson, 1974; Goldstein, 1976; Weitz *et al.*, 1978; Bangham and Sacherer, 1980; Gupta, 1980; Parkash and Malik, 1990, who put fourth some valuable pieces of suggestions in this field. In a similar attempt, I pursued enquiry on some of the issues of high altitude demography, which remained unanswered till today. The doubts that rhetorically remind me are such as—

- High altitude does not always act as a reducing agent of fertility.
- Fertility is a reproductive consequence that reflects its determination that is social, cultural and historical.
- Late onset of menarche and its early cessation at high altitude may reduce the reproductive span of women, but its control over fertility reduction seems ambiguous as marriage takes care of societal legalized union of couples initiating conception and parenthood.

- Fertility in population is not a closed circuit. Rather it is open to the decision of members concerned in the family or group for its placement and it is more or less a controlled phenomenon, whether the population is pre-literate or advanced kind.

It would be a fair and justified attempt, if altitudes (high and low) are taken as independent variables and these are compared by other associated aspects as dependent variables to adjudge the fertility pattern of populations in altitudinal settlements. Thus, incorporating several possible determinants to understand the variability pattern in high and low altitude Bhotia populations, elevates the scope of the study.

When I write down this section of my book, the people of Uttaranchal celebrates the fourth foundation anniversary. It has practically fulfilled the political dream of people after a prolonged struggle. The state has 13 districts in two broad cultural divisions *viz.*, Garhwal and Kumaon. There are seven districts, namely Uttarkashi, Chamoli, Rudraprayag, Pauri Garhwal, Tehri Garhwal, Dehradun and Hardwar in Garhwal administrative division and the rest like Nainital, Almora, Champawat, Pithoragarh, Bageswar and Udham Singh Nagar in the Kumaon administrative division. These two divisions are also marked by cultural and linguistic differentiation along with the marked developmental pace. A variety and complexity of natural ecosystems with unique geo-climatic conditions, vegetation, wildlife, soil, kaleidoscopic moods and beauty of nature, socio-economic conditions and culture altogether mark the area of the state. The population of the state of Uttaranchal accounts for less than one per cent of total population of the country with density of 159 individuals per sq. km. The area of Kumaon region is just 39.3 per cent of the state and accommodates 42 per cent of the state population with a density of 170 individuals per sq. km. The decadal growth rate for 1991-2001 of the state is 19.2 per cent and it is 16.9 per cent in the Kumaon region. The state has five tribal groups, namely, the Tharu, the Boksa, the Jaunsari, the Bhotia and the Raji. The Bhotia tribe has been spread in three districts of the state such as Uttarkashi, Chamoli and Pithoragarh. The present study focuses on the Bhotia tribe settled in the District Pithoragarh.

The Bhotias of Kumaon region like to introduce themselves as *Sauka* or *Rang* and live in the northern high altitude regions of Pithoragarh. The human settlements in the *Bhoti* (*i.e.*, the land of Bhotias) region of Kumaon are confined to four valleys, namely Johar, Darma, Chaudans and Byans. The Johar valley is in the Munsiyari tehsil and other three valleys are under the jurisdiction of tehsil Dharchula. Rivers such as Goriganga, Dhauliganga and Kaliganga drain these valleys. The impact of climatic conditions on the life of Bhotias is widely apparent. The higher reaches of these valleys remain covered by snow for nearly six months in a year. The severity of winter compels people to leave the place, and hence they come down southward to their winter homes in the warm places. Thus, transhumance becomes a regular feature of their life. The people were mercantile groups and earlier they were connecting Tibet in trans-Himalayas and the plains in India to carry forward the trade activities. It is the war with China in 1962 and the subsequent sealing of the border with China that put them partially settled at high altitude in Greater Himalayas and permanently settled at low altitude in Middle and Lesser Himalayas. Therefore, their settlement in different altitudes is a post-war phenomenon.

Demography is a discipline in which the data are collected by field survey. The field survey for this study was carried out between the year 1998 and 1999 among the Bhotias of Pithoragarh District. In order to understand the impact of altitude on the demographic structure and fertility pattern, the interview schedules were used to collect the information from people inhabiting high and low altitudes of the District Pithoragarh in Uttaranchal Himalayas. Married women, who were not divorced and had at least a child at the time of fieldwork, were selected as unit of the study. They were asked questions related to family, economy, occupation, reproductive life, etc. The genealogy method was used in order to comprehend information about the generations of a family. The cross checking was done by involving other members including their husbands in the household. Demographic data were collected from 262 households from 17 villages (7 villages from high altitude and 10 villages from low altitude). The sample size is 262 households that consist of 110 from high altitude and 152 from low altitude. The average altitude of villages consulted at high altitude is 3,433m and 1,861m at low altitude. The demographic analysis is done from two dimensions. First, population composition includes age-sex composition, sex ratio, masculinity proportion, index of ageing and dependency ratio. Second, fertility measures include pregnancy history, survival level and rates. The analysis also involves human resources like education, occupation and economy and their mobilization in the Bhotia populations at high and low altitudes of Uttaranchal Himalayas. Percentage, mean, standard error, t-test of significance are some of the statistical tools used to measure the variability and significance level among the Bhotia populations settled at high and low altitudes.

Demography as a discipline is concerned itself with the totality of people and their quantification in many ways. The categorization and analysis of high and low altitude population composition of the Bhotia tribe have been done to comprehend the understanding of interrelationship between altitude and demographic structure. Important attributes of demographic structure such as age and sex structure, family size and type, marital status, etc. have been taken up to study the variations. It is necessary to study the age and sex composition in order to understand the population dynamics in the Bhotia tribe and their settlements in Himalayan high and low altitudes. In the Bhotia population, there are 52.24 per cent males and 47.76 per cent females. Altitude-wise, no difference is observed in the male-female proportion in the Bhotia populations. The percentage of economically active population remains same for the two settlements. Some changes have been marked in the child and old age populations. Higher percentage of child population and lower percentage old age population are found in the high altitude Bhotia tribe.

Balance between sexes is an important aspect of population structure. Sex composition is an important indicator of fertility trends, family structure, and marriage pattern and to know about the status of women in the society. The study on sex composition is done with reference to sex ratio. Sex ratio in a population is the number of females to the males. Sex ratio varies considerably due to the impact of sex-selective mortality and migration. The sex ratio among the infants below one year of age is of one to one equation at high altitude and it decreases considerably in subsequent age groups and again it increases among the old age people. The sex ratio in the high altitude Bhotia population is 875 females per 1000 male population. This shows a discouraging sign for females at high altitude. Contrary to this, at low altitude the overall sex ratio is 943. Even if, the sex ratio here is low among infants, but the ratio is impressive among the child population (0-14 years) and old age population. But in the economically active population, the high and low altitude settlements have no major differences in the sex ratio.

The Bhotia population irrespective of high and low altitude settlements has more number of males than that of females. Therefore, the populations are basically masculine in nature. In the old age population, the proportion has decreased in general for both the settlements, showing more females than males. Furthermore, the index of ageing indicates that it is quite low at high altitude (10.5 per cent) than in the low altitude settlements (22.04 per cent). As there are less number of old age people, the old age dependency ratio is quite low (5.68) at high altitude than at low altitude (10.77). Young age dependency ratio is high at high altitude (54.09) than at low altitude (48.87). As far as the total dependency ratio is concerned, there is no difference found between the two altitudinal settlements.

The size of the family is classified into four categories such as small (one to three members), medium (four to six), large (between seven and nine) and very large (above 10). The average size of family is 6.39 and 6.53 at high and low altitudes respectively. At both the altitudes, Bhotia people have more nuclear families than joint families. In general, there are 59.54 per cent and 40.46 per cent nuclear and joint families respectively in the Bhotia population.

Marriage is a social phenomenon. In the Bhotia tribe, there are 50.94 per cent, 43.99 per cent and 5.07 per cent people unmarried, married and widowed respectively. At high altitude, the similar figures are 53.49 per cent, 43.81 per cent and 2.70 per cent. Widowers (0.53 per cent) are less than widows (5.18 per cent). In the low altitude, 49.14 per cent, 44.11 per cent and 6.75 per cent people are unmarried, married and widowed. There are 3.52 per cent widowers and 10.17 per cent widows. It is observed that unmarried people are comparatively found more at high altitude. However, more married and widowed people are available at low altitude.

Resource constitutes all the attributes of our environment, both material and metaphysical that can be used for meeting human demands that are economically feasible, culturally acceptable, technologically accessible, and environmentally sustainable. Availability of any substance is only a precondition for considering it as resource. To become a resource, the pattern and aspects of their mobilization are equally important. In the study, some essential aspects of the resource mobilization are incorporated to understand the resource base in the Bhotia society at high and low altitudes. For example, education is the basic resource, which changes the dimension of human life. The Bhotia tribal community displays a higher rate of literacy (83.5 per cent). This indicates 91.9 per cent male literacy and 74.1 per cent female literacy with disparity level of 17.8 points. However, low altitude has a bit of higher level of literacy. The women sections are more literate at low altitude than their high altitude counterparts. The gender gap is little widened at high altitude (20.0 points) than the low altitude (16.4 points).

In the resource mobilization, occupation structure gets a pivotal place. Agriculture is the mainstay of the Bhotia people at high altitude. Almost 32 per cent people are engaged in the agricultural activities. The participation of women in agriculture is relatively higher than that of men. Other than agriculture, people are involved in business (14.4 per cent) and service sector (14.7 per cent). Contrary to this, at low altitude, service sector accommodates 22.5 per cent compared to 21.1 per cent people in agriculture. Business sector also accommodates a significant proportion of people (15 per cent). However, women dominate the spinning and weaving industry along with household activities. Unemployment makes its appearance among the Bhotia people at both the settlements. Furthermore, the basic resource mobilization depends on the exploitation of indigenous and external resources along with technological development. The average monthly income of the Bhotia household is Rs. 2,342. The average monthly income is Rs. 2,124 at high altitude, which is below the AMI of low altitude (Rs. 2,487). The class formation in the Bhotia tribal society is a new concept. The low altitude gives wider support and exposure to earn and sustain the life better.

Fertility

Fertility is the childbearing performance of individuals, couples, groups or populations. Fertility is generally expressed in relation to mothers. Fertility is expressed in terms of the number of live births of a woman. Fertility is however, a complex system representing a set of different reproduction strategies. Though reproduction is a biological phenomenon, social norms and practices can influence the level of fertility. Some biological events bring a person closer to the reproduction activities. For women, the menarche, the first menstruation, is the potential beginning of physiological level for reproduction till its complete cessation, *i.e.*, menopause. However, in human society the marriage brings legalization of sexual unions. Therefore, fertility pattern is such a complex inner dynamics that it includes some biological and social events of women's life. The mean age at menarche of Bhotia women is 13.4 years and menopause 44.5 years. This indicates that the reproductive cycle among the Bhotia women continues for about 31.1 years. In the high altitude, the mean age at menarche is slightly delayed (13.5 years) than at the low altitude (13.3 years). The menopause comes early at high altitude *i.e.*, 44.4 years than the low altitude 44.6 years. Therefore, the reproductive life span among the women is slightly reduced at high altitude (30.9 years) than at low altitude (31.3 years). The mean age at marriage among the Bhotia women is 19.5 years. It is 19.8 years and 19.3 years at high and low altitudes respectively. The mean age at first childbirth is 21.5 years at high altitude. It is 21.1 years at low altitude. The gap between the marriage and first childbirth is 1.6 years and 1.8 years respectively at high and low altitudes. The mean age at last childbirth at high altitude is 29.4 years, while it is 27.8 years at low altitude. The gap between the first and last childbirth is 7.9 years and 6.8 years respectively.

It is found that 20 to 25 per cent of pregnancies are concentrated among the women in the age group of 35-39 years. It is 20.1 per cent at high altitude and 24.1 per cent at low altitude. Almost 95.1 per cent and 95.3 per cent pregnancies have led to live births at high and low altitudes respectively. At high altitude, the foetal deaths are found to be highest (44.4 per cent) among the women in the post-reproductive phase of life. However, maximum number of foetal deaths (26.9 per cent) is observed in the age group 35-39 years. The survival rate of the children is almost 89 per cent in the Bhotia population. In this aspect no difference exists between two altitudes. Survival rate for female is little better in low altitude (89.7 per cent) than in high altitude (85.3 per cent).

The mean number of pregnancies, live births, deceased and surviving children are higher at high altitude than at low altitude. The mean foetal death is slightly higher at low altitude. Likewise, the crude birth rate, total fertility rate, completed fertility rate, and age specific fertility rates are reduced at high altitude. Contrary to this, general fertility rate, gross reproduction rate, mean number of children and child woman ratio are elevated at high altitude. As far as the fertility-mortality nexus is concerned, higher mean fertility among the women has positive correlation with higher mean mortality level. This is the case for both the altitudes.

The relationship and association between the menarche and fertility is completely ambiguous in nature. Delay in the mean age at marriage brings down the fertility level. This pattern of association is similar in both the altitudes. Nuclear families have displayed lower fertility among the women where the pattern is uniform for both the altitudes. Illiterate mothers have higher fertility. Higher level of education is associated with lower fertility level. This is common to both the altitudes. The women who carry out agricultural or spinning and weaving activities have displayed higher fertility than housewives and service holders. This pattern is similar for both the settlements. The women of low income group have higher fertility than the high income groups have. But it is the women of middle income group who display lowest fertility than both extreme categories. Family planning method is used to control the natural fertility. Therefore, the women who use family planning methods show lower fertility level. In all cases, the pattern is uniform for both the altitudes. However, the mean fertility levels in respective aspects and categories differ, but the difference between the two altitudes (high and low) is not statistically significant. The significance level has been determined by using 't' test.

The dichotomy between the high and low altitudes among the Bhotias needs to be analysed in the context of prevailing situations. It is discussed in earlier sections of the book that the Bhotia people practice transhumance mode of existence and ways of life for a long time. Meaning thereby, they have been moving in the higher reaches of Great and trans-Himalayas in search of summer pastures (*Bugyals*) during summer months and used to move down the valleys in the Middle Himalayas during winter months. Therefore, they could not generate high altitude and low altitude responses as far as their demographic parameters are concerned. It is only in the aftermath of Indo-Sino war in 1962 that the transhumance mode of existence has been replaced by sedentary mode of existence. It is decidedly a short period of time to expect any emphatic results. However, on the basis of findings, it can only be indicated that there are tendencies towards the interrelationship between altitudes and demographic parameters. Some of these are analysed in the book.

Altitudinal Differences

There is a higher percentage of child population (0-14 years) at high altitude. This may be related to the greater demand of manpower at high altitude settlements. The difference, which exists between the two altitudes in child population, is diminished at the economically productive population (15-59 years) that is either due to the selective out migration for earning livelihood or through the loss of life at high altitude. The reduction of old age people at high altitude proves the fact that there is a constant stress-strain pressure accumulated on the population structure. The survival capacity is low among the old age population at high altitude as it puts the aged population at a constant threat of the high altitude stress and strain.

Sex ratio is 1000 among the infants at high altitude. Reduction of girl children in the population at high altitude is due to the negligence and ill treatment by the parents and other members in the family. High altitude settlements demand for more male members. This is a typical character of populations settled at high altitude. The low altitude settlements, contrary to the high altitude, are open and receptive; thus there is a tendency of equalization of gender. The loss of old male members at these settlements may be related to the early occurrence of aging process. Irrespective of altitudinal settlements, the population is masculine in nature. However, the proportion of masculinity is more at high altitude.

Higher young age dependency level at high altitude signifies higher concentration of child population. The reduction in the old age dependency at high altitude implies lower concentration of old age people, which is because of high altitude constraints acting on the old age people.

The family size is larger at low altitude. This shows that members of the family at low altitude remain together because of the facilities and entitlements available to them. Furthermore, the high altitude environment is not conducive for old age people, giving rise to reduction of family size. Contrary to the low altitude settlement, the high altitude environment limits the family size by constraints and pressure on the individuals. Collective living and group formation is an outcome of these circumstances.

Not a single instance of child marriage is found among the Bhotias. This indicates that the parents and the people in general are quite conscious about the ill effects of child marriage. At high or low altitude, almost equal percentage of people have been married. This is because of the similarity found at both the altitudes in age and sex distribution of people at economically productive stage. As marriage restriction prevails on the basis of settlements, valley-level identity often takes a dominant place as far as the matrimonial alliance is concerned, thus giving the traditional clan-based rules to operate. Social sanction restricts people to opt polygamy. At high altitude, the early male deaths give rise to higher percentage of widows than at low altitude.

As such, there is no much difference in terms of literacy rates in the two altitudinal settlements. The people have a long historical background from pure nomadic and transhumance activities to partly settled life. Their exposure and awareness are synchronized through the interaction with the people in the plains and trans-Himalayan territories as they were connecting two frontiers during these trading years. The Chinese aggression (1962) and subsequently the sealing of international border, breakdown of age old traditional trading and mercantile activities, ascribing the tribal status by the Government of India in 1967, etc. shifted the focus of people from other activities to opt for secured jobs in the Government sector. This is the motivation for their education. The gender discrepancy on educational status, which is found at high altitude, may be related to its rough and harsh climate. The people tend to give more attention to the nature for agriculture and allied occupation. The children, for parents, are the helping hands and their attention is diverted rather towards earning and doing the seasonal work. The girl children are more subject to this. This is also an outcome of the system of patriarchy in the Bhotia society.

The occupational differentiation, which exists among the people in the high and low altitude settlements, primarily connotes that the people have major agricultural holdings at high altitude. Leading a transhumance life and being traders for centuries, accumulation of major holdings are confined to the high altitude areas. The low altitude settlements are comparatively new—a post war development. Migration from plains has reduced the Bhotia landholdings in the low altitude settlements. As a matter of fact, a majority of land holdings are with the non-Bhotias at low altitude. Due to the availability of education and modern facilities, people look for occupations other than the agriculture that profits them more. Employment in service sector is taken as a defence mechanism to sustain their livelihood at low altitudes. Not having the agricultural land has shifted the attention of people to other sectors. The women in the Bhotia society basically control spinning and weaving industry. However, the traditional involvement of people in the handicraft industry has no doubt been decreased. It is found that women at low altitude are more associated with spinning and weaving, as they have more time to contribute. The growth of labour class and unemployed sections in the Bhotia society is a post-development concept. The educational attainment, not getting a job in the service sector due to competition, reluctance of youths to revert to their traditional occupations, etc. have resulted in unemployment, a by-product of all these situations.

At high altitude settlement, there is a concentration of households in the middle income groups. This is because, in this kind of settlement, natural constraints restrict opportunities of enlarging the resource basket. Therefore, the high income generation is difficult and cost intensive. At the other extreme of social ladder, there are low income groups. It is observed that at high altitude the minimum level of subsistence is essential, below which it is difficult for households to sustain. As opposed to this, at low altitude, there is relatively a greater proportion of people at the lower level of income distribution as a result of ever-shrinking low resource basket, but increasing alternative economic opportunity as a result of economic diversification.

No difference exists between the two settlements, as far as the survival rate is concerned. No doubt, high altitude possesses a number of stress-strain factors, but it is the long-term association of the population with the high altitude environment which acts as benefactor through the adaptive mechanism. Low altitude has privileges on several aspects such as health, education, awareness and other resources that make the life process easier and healthy. Therefore, the survival level is same for both the altitudes.

Mean fertility level at high altitude is higher than that found at low altitude. This finding negates the views held by earlier proponents. It has been believed by many researchers that the high altitude has a depressing effect on fertility. However, the total fertility rate (TFR) and the completed fertility rate (CFR) are reduced at high altitude in comparison to the low altitude. The crude birth rate (CBR) is also suppressed at high altitude; that indicates the present birth situation of the population. Therefore, the cursory understanding to the linkage between the fertility and altitude may be taken that higher mean fertility of the population is a defence mechanism to a higher mortality. Complete rejection of earlier observations about high altitude reduction in fertility is an academic error, as the total and completed fertility rates provide support to the reduction theory. This is again supported and substantiated by the present finding in the form of reduced crude birth rate at high altitude.

Fertility level is determined by a series of determining factors. The factors are environmental and socio-cultural. It is not just the environment which designs the population structure always, but many associated factors like socio-cultural, economic, marriage age, family planning methods, etc., influence the fertility level. The influence of these factors is similar in patterning the mean fertility level for both the altitudes as well as the population itself. Though statistically this relationship has been proved not significant, it is very much so, because of the populations at high and low altitude settlements bear ethnic and genetic similarity. Therefore, they do not display significant differences in these respects.

From the entire narratives and discourses, it is understood that the demographic structure of Bhotia populations settled at high and low altitudes shows variation. Fertility behaviour is a complex phenomenon, which is very much determined by not an individual factor but by a conglomeration of many single factors. Fertility is affected by both socio-cultural and environmental factors, though it is difficult to isolate the role of these factors. The single factor domination, particularly with respect to fertility, showing that the debilitating effects on reproduction are due not simply to hypoxia but also to ethnic and socio-cultural factors. Studies suggest that Tibetan and Bod populations have higher fertility at high altitude compared to the populations living at low altitude. The direct effect of hypoxia reducing fertility has been called into question by contradictory findings. Contrary to the above statements, the present study shows a reduction of fertility at high altitude. But the difference between the altitudes is not so emphatic. The reason is confined to the history and tradition of the process of peopling of the populations. For the Bhotia tribe in the Kumaon region, it is only after the year 1962 the settlement process began. Therefore, it is definitely a short period to expect major changes in the populations.

The entire textual debate on the altitude and demographic structure has brought curiosity in the academic discussion. The difficulties that I face to explain this kind of contradictory matters are of serious consequence. There is no single answer to satisfy the readers on these issues. Each population displays a set of characters that are unique for the population itself and the environment it is exposed to. The entire set of knowledge can be framed looking at these aspects. Therefore, it can be mentioned that knowledge has no limitation. No limitation can bring knowledge into conformity. Knowledge is unique. To compartmentalize knowledge in academic circulation is a parochial attitude. Therefore, the scope of the present book may go beyond what is presented in the text.

APPENDICES

Appendix 1

Area and Human Populations in Different Himalayan States

Himalayan Range	*Himalayan State*	*Area (sq. km.) (Per cent)*	*Popula- (In 2001) (Per cent)*	*Population Density 1991*	*2001*	*Gr. Rate (1991-2001)*	*Per-cent-age ST*
Western Himalayas	Jammu and Kashmir	101,387 (25.5)	10,143,700 (26.3)	76	100	29.0	10.9
	Himachal Pradesh	55,673 (14.0)	6,077,900 (15.9)	93	109	17.5	4.0
Central Himalayas	Uttaranchal	53,483 (13.5)	8,489,349 (22.0)	116	159	19.2	3.0
Eastern Himalayas	Sikkim	7,299 (1.8)	540,851 (1.4)	57	74	33.0	20.6
	Darjeeling District (W.B.)	3,149 (0.8)	1,605,900 (4.2)	413	510	23.5	12.7
	Arunachal Pradesh	83,743 (21.1)	1,097,968 (2.9)	10	13	26.2	64.2
	Nagaland	16,579 (4.2)	1,990,036 (5.2)	73	120	64.4	89.1
	Manipur	22,327 (5.6)	2,166,788 (5.6)	82	97	30.0	34.2
	Mizoram	21,081 (5.3)	888,573 (2.3)	33	42	29.2	94.5
	Tripura	10,486 (2.6)	3,199,203 (8.3)	263	305	15.7	31.1
	Meghalaya	22,429 (5.6)	2,318,822 (6.0)	79	103	29.9	85.9
Total	Himalayan Region	3,97,636 (100.0)	38,519,090 (100.0)	75	97	28.9	40.9
	India	3,166,414	1,028,610,328	267	324	21.3	8.2

Source: Census of India, 2001: Primary Census Abstract.

Appendix 2

Area and Population Configuration in Uttaranchal

Sl. No.	*Parameter*		*Pithora-garh*	*Kumaon Himalaya*	*Uttar-anchal*	*India*
1	Area (sq. km) %age (13.3)		7100.0 (39.3)	21034.5 (100.0)	53483.0	3,166,414
2	No. of Households %age (6.1)		98514 (42.1)	675606 (100.0)	1603242	193,579,954
3	Average Household Size		4.7	5.3	5.3	5.3
4	Density (Invs per sq. km.)		65	170	159	324
5	Population462289 %age (5.4)		3565383 (42.0)	8489349 (100.0)	1,028,610,328	
6	Sex Ratio (F/M × 1000)		1031	980	962	933
7	Decennial Population Growth (1991-2001)		10.9	16.9	19.2	21.3
8	Child Population (0-6Yr.) %age (5.3)		72080 (42.9)	583529 (100.0)	1360032 (15.9)	163,819,614
9	Sex Ratio (0-6Yr.)		902	917	908	927
10	Literacy Rate (Excluding Children 0-6 yr.)	P M F Disparity	75.9 90.1 62.1 28.0	72.4 86.0 59.5 26.5	71.6 83.3 59.6 23.7	64.8 75.3 53.7 21.6
11	Percentage of Workers	P M F	43.0 43.4 42.6	40.9 45.4 35.8	36.9 46.1 27.3	39.1 50.7 25.6
12	Percentage of Main Workers	P M F	26.8 31.1 22.7	28.7 35.5 21.4	27.4 37.9 16.4	30.4 45.1 14.7
13	Percentage of Marginal Workers	P M F	16.2 12.4 19.8	12.5 10.0 14.4	9.6 8.3 10.9	8.7 6.6 11.0
14	Percentage of Non-Workers	P M F	57.0 56.6 57.4	59.1 54.6 64.2	63.1 53.9 72.7	60.9 48.3 74.4
15	Percentage of Cultivators	P M F	67.6 47.7 87.2	59.8 44.6 77.1	50.1 34.3 77.8	31.7 31.1 32.9

(contd.)

Appendix 2 (Contd.)

Sl. No.	Parameter		Pithora-garh	Kumaon Himalaya	Uttar-anchal	India
16	Percentage of Agricultural Labour	P M F	1.3 1.2 1.3	7.1 6.6 8.7	8.3 8.5 6.1	26.5 20.8 38.9
17	Work Participation Rate (Total)		43.0	40.9	36.9	39.1
18	ST Population %age to the Total Population		19279 (4.2)	138021 (2.5)	256129 (3.0)	84,326,240 (8.2)
19	%age of ST Population to the Total ST Population of State		7.5	53.9	100.0	—
20	Sex Ratio of ST Population		1046	981	970	978
21	SC Population %age to the Total Population		106449 (23.0)	660467 (20.1)	1517186 (17.9)	166,635,700 (16.2)
22	%age of SC Population to the Total SC Population of State		7.0	43.5	100.0	—
23	Sex Ratio of SC Population		990	962	943	936

Source: Census of India, 2001: Uttaranchal District Profile.

Appendix 3

Intra-Regional Variation in levels of Development in Uttaranchal

Sl. No.	*Parameter*	*Pithoragarh*	*Kumaon Himalaya*	*Uttaranchal*
	Agriculture			
1	Operation Holding (ha/holding, 1990-91)	0.5	0.9	1.0
2	Gross Cropped Area ('000 ha, 1998-99)	72.1	665.1	1306.2
3	Gross Irrigated Area (% of GCA, 1998-99)	9.3	32.0	42.2
4	Area Under Foodgrain ('000 ha, 1999-2000)	80.5	545.7	987.8
5	Area Under Rice ('000 ha, 1999-2000)	28.2	200.2	304.1
6	Area Under Wheat ('000 ha, 1999-2000)	26.3	212.8	387.8
7	Fertilize Consumption (kg/ha, 1998-99)	5.4	48.1	101.4
8	Food Grain Production ('000 tonnes, 1999-2000)	98.7	1089.8	1791.3
9	Forest Area ('000 ha, 1998-99)	267.7 (37.7)	1124.1 (53.4)	3498.4 (65.41)
	Infrastructure			
10	Villages Electrified (No., 1997-98)	1564	5773	9868
11	Road Length (km, 1996-97)	1552	7842	17457
12	Road Density (per sq. km, 1996-97)	0.2	0.4	0.4
13	Telephone Connections (No., 2001-02)	—	—	308755
14	Post Offices (No., 1998-99)	315	1185	2683
	Banking			
15	Bank Branches (No., 2001-02)	50	343	857
16	Credit/Deposit Ratio (%, 2001-02)	17.5	28.7	26.0

(contd.)

Appendix 3 (Contd.)

Sl. No.	Parameter	Pithoragarh	Kumaon Himalaya	Uttaranchal
	Education			
17	Primary Schools (No., 2002-03)	1457	7173	16990
18	Primary Students Enrolled ('000 No., 2000-01)	106	624	1486
19	Primary School Teachers (No., 2000-01)	3041	15673	37937
20	Primary Students per Teacher (No., 2000-01)	26	25	40
21	Secondary Schools (No., 2002-03)	123	649	1589
22	Secondary Students enrolled ('000 No., 2000-01)	19	113	266
	Health			
23	Primary Health Centres (per lakh pop, 1994-95)	4.3	3.8	3.3
24	Hospital beds (per lakh pop, 1994-95)	120.7	118.9	119.5
25	Hospitals (per lakh pop, 1994-95)	14.2	11.9	12.7
	Tourism			
26	Domestic (No., 2000-01)	103976	822564	10548784
27	Foreign (No., 2000-01)	534	13620	54701

Source: Monthly Review of Uttaranchal Economy, Centre for Monitoring Indian Economy, August 2004, pp. 6-7.

Appendix 4

Bhotia Population by Age and Sex at High and Low Altitudes in Kumaon Himalaya

Age Group (in yr.)		*High Altitude*			*Low Altitude*			*Total*		
		Male	*Female*	*Total*	*Male*	*Female*	*Total*	*Male*	*Female*	*Total*
Below 1	**No.**	**8**	**8**	**16**	**13**	**11**	**24**	**21**	**19**	**40**
	%	**1.14**	**1.14**	**2.28**	**1.31**	**1.11**	**2.42**	**1.24**	**1.12**	**2.36**
0-4	No.	41	39	80	59	48	107	100	87	187
	%	5.83	5.55	11.38	5.94	4.83	10.78	5.90	5.13	11.03
5-9	No.	42	36	78	44	64	108	86	100	186
	%	5.97	5.12	11.10	4.43	6.45	10.88	5.07	5.90	10.97
10-14	No.	43	37	80	47	42	89	90	79	169
	%	6.12	5.26	11.38	4.73	4.23	8.96	5.31	4.66	9.96
0-14	**No.**	**126**	**112**	**238**	**150**	**154**	**304**	**276**	**266**	**542**
	%	**17.92**	**15.93**	**33.85**	**15.11**	**15.51**	**30.61**	**16.27**	**15.68**	**31.96**
15-19	No.	54	38	92	50	41	91	104	79	183
	%	7.68	5.41	13.09	5.04	4.13	9.16	6.13	4.66	10.79
20-24	No.	33	35	68	55	49	104	88	84	172
	%	4.69	4.98	9.67	5.54	4.93	10.47	5.19	4.95	10.14
25-29	No.	39	28	67	47	41	88	86	69	155
	%	5.55	3.98	9.53	4.73	4.13	8.86	5.07	4.07	9.14
30-34	No.	27	24	51	41	34	75	68	58	126
	%	3.84	3.41	7.25	4.13	3.42	7.55	4.01	3.42	7.43
35-39	No.	19	24	43	32	42	74	51	66	117
	%	2.70	3.41	6.12	3.22	4.23	7.45	3.01	3.89	6.90
40-44	No.	25	13	38	41	26	67	66	39	105
	%	3.56	1.85	5.41	4.13	2.62	6.75	3.89	2.30	6.19
45-49	No.	18	19	37	23	28	51	41	47	88
	%	2.56	2.70	5.26	2.32	2.82	5.14	2.42	2.77	5.19
50-54	No.	9	13	22	23	16	39	32	29	61
	%	1.28	1.85	3.13	2.32	1.61	3.93	1.89	1.71	3.60
55-59	No.	13	9	22	17	16	33	30	25	55
	%	1.85	1.28	3.13	1.71	1.61	3.32	1.77	1.47	3.24
15-59	**No.**	**237**	**203**	**440**	**329**	**293**	**622**	**566**	**496**	**1062**
	%	**33.71**	**28.88**	**62.59**	**33.13**	**29.51**	**62.64**	**33.37**	**29.25**	**62.62**

(contd.)

Appendix 4 *(Contd.)*

Age Group (in yr.)		*High Altitude*			*Low Altitude*			*Total*		
		Male	*Female*	*Total*	*Male*	*Female*	*Total*	*Male*	*Female*	*Total*
60-64	No.	4	8	12	11	17	28	15	25	40
	%	0.57	1.14	1.71	1.11	1.71	2.82	0.88	1.47	2.36
65+	No.	8	5	13	21	18	39	29	23	52
	%	1.14	0.71	1.85	2.11	1.81	3.93	1.71	1.36	3.07
60+	**No.**	**12**	**13**	**25**	**32**	**35**	**67**	**44**	**48**	**92**
	%	**1.71**	**1.85**	**3.56**	**3.22**	**3.52**	**6.75**	**2.59**	**2.83**	**5.42**
All Ages	**No**	**375**	**328**	**703**	**511**	**482**	**993**	**886**	**810**	**1696**
	%	**53.34**	**46.66**	**100.00**	**51.46**	**48.54**	**100.00**	**52.24**	**47.76**	**100.00**

Source: Primary Data.

Appendix 5

Educational Structure of the Bhotia Tribe (Number and Percentage) at High and Low Altitudes in Kumaon Himalaya

Age Group		*Illiterate*			*Literate*																					*Total*		
					Informal Education			*Elementary Education*			*Under-Matricu-lation*			*Matricu-lation*			*Higher Secondary*			*Above Higher Secondary*			*Total*					
		M	*F*	*T*	*M*	*F*	*T*	*M*	*F*	*T*	*M*	*F*	*T*	*M*	*F*	*T*	*M*	*F*	*T*	*M*	*F*	*T*	*M*	*F*	*T*	*M*	*F*	*T*
6-14	No.	1	1	2	—	—	—	64	52	116	13	10	23	—	—	—	—	—	—	—	—	—	77	62	139	78	63	141
	%	1.3	1.6	1.4				83.1	83.9	83.5	16.9	16.1	16.5										98.7	98.4	98.6	55.3	44.7	23.3
15-59	No.	21	69	90	4	11	15	35	47	82	68	33	101	39	15	54	41	19	60	29	9	38	216	134	350	237	203	440
	%	8.9	34.0	20.5	1.9	8.2	8.3	16.2	35.1	23.4	31.5	24.6	28.9	18.1	11.2	15.4	19.0	14.2	17.1	13.4	6.7	10.9	91.1	66.0	79.5	53.9	46.1	72.6
60+	No.	5	9	14	4	4	8	2	—	2	1	-	1	—	—	—	—	—	—	—	—	—	7	4	11	12	13	25
	%	41.7	69.2	56.0	57.1	100	72.7	28.6		18.2	14.3		9.1										58.3	30.8	44.0	48.0	52.0	4.1
Total	No.	27	79	106	8	15	23	101	99	200	82	43	125	39	15	54	41	19	60	29	9	38	300	200	500	327	279	606
	%	8.3	28.3	17.5	2.7	7.5	4.6	33.7	49.5	40.0	27.3	21.5	25.0	13.0	7.5	10.8	13.7	9.5	12.0	9.7	4.5	7.6	91.7	71.7	82.5	54.0	46.0	100
6-14	No.	—	—	—	—	—	—	67	71	138	14	17	31	—	—	—	—	—	—	—	—	—	81	88	169	81	88	169
	%							82.7	80.7	81.7	17.3	19.3	18.3										100	100	100	47.9	52.1	19.7
15-59	No.	23	70	93	2	15	17	38	63	101	72	42	114	61	37	98	56	41	97	77	25	102	306	223	529	329	293	622
	%	7.0	23.9	15.0	0.7	6.7	3.2	12.4	28.3	19.1	23.5	18.8	21.6	19.9	16.6	18.5	18.3	18.4	18.3	25.2	11.2	19.3	93.0	76.1	85.0	2.9	47.1	72.5

(contd.)

Appendix 5 *(Contd.)*

Age Group		*Illiterate*			*Literate*																					*Total*		
					Informal Education			*Elementary Education*			*Under-Matriculation*			*Matriculation*			*Higher Secondary*			*Above Higher Secondary*			*Total*					
		M	*F*	*T*	*M*	*F*	*T*	*M*	*F*	*T*	*M*	*F*	*T*	*M*	*F*	*T*	*M*	*F*	*T*	*M*	*F*	*T*	*M*	*F*	*T*	*M*	*F*	*T*
60+	No.	12	31	43	8	4	12	9	—	9	2	—	2	1	—	1	—	—	—	—	—	—	20	4	24	32	35	67
	%	37.5	88.6	64.2	40.0	100	50.0	45.0		37.5	10.0		8.3	5.0		4.2							62.5	11.4	35.8	47.8	52.2	7.8
Total	No.	35	101	136	10	19	29	114	134	248	88	59	147	62	37	99	56	41	97	77	23	102	406	315	722	442	416	858
	%	7.9	24.3	15.8	2.5	6.0	4.0	28.0	42.5	34.3	21.6	18.7	20.4	15.2	11.7	13.7	13.8	13.0	13.4	18.9	7.3	14.1	92.1	75.7	84.2	51.5	48.5	100
Total																												
6-14	No.	1	1	2	—	—	—	131	123	254	27	27	54	—	—	—	—	—	—	—	—	—	158	150	308	159	151	310
	%	0.6	0.7	0.6				82.9	82.0	82.5	17.1	18.0	17.5										99.4	99.3	99.4	51.3	48.7	21.2
15-59	No.	44	139	183	6	26	32	73	110	183	140	75	215	100	52	152	97	60	157	106	34	140	522	357	879	566	496	1062
	%	7.8	28.0	17.2	1.1	7.3	3.6	14.0	30.8	20.8	26.8	21.0	24.5	19.2	14.6	17.3	18.6	16.8	17.9	20.3	9.5	15.9	92.2	72.0	82.8	53.3	46.7	72.5
60+	No.	17	40	57	12	8	20	11	—	11	3	—	3	1	—	1	—	—	—	—	—	—	27	8	35	44	48	92
	%	38.6	83.3	62.0	44.8	100	57.1	40.7		31.4	11.1		8.6	3.7		2.9							61.4	16.7	38.0	47.4	52.2	63
Total	No.	62	180	242	18	34	52	21.5	233	448	170	102	272	101	52	153	97	60	157	106	34	140	707	515	1222	769	695	1464
	%	8.1	25.9	16.5	2.5	6.6	4.3	30.4	45.2	36.7	24.0	19.8	22.3	14.3	10.1	12.5	13.7	11.7	12.8	15.0	6.6	11.5	91.9	72.1	83.5	52.5	47.5	100

Note: Informal Education means the educational attainment without attending the school or any institution; Elementary Education means up to Class VIII; Under Matriculation means those have not completed Class X; Above Higher Secondary = It includes Graduation, Post Graduation and Professional Courses like medical, Engineering, Computer Professionals etc.

Source: Primary Data

Appendix 6

Occupational Structure of the Bhotia Tribe (Number and Percentage) at High and Low Altitudes in Kumaon Himalaya

Age Group		*Agriculture*			*Business*			*Service*			*House Wife/ Household Work*			*Spinning Weaving*			*Animal Husbandry/ Herding*			*Labourer*			*Unemployed*			*Total*		
		M	*F*	*T*	*M*	*F*	*T*	*M*	*F*	*T*	*M*	*F*	*T*	*M*	*F*	*T*	*M*	*F*	*T*	*M*	*F*	*T*	*M*	*F*	*T*	*M*	*F*	*T*
High Altitude																												
15-59	No.	48	60	108	48	3	51	46	7	53	—	66	66	1	28	29	7	6	13	12	1	13	9	2	11	171	173	344
	%	28.1	34.7	31.4	28.1	1.7	14.8	26.9	4.0	15.4		38.2	19.2	0.6	16.2	8.4	4.1	3.5	3.8	7.0	0.6	3.8	5.3	1.2	3.2	49.7	50.3	95.3
60+	No.	7	1	8	—	1	1	—	—	—	—	—	—	1	7	8	—	—	—	—	—	—	—	—	—	8	9	17
	%	87.5	11.1	47.1		11.1	5.9							12.5	77.8	47.1										47.0	53.0	4.7
Total	No.	55	61	116	48	4	52	46	7	53	—	66	66	2	35	37	7	6	13	12	1	13	9	2	11	179	182	361
	%	30.7	33.5	32.1	26.8	2.2	14.4	25.7	3.8	14.7		36.3	18.3	1.1	19.2	10.2	3.9	3.3	3.6	6.7	0.5	3.6	5.0	1.1	3.0	49.6	50.4	100
Low Altitude																												
15-59	No.	41	54	95	58	13	71	100	17	117	—	98	98	2	54	56	3	5	8	15	2	17	10	3	13	229	246	475
	%	17.9	22.0	20.0	25.3	5.3	14.9	43.7	6.9	24.6		39.8	20.6	0.9	22.0	11.8	1.3	2.0	1.7	6.6	0.8	3.6	4.4	1.2	2.7	48.2	51.8	91.2
60+	No.	7	8	15	5	2	7	—	—	—	—	—	—	4	20	24	—	—	—	—	—	—	—	—	—	16	30	46
	%	43.8	26.7	32.6	31.3	6.7	15.2							25.0	66.7	52.2										3.5	6.5	8.8
Total	No.	48	62	110	63	15	78	100	17	117	—	98	98	6	74	80	3	5	8	15	2	17	10	3	13	245	276	521
	%	19.6	22.5	21.1	25.7	5.4	15.0	40.8	6.2	22.5		35.5	18.8	2.4	26.8	15.4	1.2	1.8	1.5	6.1	0.7	3.3	4.1	1.1	2.5	47.0	53.0	100

(contd)

Appendix 6 (Contd.)

Age Group		*Agriculture*			*Business*			*Service*			*House Wife/ Household Work*			*Spinning Weaving*			*Animal Husbandry/ Herding*			*Labourer*			*Unemployed*			*Total*		
		M	*F*	*T*	*M*	*F*	*T*	*M*	*F*	*T*	*M*	*F*	*T*	*M*	*F*	*T*	*M*	*F*	*T*	*M*	*F*	*T*	*M*	*F*	*T*	*M*	*F*	*T*
														Total														
15-59	No.	89	114	203	106	16	122	146	24	170	—	164	164	3	82	85	10	11	21	27	3	30	19	5	24	400	419	819
	%	22.3	27.2	24.3	26.5	3.8	14.9	36.5	5.7	20.8		39.1	20.0	0.8	19.6	10.4	2.5	2.6	2.6	6.8	0.7	3.7	4.8	1.2	2.9	48.8	51.2	92.9
60+	No.	14	9	23	5	3	8	—	—	—	—	—	—	5	27	32	—	—	—	—	—	—	—	—	—	24	39	63
	%	58.3	23.1	36.5	20.8	7.7	12.7							20.8	69.2	50.8										38.1	61.9	7.1
Total	No.	103	123	226	111	19	130	146	24	170	—	164	164	8	109	117	10	11	21	27	3	30	19	5	24	424	458	882
	%	24.3	26.9	25.6	26.2	4.1	14.7	34.4	5.2	19.3		35.8	18.6	1.9	23.8	13.3	2.4	2.4	2.4	6.4	0.7	3.4	4.5	1.1	2.7	48.1	51.9	100

Source: Primary Data.

Appendix 7

Reproductive History of the Bhotia Women at High Altitude in Kumaon Himalaya

Age Group (Yrs.)	Mothers	Live Births			Foetal Deaths					Deceased Children			Surviving Children			Pregnancies
					Stillbirth			Abortion	Total							
		M	F	T	M	F	T			M	F	T	M	F	T	
20-24	23 29.9	20 5.1	22 5.6	42 10.8	—	—	—	1 9.1	1 5.6	—	1 2.3	1 2.3	20 5.8	21 6.1	41 11.8	43 10.5
25-29	15 13.6	23 5.9	20 5.1	43 11.0	1 14.3	—	1 14.3	3 27.3	4 22.2	—	5 11.4	5 11.4	23 6.6	15 4.3	38 11.0	47 11.5
30-34	20 18.2	46 11.8	30 7.7	76 19.5	1 14.3	—	1 14.3	1 9.1	2 11.1	4 9.1	2 4.5	6 13.6	42 12.1	28 8.1	70 20.2	78 19.1
35-39	20 18.2	40 10.3	41 10.5	81 20.8	1 14.3	—	1 14.3	—	1 5.6	3 6.8	7 15.9	10 22.7	37 10.7	34 9.8	71 20.5	82 20.1
40-44	10 9.1	29 7.4	20 5.1	49 12.6	—	—	—	1 9.1	1 5.6	4 9.1	3 6.8	7 15.9	25 7.2	17 4.9	42 12.1	50 12.3
45-49	11 10.0	27 6.9	28 7.2	55 14.1	—	—	—	1 9.1	1 5.6	4 9.1	7 15.9	11 25.0	23 6.6	21 6.1	44 12.7	56 13.7
50+	11 10.0	21 5.0	23 5.9	44 11.3	3 42.3	1 14.3	4 57.1	4 36.4	8 44.4	2 4.5	2 4.5	4 9.1	19 5.5	21 6.1	40 11.6	52 12.7
Total	110 100.0	206 52.8	184 47.2	390 100.0	6 85.7	1 14.3	7 100.0	11 100.0	18 100.0	17 38.6	27 61.4	44 100.0	189 54.6	157 45.4	346 100.0	408 100.0

Note: Second figure in each cell is the percentage.
Source: Primary Data.

Appendix 8

Reproductive History of the Bhotia Women at Low Altitude in Kumaon Himalaya

Age Group (Yrs.)	*Mothers*	*Live Births*			*Foetal Deaths*					*Deceased Children*			*Surviving Children*			*Pregnancies*
					Stillbirth			*Abortion*	*Total*							
		M	*F*	*T*	*M*	*F*	*T*			*M*	*F*	*T*	*M*	*F*	*T*	
20-24	20 13.2	16 3.2	20 4.0	36 7.2	—	—	—	3 18.8	3 11.5	—	—	—	16 3.6	20 4.5	36 8.1	39 7.4
25-29	24 17.8	32 6.4	29 5.8	61 12.2	—	2 20.0	2 20.0	1 6.3	3 11.5	1 1.8	—	1 1.8	31 7.0	29 6.5	60 13.5	64 12.1
30-34	23 15.1	35 7.0	36 7.2	71 14.1	2 20.0	1 10.0	3 30.0	1 6.3	4 15.4	5 8.8	3 5.3	8 14.0	30 6.7	33 7.4	63 14.2	75 14.2
35-39	32 21.1	61 12.2	59 11.8	120 23.9	1 10.0	1 10.0	2 20.0	5 31.3	7 26.9	4 7.0	8 14.0	12 21.1	57 12.8	51 11.5	108 24.3	127 24.1
40-44	18 11.8	39 7.8	26 5.2	65 12.9	1 10.0	—	1 10.0	—	1 3.8	6 10.5	2 3.5	8 14.0	33 7.4	24 5.4	57 12.8	66 12.5
45-49	21 13.8	44 8.8	59 11.8	103 20.5	—	1 10.0	1 10.0	3 18.8	4 15.4	9 15.8	9 15.8	18 31.6	35 7.9	50 11.2	85 19.1	107 20.3
50+	11 7.2	23 4.6	23 4.6	46 9.2	1 10.0	—	1 10.0	3 18.8	4 15.4	6 10.5	4 7.0	10 17.5	17 3.8	19 4.3	36 8.1	50 9.5
Total	152 100.0	250 49.8	252 50.2	502 100.0	5 50.0	5 50.0	10 100.0	16 100.0	26 100.0	31 54.4	26 45.6	57 100.0	219 49.2	226 50.8	445 100.0	528 100.0

Note: Second figure in each cell is the percentage.
Source: Primary Data.

Appendix 9

Reproductive History of the Sample Bhotia Women in Kumaon Himalaya

Age Group (Yrs.)	Mothers	Live Births			Foetal Deaths					Deceased Children			Surviving Children			Pregnancies
					Stillbirth			Abortion	Total							
		M	F	T	M	F	T			M	F	T	M	F	T	
20-24	43 16.4	36 4.0	42 4.7	78 8.7	—	—	—	4 14.8	4 9.1	0	1 1.0	1 1.0	36 4.6	41 5.2	77 9.7	82 8.8
25-29	42 16.0	55 6.2	49 5.5	104 11.7	1 5.9	2 11.8	3 17.6	4 14.8	7 15.9	1 1.0	5 5.0	6 5.9	54 6.8	44 5.6	98 12.4	111 11.9
30-34	43 16.4	81 9.1	66 7.4	147 16.5	3 17.6	1 5.9	4 23.5	2 7.4	6 13.6	9 8.9	5 5.0	14 13.9	72 9.1	61 7.7	133 16.8	153 16.3
35-39	52 19.8	101 11.3	100 11.2	201 22.5	2 11.8	1 5.9	3 17.6	5 18.5	8 18.2	7 6.9	15 14.9	22 21.8	94 11.9	85 10.7	179 22.6	209 22.3
40-44	28 10.7	68 7.6	46 5.2	114 12.8	1 5.9	—	1 5.9	1 3.7	2 4.5	10 9.9	5 5.0	15 14.9	58 7.3	41 5.2	99 12.5	116 12.4
45-49	32 12.2	71 8.0	87 9.8	158 17.7	—	1 5.9	1 5.9	4 14.8	5 11.4	13 12.9	16 15.8	29 28.7	58 7.3	71 9.0	129 16.3	163 17.4
50+	22 8.4	44 4.9	46 5.2	90 10.1	4 23.5	1 5.9	5 29.4	7 25.9	12 27.3	8 7.9	6 5.9	14 13.9	36 4.6	40 5.1	76 9.6	102 10.9
Total	26 100.0	456 51.1	436 48.9	892 100.0	11 64.7	6 35.3	17 100.0	27 100.0	44 100.0	48 47.5	53 52.3	101 100.0	408 51.6	383 48.4	791 100.0	936 100.0

Note: Second figure in each cell is the percentage.
Source: Primary Data.

Appendix 10

Mean Value of the Reproductive History of the Sample Bhotia Women in Kumaon Himalaya

Age Group	*Live birth*			*Foetal Death*			*Deceased Children*			*Servicing Children*			*Pregnancy*		
	HA	*LA*	*Total*	*HA*	*LA*	*Total*	*HA*	*LA*	*Total*	*HA*	*LA*	*Total*	*HA*	*LA*	*Total*
20-24	1.83	1.80	1.81	0.04	0.15	0.09	0.04	—	0.02	1.78	1.80	1.79	1.87	1.95	1.91
25-29	2.87	2.26	2.48	0.27	0.11	0.17	0.33	0.04	0.14	2.53	2.22	2.33	3.13f	2.37	2.64
30-34	3.80	3.09	3.42	0.10	0.17	0.14	0.30	0.35	0.33	3.50	2.74	3.09	3.90	3.26	3.56
35-39	4.05	3.75	3.87	0.05	0.22	0.15	0.50	0.38	0.42	3.55	3.38	3.44	4.10	3.97	4.02
40-44	4.90	3.61	4.07	0.10	0.06	0.07	0.70	0.44	0.54	4.20	3.17	3.54	5.00	3.67	4.14
45-49	5.00	4.90	4.94	0.09	0.19	0.16	1.00	0.86	0.91	4.00	4.05	4.03	5.09	5.10	5.09
50+	4.00	4.18	4.09	0.73	0.36	0.55	0.36	0.91	0.64	3.64	3.27	3.45	4.73	4.55	4.63
Total	3.55	3.30	3.40	0.16	0.17	0.17	0.40	0.38	0.39	3.15	2.93	3.02	3.71	3.47	3.57

Note: HA = High Altitude, LA = Low Altitude.
Source: Primary Data.

Appendix 11

Mean Live Births Reported in Different Populations of Himalayan Regions in India

Himalayan Region	*State*	*Population*	*Mean Live Births*	*Author(s)*
Eastern	Arunachal Pradesh	Khamti	3.57 ± 0.09	Choudhury *et al.*, 1991
		Apatani (Rural)	5.82	Padmanavam, 1982
		Apatani (Mite)	5.72	
		Singpho	5.6	Padmanavam 1998
	Assam	Khamti	5.11 ± 0.34	Barua *et al.*, 1994
		Hindu Oraon	6.13	Sengupta and
		Christian Oraon	5.54	Gogoi, 1997
		Sonowal Kachari	7.04	Deka, 1978
	Manipur	Pangal Muslim	4.01	Choudhury and Devi, 1997
		Meitei	4.63	
	Meghalaya	War Khasi	4.03 ± 0.17	Khongsdier and Ghosh, 1994
		Hajong	6.8	Barua, 1983
		Non-Christian Khasi	5.7	Nag, 1965
		Christian Khasi	4.1	
		Punjabi Sonar	5.69	Joswal and Dutta Choudhury, 1984
	Sikkim	Lepcha	6.02 ± 0.33	Bhasin and
		Bhutia	5.41 ± 0.29	Kshatriya, 1990
		Sherpa	5.64 ± 0.75	
		Tamang	6.71 ± 0.60	
		Brahman	7.27 ± 0.72	
		Chhetri	6.52 ± 0.47	
		Newar	7.23 ± 0.52	
		Rai	5.95 ± 0.42	
		Limboo/Subba	5.25 ± 0.84	
		Gurung	6.89 ± 0.65	
		Mangar	6.08 ± 0.52	
		Scheduled Caste	5.85 ± 0.61	
Western	Himachal Pradesh	Gaddis in Himalayan Zone	4.8	Bhasin and Bhasin, 1993
		Gaddis in Inner Himalayan Zone	4.5	
Central	Uttaranchal	Bhoksa	6.4	Garg *et al.*, 1980
		Bhotia	3.40 ± 0.40	**Present Study***

Source: Primary* and Secondary Data

BIBLIOGRAPHY

Abelson, A.E. (1976): Altitude and Fertility. *Human Biology*, 48 (1): 83-92.

Abelson, A.E. (1984): Comment on Goldstein, Tsarong, and Beall. *American Anthropologist*, 86 (3): 702-3.

Abelson, A.E.; T.S. Baker and P. T. Baker (1974): Altitude, Migration and Fertility in the Andes. *Social Biology*, 21 (1): 12-27.

Aggarwala, S.N. (1977): *India's Population Problems*. Tata McGraw Hill Publishing Co. Ltd., New Delhi.

Atkinson, E.T. (1972): *The Himalayan Gazetteer*, Vol. I-VI (First Ed. 1882), Cosmos Publication, New Delhi.

Baker P.T. (1969): Human Adaptation to High Altitude. *Science*, Washington, 163: 1149-56.

Baker P.T. (1978): The Adaptive Fitness of High-altitude Populations. In: *The Biology of High-altitude Peoples* (Ed.) P.T. Baker, Cambridge University Press, London, pp.317-50.

Baker, P.T. and J.S. Dutt (1972): Demographic Variables as Measures of Biological Adaptation: A Case Study of High Altitude Human Populations. In: *The Structure of Human Populations* (Eds.) G.A. Harrison and A.J. Boyce. Clarendon Press, Oxford. pp. 352-78.

Balgir, R.S. (1991): Bio-demographic Studies among the Hindu and Muslim Gujjars of Northwestern India. *J. Hum. Ecol.*, 2 (2): 173-79.

Bangham, C.R.M. and J. M. Sacherer (1980): Fertility of Nepalese Sherpas at Moderate Altitude: Comparison with High-altitude Data. *Ann. Hum. Biology*, 7(4): 323-30.

Bangham, C.R.M. and J.M. Sacherer (1981): 'A reply by Drs. Bangham and Sacherer to Charles Weitz' (As Letter to the Editor). *Ann. Hum. Biology*, 8 (4): 385-6.

Barua, S.; R. Th. Varte and N.C. Sarkar (1994): Fertility and Mortality Differentials among the Khamti of Assam and Arunachal Pradesh: A Study on the Effect of Migration. *J. Indian Anthrop. Soc.*, 29 (1 and 2): 137-42.

Basu, A. (1993): Tribal Demography and Health: Some Concepts, Issues and Observations. In: *Continuity and Change in Tribal Society* (Ed.) Mrinal Miri. Indian Institute of Advanced Study, Shimla.

Basu, A. and R. Gupta (1984): Comments on 'High Altitude Hypoxia, Culture, and Human Fecundity/Fertility'. *American Anthropologist*. 86 (4): 994-6.

Basu, A.; R. Gupta and S.K. Bhattacharya (1979): Altitude and Biology in the Sherpa: An Alternative Approach to the Study of High Altitude Biology in the Context of the Eastern Himalayan Situation. *J. Indian Anthrop. Soc.*, 14 (2): 139-48.

Basu, A.M. (1991): Demand and Its Socio-cultural Context. In: *The Demographic Challenge: A Study of Four Large Indian States*, (Eds.) J. K. Satia and S.J. Jejeebhoy. Oxford University Press, Bombay, pp. 77-113.

Beall, C.M. (1983): Ages at Menopause and Menarche in a High Altitude Himalayan Population. *Ann. Human Biology*, 10 (4): 365-70.

Beard, R.J. (Ed.) (1976): *The Menopause*. MTP Press, London.

Bhasin, M.K. and G. Kshatriya (1990): Fertility and Mortality Differentials Among the Different population Groups of Sikkim, India. *J. Hum. Ecol.*, 1 (3): 267-76.

Bhasin, M.K. and V. Bhasin (1997): Population Study: Measures. In: *Human Ecological Studies—Schedules and Programme*. Kamla-Raj Enterprises, Delhi.

Bhasin, M.K.; H. Walter and H. Danker-Hopfe (1994): *People of India: An Investigation of Biological Variability in Ecological, Ethno-economic and Linguistic Groups*. Kamla-Raj Enterprises, Delhi.

Bhasin, V. and M.K. Bhasin (1993): Ecology, Population Dynamics among Transhumants of Himalayas: A Case Study of Gaddis of Himachal Pradesh. *J. Hum. Ecol.*, 4 (3): 171-219.

Biswas, S. (1994): Interethnic Relations, Ethnicity and Social Stratification: Emerging Trends in North-East India. *J. Indian Anthrop. Soc.* 29 (1 and 2):25-32.

Bradley, C. (1996): Demography. In: *Encyclopaedia of Cultural Anthropology*, (Ed.) L. David and M. Ember. Henry Holt and Company, New York, (A-D):319-23.

Bradshaw, B.S. (1969): Fertility Differences in Peru: A Reconsideration. *Population Studies*, 23 (1): 5-19.

Brown, P.E. (1966): The Age at Menarche. *British Journal of Preventive and Social Medicine*, 20: 9-14.

Brudevoll, J.E.; K. Liestol and L. Walloe (1979): Menarchial Age in Oslo during the Last 140 years. *Ann. Hum. Biology*, 6 (5): 407-16.

Brundtland, G.H. and L.Walloe (1973): Menarchial Age in Norway: Halt in the Trend Towards Earlier Maturation. *Nature*, 241:478-9.

Buck, A.A.; T.T. Sasaki and R.I. Anderson (1968): *Health and Disease in Four Peruvian Villages: Contrasts in Epidemology*. Johns Hopkins Press, Baltimore.

Butola, B.S. (1992): *Political Economy of Underdevelopment*. Har-Anand Publication and Vikas Publishing House Pvt. Ltd. New Delhi.

Carter, H.A. (1992): Himalaya. In: *The Encyclopaedia Americana (International Edition)*. Grolier Incorporated, U.S.A., 14: 200-1.

Census of India (2001): *Provisional Population Totals, India*. Series-1 (Paper-1 of 2001).

Chachra, S.P. and M.K. Bhasin (1998): Anthropo-Demographic Study among the Caste and Tribal Groups of Central Himalayas: 1. Population Structure. *J. Hum. Ecol.*, 9 (5): 405-16.

Chachra, S.P. and M.K. Bhasin (1998a): Anthropo-Demographic Study among the Caste and Tribal Groups of Central

Himalayas: 2. Fertility Differentials and Determinants. *J. Hum. Ecol.*, 9 (5): 417-29.

Chachra, S.P. and M.K. Bhasin (1998b): Anthropo-Demographic Study among the Caste and Tribal Groups of Central Himalayas: 5. Family Planning. *J. Hum. Ecol.*, 9 (5): 445-50.

Chachra, S.P. and M.K. Bhasin (1998c): Anthropo-Demographic Study among the Caste and Tribal Groups of Central Himalayas: 6. Fertility, Child Mortality and Family Planning. *J. Hum. Ecol.*, 9 (5): 451-5.

Chatterjee, S. (1994): Menarche, Menopause, and Fertility in Pashatya Vaidik Brahman Women of West Bengal. *Man in India*, 74 (3): 271-78.

Choudhury, R.H. (1984): The Influence of Female Education, Labour Force Participation, and Age at Marriage on Fertility Behaviour in Bangladesh. *Social Biology*, Vol. 31.

Chowdhury, B. and M. Devi (1997): Fertility Differentials in Manipur: A Study on the Meiteis and the Muslims. *J. Hum. Ecol.*, 8(1): 51-9.

Clegg, E. G.; G.A. Harrison and P.T. Baker (1970): The Impact of High Altitudes on Human Populations. *Human Biology*, 42: 486-518.

Crooke, W. (1974): *The Tribes and Castes of Northwestern India*, Vols: I-IV, Delhi.

Cruz-Coke, R. (1978): A Genetic Description of High-altitude Populations. In: *The Biology of High-altitude Peoples, (IBP-14)*, (Ed.) P.T. Baker. Cambridge University Press, Cambridge, pp.47-63.

Cruz-Coke, R.; A.P. Cristoffanini; M. Aspillaga and F. Biancani (1966): Evolutionary Forces in Human Populations in an Environmental Gradient in Arica, Chile. *Human Biology*, 38 (4): 421-38.

Das, J.C. (1982): From Trade to Agriculture—A Case Study of the Bhotia of Pithoragarh. In: *Economies of the Tribes and Their Transformation*, (Ed.) K.S. Singh. Concept Publishing Company, New Delhi, pp.208-15.

Das, J.K. (2001): *Human Rights and Indigenous Peoples*. A.P.H. Publishing Corporation, New Delhi.

Das, S.K.; P.P. Majumdar and A. Basu (1982): Demography and Demographical Genetics of Two Isolated Mountain Villages of Northern Sikkim, Eastern Himalaya. *J. Indian Anthrop. Soc.*, 17 (2): 155-62.

Dasgupta, B. (1997): India's Tribal Population: An Overview. *J. Indian Anthrop. Soc.*, 32: 99-138.

Dash, C. and J. Kanungo (2002): Altitude and Fertility: A Study on the Bhotia Tribe of Kumaon Himalaya, Uttaranchal, India. *J. Indian Anthrop. Soc.*, 37(2):141-50.

Davis, K. (1951): *The Population of India and Pakistan*. Princeton Press, Princeton.

Davis, K. (1964): Human Fertility in India. *American Journal of Sociology*, Vol. 52: 1946-7.

Davis, K. and J. Blake (1956): Social Structure and Fertility: An Analytical Framework. *Economic Development and Cultural Change*, 4: 211-35.

Davis, K. and P.O.D. Oever (1986): Demographic Foundations of New Sex Roles. In: *Fertility and Mortality: Theory, Methodology and Empirical Issues*, (Ed.) K. Madhavan. Sage Publication, New Delhi, pp. 13-29.

De Jong, G.F. (1970): Demography and Research with High Altitude Populations. *Social Biology*, 17 (2): 114-19.

Dhoundiyal, N.C. and V.R. Dhoundiyal (1997): Kumaon: Land and Its People. In: *Studies on Kumaun Himalaya*, (Eds.) S.K. Sharma and N.C. Dhoundyial. Indus Publishing Company, New Delhi. pp.17-27.

Driver, E.D. (1963): *Differential Fertility in Central India*. Princeton University Press, Princeton, New Jersey.

Dube, D.K. and H. Singh (1997): The Collapse of Indo-Tibetan Trade and Its Impact on the Demographic Structure of Border Area—A Case Study of Bhotia Valleys of Kumaon. In: *People of the Himalayas: Ecology, Culture, Development and Change*, (Ed.) K.C. Mahanta. Kamla-Raj Enterprises, Delhi, pp. 279-84.

Dutt, J.S. (1976): Altitude and Fertility and Early Childhood Mortality: The Bolivian Example. *Am. J. Phys. Anthrop.*, 44 (1): 175.

Dutt, J.S. (1980): Altitude and Fertility: The Confounding Effect of Childhood Mortality—A Bolivian Example. *Social Biology*, 27 (2): 101-13.

Dutta, A. and S. Sinha (1997): Gender Disparities in Social Well-being: An Overview. *Indian Journal of Gender Studies*, 4 (1): 51-65.

Frisancho, A.R. (1970): Developmental Responses to High Altitude Hypoxia. *Am. J. Phys. Anthrop.*, 32: 401-8.

Frisancho, A.R.(1975): Functional Adaptation to High Altitude Hypoxia. *Science*, 187: 313-19.

Frisancho, A.R. (1978): Human Growth and Development. In: *The Biology of High-altitude Peoples (IBP-14)*, (Ed.) P.T. Baker. Cambridge University Press, Cambridge, London, pp.117-70

Frisancho, A. R. and P.T. Baker (1970): Altitude and Growth: A Study of the Patterns of Physical Growth of a High Altitude Peruvian Quechua Population. *Am. J. Phys. Anthrop.*, 32: 279-92.

Frish, R.E. (1975): Demographic Implications of Female Fecundity. *Social Biology*, 22: 17-22.

Furer-Haimendorf, Von C. (1981): Introduction. In: *Asian Highland Societies*, (Ed.) Von C. Furer-Haimendorf, Sterling Publishers, New Delhi.

Gangopadhyay, P. and S. Kundu (1989): A Note on Hormonal Changes among the Females under Pre and Post-menopausal Conditions. *Man in India*, 69(3): 272-77.

Garg, S.K.; D. Tyagi and A.R. Sankhyan (1981): Reproductive Life of Bhoksa Women. *Ann. Hum. Biol.*, 8: 361-70.

Ghosh, B.R. (1995): Society and Culture among the People of Himalayan Border Area. In: *The People of the Himalayas*, (Ed.) M.K. Raha. Anthropological Survey of India, Calcutta, pp.1-9.

Godelier, M. (1986): *The Mental and Material: Thought Economy and Society*. England: Verso.

Goldstein, M. (1976): Fraternal Polyandry and Fertility in a High Himalayan Valley in Northwest Nepal. *Human Ecology*, 4: 223-33.

Goldstein, M.C. (1981): New Perspective on Tibetan Fertility and Population Decline. *American Ethnologist*, 8(4): 721-29.

Goldstein, M.C.; C. M. Beall and P. Tsarong (1984): On Studying Fertility at High Altitude: A Rejoinder to Hoff. *American Anthropologist*, 86(2): 419-23.

Goldstein, M.C.; C. M. Beall and P. Tsarong (1984a): Response to Abelson's Comment on Goldstein, Tsarong and Beall. *American Anthropologist*, 86 (3): 703-5.

Goldstein,M.C.; C. M. Beall and P. Tsarong (1984b): Response to Basu and Gupta. *American Anthropologist*, 86 (4): 996-97.

Goldstein,M.C.; P. Tsarong and C. M. Beall (1983): High Altitude Hypoxia, Culture, and Human Fecundity/Fertility: A Comparative Study. *American Anthropologist*, 85 (1): 28-49.

Guha, R. (1994): *Social Ecology*. (Ed.) Ramachandra Guha. Delhi: Oxford University Press.

Guha, P.K. (1997): The Bhotiya of Mana Village: A Study on Some Aspects of Demography. *Man in India*, 77 (1): 63-70.

Gupta, R. (1978): *A Comparative Demographic Study of the Sherpas of Upper Khumbu (Above 10,000ft.), Darjeeling District, West Bengal*. Biological Science Division of the Indian Statistical Institute, Calcutta.

Gupta, R. (1980): Altitude and Demography among the Sherpas. *J. Biosoc. Sci.*, 12: 103-14.

Gupta, R.; A. Basu; I. G. Pawson; P. Bharti; B. Mukhopadhayay; S. Mukhopadhayay; S.K. Roy; P.P. Majumdar; S.K. Bhattacharya; K.K. Bhattacharya and S.K. Das (1987): Altitude and Human Biology: A Comparative Study of Himalayan, Andian and Ethiopian Data. *J. Indian Anthrop. Soc.*, 22: 101-80.

Harrison, G.A. (1969): The Race Concept in Human Biology. *J. Biosoc. Sci.*, Suppl., 1: 129-41.

Harrison, G.A.; C.F. Kuchemann; M.A.S. Moore; A.J. Boyce; T. Baju; A.E. Mourant; M.J. Godber; B.G. Glasgow; A.C. Kopec; D.Tills and E.J. Clegg (1969): The Effects of Altitudinal Variation in Ethiopian Populations. *Philosophical Transactions of the Royal Society of London*, 256 (B): 147-82.

Hauser, P.M. (1976): Ageing and Worldwide Population Change. In: *Handbook of Ageing and the Social Sciences*, (Eds.) R.H. Binstock and E.Shanas. Van Nostrand Reinhold, New York. pp. 59-86.

Hauser, P.M. and O.D. Duncan (1972): Overview. In: *The Study of Population: An Inventory and Appraisal*, (Eds.) P.M. Hauser and O.D. Duncan. The University of Chicago Press, Chicago, pp. 1-26.

Hoff, C. (1984): Is There Significant Hypoxic Depression of Fertility among Andean Natives? A Reply to Goldstein, Tsarong and Beall. *American Anthropologist*, 86 (2): 417-9.

Hoon, V. (1996): *Living on the Move: Bhotiyas of the Kumaon Himalaya*. Sage Publications, New Delhi.

Howley, A. H. (1968): Human Ecology. In: *International Encyclopedia of the Social Sciences*, Vol.4 (Ed.) David L. Sills. The Macmillan Company and The Free Press.

Hurtado, A. (1964): Acclimatization to High Altitudes. In: *The Physiological Effects of High Altitude*, (Ed.) W. H. Weihe. Pergamon Press, London, pp.1-17.

James, W.H. (1966): The Effect of Altitude on Fertility in Andian Countries. *Population Studies*, 20 (2): 97-101.

Jones, D.L. (1974): *Human Reproduction and Society*. Faber and Faber, London.

Joshi, M.P. and C.W. Brown (1986): Some Dynamics of Indo-Tibetan Trade through Kumaun Garhwal. In: *Ecology, Economy and Religion of Himalayas*, (Eds) L.P. Vidyarthi and Makhan Jha. Orient Publications, Delhi, pp.59-71.

Joshi, N. (1996): India. In: *Encyclopedia of the Future*, (Ed.) G. T. Kurian and G.T.T. Molitor. Simon and Schuster Macmillan, New York, 1:467-70.

Joshi, P. and P.C. Pande (1997): Ethno-botany of the Bhotia Tribe of Kumaon Himalaya. In: *Studies on Kumaon Himalaya*. (Ed.) S.K. Sharma and N.C. Dhondiyal. Indus Publishing Company, New Delhi, pp.63-89.

Kanungo, J. (1982): *Fertility Variation among the Oriya Castes in Urban Communities*. Ph.D. Thesis. Department of Anthropology, Utkal University, Bhubaneswar.

Kashiwazaki, H.; T. Suzuki and T. Takemoto (1988): Altitude and Reproduction of the Japanese in Bolivia. *Human Biology*, 60 (6): 831-45.

Kashyap, L.K. (1998): Issues in Scheduling of Tribes: The Bhotia Case. In: *Perspectives in Tribal Development—Focus on Uttar Pradesh*, (Eds.) H. S. Saksena, B.R.K. Sukla, P.K. Tiwari and P.N. Sharma. EFCS, Lucknow, pp. 33-42.

Khongsidier, R. and A.K. Ghosh (1994): Bio-demographic Study among the War Khasi of Meghalaya. *J. Indian Anthrop. Soc.*, 29 (1and2): 195-202.

Kreager, P.C. (1993): The Changing Case for Demographic Moderation. *Current Anthropology*, 34 (3): 334-8.

Laurenson, I.F.; M. A. Benton; A.J. Bishop and C.G.N. Mascie-Taylor (1985): Fertility at Low and High Altitude in Central Nepal. *Social Biology*, 32 (1 and 2): 65-70.

Mahanta, K.C. (1997): Preface. In: *People of Himalayas: Ecology, Culture, Development and Change*, (Ed.) K.C. Mahanta. Kamla-Raj Enterprises, Delhi, pp. 3-7.

Majumdar, D.M. (1960): *Social Contours of an Industrial City: Social Survey of Kanpur*. Asia Publishing House, Delhi.

Mazess, R.B. (1975): Human Adaptation to High Altitude. In: *Physiological Anthropology*, (Ed.) A. Damon, Oxford University Press, London, pp.167-209.

Mehra, J. D. and S. C. Tiwari (1955): The Bhotias of Almora District. *Vanyajati*, III (1): 10-6.

Meillassoux, C. (1972): From Reproduction to Production. *Economy and Society*, 1 (1): 93-105.

Meillassoux, C. (1981): *Maidens, Meals and Money: Capitalism and Domestic Community*, Cambridge: Cambridge University Press.

Mencher, J.P. (1994): Ecological and Social Structure: A Comparative Analysis. In: *Social Ecology* (Ed.) Ramachandra Guha. Delhi: Oxford University Press.

Michelson, N. (1944): Studies in the Physical Development of Negroes: IV Onset of Puberty. *Amer. J. Phys. Anthrop.*, 2: 151-66.

Monge, C. (1942): Life in the Andes and Chronic Mountain Sickness. *Science*, 95 (2456): 79-84.

Monge, C. (1948): *Acclimatization in the Andes*. Johns Hopkins Press, Baltimore.

Moore, L.G. and J. G. Regensteiner (1983): Adaptation to High Altitude. *Ann. Rev. of Anthropol.*, 12: 285-304.

Pandey, A.K. (1991): *Ecology and Tribal Demography: A Comparative Study of Idu and Digaru Mishmis of Arunachal Pradesh*. Ph.D. Thesis. Department of Anthropology, Delhi University, Delhi.

Pandey, G.D. and P.P. Talwar (1987): Some Aspects of Marriage and Fertility in Rural Uttar Pradesh. *Demography India*, 2: 301-9.

Parkash, M. (1990): *Comparative Demographic Study of High Altitude and Low Altitude Bods of Himachal Pradesh*. Ph.D. Thesis, Department of Anthropology, University of Delhi, Delhi.

Parkash, M. and S.L. Malik (1990): Differences in Fertility in Highlander and Lowlander Bods of Himachal Pradesh. *J. Hum. Ecol.*, 1 (2): 175-80.

Pathy, S. (2003): Destitute, Deprivation and Tribal 'Development'. *Economic and Political Weekly*, XXXVIII(27): 2832-6.

Patnaik, M.M. (1985): *Socio-economic, Cultural and Demographic Rationality of Fertility Behaviour*. Janaki Prakashan, New Delhi.

Patra, P.K. and A.K. Kapoor (1996): Some Demographic Traits among the Dalu of West Garo Hills, Meghalaya. *Man in India*, 76 (3): 273-8.

Paul, R.C. (2000): *Situation of Human Rights in India*. Commonwealth, New Delhi.

Paul, S. (1997): *Anthropo-Demographic Study among the Kumauni Caste Groups and Bhotia Tribal Groups of Uttarakhand*. Ph.D. Thesis. Department of Anthropology, University of Delhi, Delhi.

Pawson, I.G. and C. Jest (1978): The High-altitude Areas of the World and Cultures. In: *The Biology of High-altitude Peoples*, (Ed.) P.T. Baker. Cambridge: Cambridge University Press, London, pp. 17-45.

Planning Commission (1993): *National Policy for Integrated Development in the Himalayas: Report of the Expert Group (1993)*. Planning Commission, Government of India, New Delhi.

Pressat, R. (1972): *Demographic Analysis: Methods, Results, Applications*. Edward Arnold, London.

Pressat, R. (1985): *The Dictionary of Demography* (Ed.) C. Wilson. Blackwell, Oxford, London.

Raha, M.K. (1987): Introduction. In: *The Himalayan Heritage*, (Ed.) M.K. Raha. Gian Publishing House, Delhi.

Raha, M.K. (1995): Introduction. In: *The People of the Himalayas*, (Ed.) M.K. Raha. Anthropological Survey of India, Calcutta.

Raipa, R.S. (1974): *Shauka: Seemawarti Janjati (Samajik Avam Sanskritik Adhyayan)*, Raipa Brothers, Dharchula, Pithoragarh, India (Hindi).

Rajangam, S. and I. M. Thomas (1987): Menarche and Menopause in Tamil Brahmins of India. *Man in India*, 67 (3): 264-75.

Randhawa, M.S. (1970): *Kumaon Himalayas*. Oxford and IBH Pub. Co., New Delhi.

Raypa, R. S. (1992): Ecological Adaptation of the Bhotias of Kali Basin of U.P. Hills. In: *The Himalayas and The Himalayans*, (Ed.) M.K. Raha. Anthropological Survey of India, Calcutta, pp. 71-87.

Read, C.D. and D. H. McLeord (1955): *Gynaecology*. Churchill, London.

Robinson, K. (2001): Government Agency, Women's Agency: Feminisms, Fertility and Population Control. In: *Borders of Being* (Eds.) Margaret Jolly and Kalpana Ram. Ann Arbor: The University of Michigan Press.

Ryder, N.B (1959): Fertility. In: *The Study of Population: An Invention and Appraisal*, (Eds.) P.M. Hauser and O.D. Duncan. University of Chiacago Press, Chicago.

Sachidananda and R.R. Prasad (1996): Introduction. In: *Encyclopedic Profile of Indian Tribes*, (Eds.) Sachidananda and R.R. Prasad. Discovery Publishing House, New Delhi, Vol.1 (A-E).

Sarkar, R.M. (1993): Bio-cultural Traditions in Anthropology with Special Reference to India. *Man in India*, 73 (3): 295-305.

Satyanarayana, K. and A.N. Naidu (1979): Nutrition and Menarche in Rural Hyderabad. *Ann. Hum. Biol.*, 6: 163-65.

Saxena, G.B. (1965): Differential Fertility in Rural Hindu Communities: A Sample Survey of Rural Uttar Pradesh, India. *Eugenic Quarterly*, Vol. 12.

Sayers, J. (1982): *Biological Politics: Feminist and Anti-Feminist Perspectives*, London and New York: Tavistock.

Sen, A.K. (2001): *Development as Freedom*. London: Oxford University Press.

Sengupta, S. and A. Gogoi (1997): Effects of Socio-cultural Factors on Fertility and Mortality Among the Oraons of Assam: A Preliminary Study. In: *People of the Himalayas: Ecology, Cultural, Development and Change*, (Ed.) K.C. Mahanta. Kamla-Raj Enterprises, Delhi, India, pp. 335-41.

Sherring, C.A. (1906): *Western Tibet and British Borderland*, Edward Arnold, London.

Shrivastava, R.P. (1966): Tribe-Caste Mobility in India and the Case of Kumaon Bhotias: Part-1. In: *Caste and Kin in Nepal, India and Cylon: Anthropological Studies in Hindu-Buddhist Contact Zones*, (Ed.) Christoph Von Furer-Heimendorf. Asian Publishing House, Bombay, pp. 161-212.

Singh, K.P. (1986): *Correlates of Fertility Behaviour: A Study of Rural Community in Punjab and Haryana*. Concept Publishing Company, New Delhi.

Singh, R. L. (1971): *Regional Geography of India*. National Geographical Society of India, Varanasi.

Southall, A. (1996): Tribes. In: *Encyclopedia of Cultural Anthropology*, (Eds.) D. Levinson and M. Ember. Henry Holt and Company, New York, 4(S-Z):1329-36.

Srinivasan, K. (1991): Fertility and Proximate Determinants. In: *The Demographic Challenge: A Study of Four Large Indian States*, (Eds.) J.K. Satia and S.J. Jejeebhoy. Oxford University Press, Bombay, pp.36-76.

Srinivasan, K.; S.J. Jejeebhoy; R.A. Easterlin and E.M. Crimmins (1984): Factors Affecting Fertility Control in India. *Pop. Develop. Rev.*, 10: 273-96.

Srivastava, A.R.N. (1994): On Demography and Social Structure. *Current Anthropology*, 35 (4): 434-5.

Steward, J. H. (1968): Cultural Ecology. In: *International Encyclopedia of the Social Sciences*, Vol.4 (Ed.) David L. Sills. The Macmillan Company and The Free Press.

Stycos, J.M. (1963): Culture and Differential Fertility in Peru. *Population Studies*, 16: 257-70.

Tanner, J.M. (1962): *Growth at Adolescence.* Blakewell Scientific Publication, Oxford, London.

Thompson, W.S. and D.T. Lewis (1965): *Population Problems.* McGraw-Hill Book Company, New York.

United Nations (1998): *World Population Prospects: The 1996 Revision.* Economic and Social Affairs Population Division, United Nations, New York, pp. 6-52.

Uppreti, H.C (1968): The Social Life of Bhotias. *Vanyajati*, Vol. XVI(1):15-20.

Valsik, J.A. (1965): The Seasonal Rhythm of Menarche: A Review. *Human Biology*, 37 (2): 75-90.

Valsik, J.A.; R. S. Stukovasky and N. Janku (1973): Factors Influencing Menarche. In: *Physical Anthropology and its Extending Horizons*, (Eds.) A. Basu, A.K. Ghosh, S.K. Biswas and R. Ghosh. Orient Longman, Calcutta, pp. 99-108.

Walton, H.G. (1911): Almora: A Gazetteer. In: *District Gazetteers of United Province of Agra and Dudh.* Government Press, Allahabad, Vol. XXXV.

Weitz, C. (1981): Fertility of Nepalese Sherpas at Moderate Altitudes: Comparisions with High-altitude Data. *Ann. Hum. Biology*, 8(4): 383-85.

Weitz, C.A.; I.G. Pawson; M.V. Weitz; S.D.R. Lang and A. Lang (1978): Cultural Factors Affecting the Demographic Structure of a High Altitude Nepalese Population. *Social Biology*, 25 (5): 179-95.

Whitehead, L. (1968): Altitude, Fertility and Mortality in Andean Countries. *Population Studies*, 22 (3): 335-46.

Wood, J. W. (1990): Fertility in Anthropological Populations. *Annu. Rev. Anthropol.*, 19: 211-42.

INDEX